Activity-Based Costing for Small and Mid-Sized Businesses

Activity-Based Costing for Small and Mid-Sized Businesses:

An Implementation Guide

Douglas T. Hicks

JOHN WILEY & SONS, INC.

New York • Chichester • Weinheim • Brisbane • Singapore • Toronto

Copyright © 1992 by John Wiley & Sons, Inc.

Library of Congress Cataloging-in-Publication Data:

Hicks, Douglas T.
    Activity-based costing for small and mid-sized businesses : an
implementation guide / Douglas T. Hicks.
        p.   cm.
    Includes bibliographical references.
    ISBN 0-471-19627-4 (paper)
    1. Cost accounting. 2. Small business-Accounting   I. Title.
HF5686.C8H49   1992   91-47902
657' .42–dc20

Printed in the United States of America

10 9 8 7 6 5 4 3 2 1

To my parents,
Theron and Jane Hicks,
an unwavering source of love, support, and encouragement

Preface

The concept of activity-based costing (ABC) has grown faster than any new accounting concept in recent history. Only a decade ago, the vast majority of executives and accountants accepted the cost information provided by their organizations' systems as being accurate and relevant. As the 1980s closed, however, very few still believed this information to be reliable. The "bashing" of traditional cost accounting has been successful, and the concept of ABC has come to be generally accepted as the more accurate and relevant way to view costs. Unfortunately, ABC remains only a concept for most organizations.

Most current approaches to ABC are based on concepts developed by the Computer Aided Manufacturing–International (CAM-I) Project, sponsored by organizations such as General Dynamics, McDonnell Douglas, Westinghouse, TRW, Allison Gas Turbine Division of General Motors, Hughes Aircraft, Lockheed, and the "Big 6" public accounting firms. The project's researchers developed a much improved approach to cost accounting and cost management in general. The ideas and implementation approaches they developed have been right in line with the needs of the project's sponsors.

However, most organizations are not megacorporations such as General Dynamics, Westinghouse, or General Motors. Implementation of the solutions developed for these industrial giants is far beyond the resources of small and mid-sized businesses.

Nevertheless, these smaller businesses need to understand their product and process costs every bit as well as CAM-I's sponsors do.

This book describes an alternative to the "big guys'" approach to activity-based costing. To differentiate this approach from the ABC of larger organizations, I refer to it as abc, in lowercase letters. It was not developed in a sponsored "think tank" that was developing answers for a specific audience. It is also not simply a scaled-down version of ABC. The abc system developed as a series of solutions to actual cost accounting problems at real-world organizations. These solutions were eventually consolidated into an overall methodology that can be applied to any organization. For small and mid-sized organizations, it is not merely "as good as ABC"; I believe it is "better than ABC."

The sponsors of abc are the clients with whom D. T. Hicks & Co. has worked during the past six years to solve their cost accounting problems. These organizations included:

- A $6 million manufacturer of composite structures
- A $24 million stamper and assembler of automotive components
- A $2 million commercial printer
- A $45 million, multilocation manufacturer of extruded and assembled automotive components
- A $5 million prototype and tool building facility
- A $15 million manufacturer of hot-formed, machined, and assembled aircraft components
- A $35 million precision forger of aircraft and gas turbine blades.

These and many other organizations obtained improved cost information through the theories and techniques described in this book.

The book is divided into three sections. The first section addresses some of the general issues regarding abc at small and mid-sized organizations. I begin the text by discussing the need for a different approach to activity-based costing at the small and mid-sized firm (Chapter 1). I then briefly describe how cost accounting grew to become so "irrelevant" (Chapter 2), what types of problems can be caused by a dysfunctional cost system (Chapter 3), and how problem cost systems can be identified (Chapter 4). I conclude with a discussion of activity-based costing as a solution to the cost accounting problem and the key concepts that are needed to implement abc (Chapter 5).

The second section of the book is about implementing abc. I begin by outlining the steps that are required to establish an activity-based system (Chapter 6). I then describe how the organization can develop an effective cost flow pattern (Chapter 7), tools to use in designing the mechanics for implementing the cost flow pattern (Chapter 8), a process for planning a cost model of the organization (Chapter 9), and an outline for gathering data necessary to drive the cost model (Chapter 10). In Chapters 11 through 14, I describe the techniques for putting together the concepts and tools into a personal computer–based cost accumulation model that simulates the flow of costs through the organization to its products and services. To more clearly present a "blueprint" for implementing an abc system, I use the example of Costa Manufacturing Company, a hypothetical organization that is a composite of several clients of D. T. Hicks & Co. The end of this section provides a summary of what has been accomplished thus far (Chapter 15) and two examples of how the concepts and techniques described for Costa Manufacturing can also be used to implement abc systems at service organizations (Chapter 16).

In the book's third section, I explain how the activity-based cost accumulation model developed in the previous section can be used to improve the organization's decision-making process. Again using Costa Manufacturing as an example, the cost accumulation model is used to perform product costing and assess product line profitability (Chapter 17), identify and analyze cost reduction opportunities (Chapter 18), and calculate the benefit of possible capital expenditures and evaluate the decision between extra overtime and additional employees (Chapter 19). This section also shows how an organization can develop cost estimates and evaluate pricing strategies for multi-year programs (Chapters 20 through 24). The section and book conclude with a review of the improvements that were made possible in Costa's cost information through the use of the abc methodology (Chapter 25).

An activity-based approach to cost accounting is not an option for organizations hoping to compete in the 1990s. It is a requirement. Knowledge of product and process cost is critical for any organization hoping to maintain, or improve, its competitive position. The question is not *whether* the organizations will change, but *when*. The methodology described in this book will enable small and mid-sized organizations to benefit from this new management concept today, thereby strengthening the probability of their continued success tomorrow.

I have become indebted to many in the preparation of this work. One of my largest debts is to Gordon Nelson, who suggested many improvements in the manuscript and kept reminding me that I am neither Charles Horngren nor Charles Dickens. I am also indebted to Jerry D. Pierick, who helped me change from a financial accountant into a management accountant; Alex Jackson III, whose seemingly off-the-wall questions often resulted in concepts that have been critical in the development of the abc approach; and Robert L. Keck and Terry J. Nicholson, two mentors and friends who have always been willing to discuss (and debate) with me some of my more unusual accounting theories. Finally, I am indebted to my son, Jonathan D. Hicks, whose computer graphics skills made possible many of the methods used to visualize the abc concepts and techniques presented in this book.

Douglas T. Hicks

Farmington Hills, Michigan
February 1992

Contents

Part I

———

Activity-Based Costing

1

Activity-Based Costing for the Small and Mid-Sized Organization

As we enter the last decade of the century, activity-based costing has become the hottest topic in management accounting. In the early 1980s, academics such as Robert Kaplan of the Harvard Business School and Carnegie-Mellon University and H. Thomas Johnson, then of Pacific Lutheran University, began questioning the relevance of traditional cost accounting practices.[1] Others, such as Eli Goldratt, author of *The Goal*, accused management accounting practices of being one of the major reasons for the deterioration of U.S. productivity.[2] Motivated by the valid points raised in their criticisms, individuals (including Kaplan and Johnson) and organizations began developing ideas and techniques for rectifying the longstanding deficiencies in traditional cost accounting.

By the end of the 1980s, organizations such as Computer Aided Manufacturing–International (CAM-I) and the National

---

[1] Both gentlemen wrote extensively on the subject culminating in their co-authored, *Relevance Lost: The Rise and Fall of Management Accounting* (Boston: Harvard Business School Press, 1987).

[2] Eliyhau M. Goldratt and Jeff Cox, *The Goal* (Croton-on-Hudson, NY: North River Press, 1984).

Association of Accountants had introduced activity-based costing (ABC for those inclined to add all management theories to the pot of management alphabet soup). This cost accounting technique methodically charges all of an organization's indirect costs to the "activities" that make the costs necessary and then distributes the activities' costs to the products that make the activities necessary.

As is inevitable during the early days of any new concept, the developers of activity-based costing have moved it toward its most theoretically pure form. The theories and suggested methods of implementation found in today's literature and taught in current seminars are the result of work performed or sponsored by academics, multibillion dollar corporations, and the "Big 6" public accounting firms. The practices being advocated are valid and will result in much more relevant cost information for management's use. Unfortunately, they are also too complex and expensive for effective implementation by small and mid-sized organizations, a group whose needs are every bit as critical as those of the multibillion dollar organizations that can afford to implement full-scale activity-based costing.

The concepts and techniques suggested in this book provide a simpler, more cost-effective way for organizations that cannot afford thousands of hours of employee time and six-figure consulting fees to abandon traditional cost accounting practices and benefit from the application of the much superior theories of activity-based costing.

Philosophical Foundations

In developing activity-based costing for small and mid-sized organizations, which I label abc (using lowercase letters) to differentiate it from the larger organizations' ABC (with capital letters), I have kept in mind three ideas—its philosophical foundations if you will.

> *Philosophical Foundations of*
> *Activity-Based Costing (abc) for*
> *Small and Mid-Sized Organizations*
>
> 1. Although management theories and concepts and the language used to describe them may be universal, implementation at a smaller organization cannot be simply the downsized version of a large organization's methods.
> 2. A great management accounting system will not itself make an organization great, but an inadequate and/or misleading system will keep one from becoming great or, worse yet, cause it to fail.
> 3. It is better to be approximately correct than to be precisely wrong. Accuracy is preferable to precision.

We discuss each of these points in detail.

1. Although management theories and concepts and the language used to describe them may be universal, implementation at a smaller organization cannot be simply the downsized version of a large organization's methods. Consider two manufacturers, one a $120 million organization with 400 metal-stamping presses and the other a $5 million organization with 15 presses. As part of a preventive maintenance program, each organization wants to collect sufficient information to know when to perform maintenance on each machine so as not to lose production time due to an unexpected, prolonged shutdown.

To accomplish this in the $120 million organization, a plantwide network of data collection devices might be installed in such a manner that one is readily accessible from any press. Any change in the status of a press is entered by the operator. These data are then processed by the organization's mainframe computer which, in turn, generates a myriad of statistical reports showing such data as press uptime percentages, downtime by cause, and mean time between failures. The computer even uses predetermined and historical data to issue warnings when each press is within a preset time of its next expected failure.

The $5 million organization cannot afford such an elaborate system. In fact, its size makes most of the data available from the larger organization's system unnecessary. Each day, the smaller organization's plant manager and/or maintenance supervisor can see and touch each press. The presses are not 400 "subjects of the realm," but are 15 "members of the family." Thus, the same level of information can be maintained by manually collecting data for certain key presses and through the observation, knowledge, and experience of the plant's key personnel for the others.

In each case, the same objective is reached: Sufficient information is gathered to know when to perform maintenance and avoid production stoppages due to unexpected, prolonged press shutdowns. The manufacturing theory being followed is the same, but each plant uses different approaches that are, to a great extent, determined by the plant's size. Thus, a small to mid-sized organization can gain superior knowledge of its costs without implementing a downsized version of the theoretically correct, complex, and expensive system that may be necessary in a large facility.

2. A great management accounting system will not itself make an organization great, but an inadequate and/or misleading system will keep one from becoming great or, worse yet, cause it to fail. Organizations are great because they provide competitively priced, quality products and services that are needed by the markets they serve. Without these factors, the greatest management accounting system in the world cannot make an organization successful.

However, competitively priced, quality products and services and a receptive market do not ensure success. For example, one manufacturer produced two distinct product lines in the same facility. One was proprietary (being designed by the manufacturer and protected by a patent) and the other was built to the customer's print. Traditional cost accounting techniques indicated that the manufactured cost of each product (cost before general, selling, and administrative expenses) was about $7.50 per unit. Each unit sold for $8.00. Conventional wisdom would conclude that each product was equally profitable as each contributed $.50 per unit to gross margin.

Applying more relevant activity-based accounting theory to the products had different results. Using abc, the cost of the proprietary product was determined to be approximately $6.50; the build-to-print product's cost was about $8.50. Clearly, these two product lines were not equal in profitability. Unfortunately, the build-to-print product's original price, established several years earlier, was based on a cost estimate developed using traditional methods. The manufacturer's customer demanded annual price reductions of 5% and would not, for any reason, accept a price increase. The company's options were to continue producing the product line at a loss, or to drop the product line and concentrate efforts on the proprietary products.

This example is not a fictional depiction. The facts presented are the simplification of an actual project I undertook in 1987. Fortunately, the company selected the second option and, despite the lower sales volume, returned to levels of profitability in 1988 that it had not seen since the early 1980s. In this case, a faulty management accounting system kept a corporation producing quality products from reaching its potential. If the organization had developed accurate and relevant cost data earlier, it could have either avoided the problem altogether by properly pricing the product initially or corrected the situation by phasing out the product line sooner. In either case, earlier recognition and correction of its cost problems would have saved the company millions of dollars.

3. It is better to be approximately correct than to be precisely wrong. Accuracy is preferable to precision.   Historically, accountants have been enamored by precision. To many, precision and accuracy were synonymous. To calculate the unit cost of a product to six decimal places instead of only four made it that much more accurate. This practice provided a great deal of false comfort to the accountant, but it was, unfortunately, as dangerous as it was foolish.

The manufacturer in the earlier example calculated its unit costs to four decimals. What was gained by showing that a product costs exactly $7.4983 to manufacture when actually it costs approximately $8.50, more than $1.00 more? Nothing was gained but false confidence in management information that almost led to disaster.

On the other hand, what would be gained if the manufacturer had installed a full-blown, theoretically perfect ABC system to learn that the product costs approximately $8.42 or $8.58 instead of approximately $8.50? Not enough would be gained to justify the additional cost involved. Note that in both cases, the unit costs were approximate. No cost accounting system provides an organization with precision. *All* product costing is approximate. *All* cost systems contain too many estimates and allocations to be precise. It is important to remember that, in putting together a small or mid-sized organization's approach to activity-based costing, the goal of accuracy, not precision, should be kept in mind.

The Cost Accumulation Model

At the heart of abc is the cost accumulation model. This model can be built using almost any business-oriented spreadsheet software. It consists of a series of single-purpose schedules that integrate to form one larger worksheet. The integrated worksheet simulates the flow of costs through the entire facility being modeled. Although I refer to the worksheet as being large, the most complex one I have developed to date (for a manufacturer with sales in excess of $45 million) required less than 250K of random-access memory (RAM). These worksheets require no complex mathematical calculations and can be built without using "higher level" spreadsheet functions. One need only to develop an effective cost flow pattern; gather the necessary cost and operating information; and then add, subtract, multiply, and divide through the formation of the model.

Once developed, the model has a myriad of uses in addition to product costing, the purpose for which it is usually built. It can assist in making capital expenditure decisions, developing budgets and forecasts, and formulating short- and long-term plans. It can take the guesswork out of long-term pricing decisions, test alternative courses of action, direct process value analysis efforts, and assist with many similar management activities. Organizations that already have these models often develop their own ways of using them to improve management information and to make decision making more effective and easier.

Because the model is the key to abc, much of our discussion of the concepts included in abc will be demonstrated in terms of their worksheet representation. To some, a picture is worth a thousand words. To accountants, a worksheet can often explain a concept that cannot be adequately expressed in ten thousand words. As a result, worksheet representations are used frequently.

Which Organizations Are Small and Mid-Sized?

This question does not have a clear-cut answer. Some $20 million organizations might be so complex that the modeling technique described in this book might not be adequate. On the other hand, a $250 million facility might find abc to be the greatest management tool it has added in decades.

For the purposes of this book, a small or mid-sized organization is an autonomous business unit that needs improved cost information but that believes that thousands of hours of employee and/or consulting time for development and untold additional hours for maintenance is too great a price to pay for that improvement. In my experience, the investment required to implement abc systems has ranged from 80 hours for a small commercial printer to 500 hours for a large automotive supplier with very poor historical financial and operating records. This contrasts with ABC implementations, which may require assembling an interdisciplinary task force, dedicating personnel to this task force full time for many months, and incurring consulting fees reaching into six figures.

Even very large organizations may find abc preferable to ABC. Major corporations often comprise many autonomous operating subsidiaries and divisions. Some, if not all, of these locations may be ideal candidates for using abc.

Although I usually use examples of manufacturers in describing the concepts and techniques of abc, the system will work just as well for a chemical company, a retailer, an insurance company, a bank, an automobile dealer, or a consulting firm. The principles are valid and useful in any organization with more than the most rudimentary business structure and a variety of operating activities. To demonstrate this, Chapter 16 includes two examples of the application of abc in service organizations.

Changing the Way We Think about Costs

Often, the exercise of thinking through a problem is more valuable than the solution developed. The introspection required in developing a sound business plan usually provides more benefits than the plan itself. In the same way, some organizations may find that the process of thinking through an activity-based cost system proves to be even more valuable than the resulting system itself.

We all have artificial constraints built into our thinking. Our experience has usually been in an environment in which someone else has already developed the concepts and our job has been to see that they were implemented effectively. As a result, we take certain things for granted that are not necessarily true.

One major example of this is a misconception that I discuss in greater detail later in this book. That misconception is that the cost accounting system must support the financial reporting system. Also included is the corollary: One cost system must be used for all of the organization's cost accounting needs. Is this constraint true? Definitely not! Even in organizations where outside rules demand consistency between cost accumulation and day-to-day accounting (such as with most government contractors), the constraint is an artificial one.

As valuable a tool as the cost accumulation model will prove to be, the efforts that go into its development may prove to be the most important and long-lasting part of implementing an activity-based approach to costing.

2

How Cost Accounting Grew to Its Current Level of Underdevelopment

"If it ain't broke, don't fix it!" How many times has that remark been repeated? At first glance, it makes sense. If something is working well, why make changes that might complicate it to the extent that it no longer works? On the other hand, how can you tell when something really is "broke"?

In some instances, a problem becomes obvious when a business system or strategy no longer works. If surplus and/or obsolete inventory builds up, it seems obvious that the inventory control system needs repair. If sales fall off, it appears that the marketing strategy needs rethinking. If products begin to fail in the field, then something needs to be done to improve quality. But how about cost accounting? How can an organization tell if its cost system is "broke"?

To answer this question, one first must have a basic understanding of how traditional cost accounting practices attained their current level of development. I attempt to provide this information through a short "allegorical history" of cost accounting.

Many years ago, an entrepreneur (whom I call A) could buy a product (rectangles sound good) and, in turn, sell it to a customer (whom I call B). Cost accounting for this type of transaction was fairly simple; the only cost involved was both variable and direct. Outside of the material cost and A's time and effort, for which A was compensated by profit, no other costs or activities were involved.

As time passed, A found that he could enhance the value of his rectangles if he purchased three asterisks, assembled them with each rectangle, and sold the assembly to B. Again, A expected to be compensated by the profit from his transactions, so the only costs involved, material costs, were both direct and variable.

This business was so successful for A that he decided to pay someone to do the assembly work. C was hired, on a piece-rate basis, to assemble the rectangles and asterisks at a location he had to provide himself. Cost accounting for this arrangement remained fairly simple. Both the material and labor costs were direct and both varied directly with the number of products being assembled.

As business continued to grow, C was no longer able to find the space to assemble the product on his own. As a result, A found lease space in which C could work. In addition to the monthly rental, A was responsible for paying the cost of heating and lighting the facility.

At this point, a cost accounting problem presented itself. The rental, heating, and lighting costs were directly attributable not to each individual product, but to the general operation of the business. In addition, all costs no longer varied with the number of products produced. The rental cost remained fixed no matter what occurred; the heating cost depended on how cold it was outside; and the lighting cost consisted of a small fixed amount per month, plus a cost for every hour the lights were turned on.

To determine the cost of each rectangle/asterisk assembly, A had to include these indirect costs. Because these costs were small compared with the material and labor costs, it was unlikely that a simple method would cause much distortion in the unit cost, so A could have used the labor, material, or combination of the two as a basis for allocating these indirect costs to the final product. Like the majority of manufacturers, he selected labor.

As volume continued to increase, A found it necessary to mechanize the assembly process to keep up with demand. He purchased an assembly machine for C to operate.

This addition further complicated A's attempts to determine the cost of each product produced. Depreciation, maintenance, and power, all indirect costs, were added to those necessary to operate his business. Unfortunately, none of these costs varied directly with the number of units produced. Depreciation was an arbitrary allocation of the cost of the purchased equipment to future periods. Power consisted of a fixed monthly service charge plus additional amounts for the power actually consumed. Maintenance was an irregular cost, incurred as service was needed.

Because A still needed to know the cost of an individual assembly, he continued to use labor as the basis for charging the growing (and no longer insignificant) group of indirect costs to individual units. At this point, A's operation and cost accounting system were typical of manufacturing firms in the early part of this century. In fact, his cost accounting system was typical of those still in existence at most manufacturers as this century draws to a close.

Recently, A decided that to continue his success, he needed to reduce the labor content of his product. His solution was to purchase an industrial robot that could replace his long-time employee, C. As a result, A now records more depreciation, incurs more power and maintenance costs, and has less heating and lighting cost. In addition, he has totally eliminated labor as a cost.

A's problem became apparent when he tried to determine the new cost of a product. His basis for charging his indirect production costs was gone. Labor could no longer be used as a basis because it was no longer a factor.

The situation for A's organization is not unlike that facing many companies today, although it is unlikely that most organizations will be able to totally eliminate labor from manufacturing costs. Entrepreneur A knew he had a problem because his indirect cost allocation basis disappeared completely. In most organizations, labor has not disappeared. Instead, it has gradually become a less significant portion of total cost. Unfortunately, direct labor continues to be the primary base on which the indirect costs are charged to products. The cost accounting practice of using direct labor as a basis for charging indirect costs to products is "broke," but the damage caused is not always obvious to the organization.

During this century, several key events have caused cost accounting practices to fall behind the development of the business operations they are supposed to reflect. As the century began, specialized branches were not necessary in accounting. When the first decade introduced a federal income tax, a new specialized area began, namely, tax accounting. In the 1930s, when the Securities and Exchange Acts placed a greater emphasis on financial accounting, cost accounting was split off as a separate discipline with financial accounting surviving as the mainstream of accounting. Because tax and financial accounting practices are mandated by law or regulation, compliance with them is not optional. As a result, organizations spent most of their accounting resources on these two areas. Cost accounting was made a stepchild and relegated to a role of supporting its two, law- and regulation-backed, siblings.

As the century continued, events such as the compilation of the Internal Revenue Code in 1954 and the creation of the Financial Accounting Standards Board in the early 1970s, placed even greater emphasis on the compliance aspects of accounting, aspects served by financial and tax accounting. Cost accounting developed somewhat during this period but, being securely belted into the backseat, was severely limited in its ability to keep up with changing times.

Perhaps the complacency of a United States growing into an industrial giant while other countries' economies were being decimated by two World Wars also suppressed any interest in the development of cost accounting. U.S. companies did not need to know their costs very well because the United States was the only nation with companies capable of mass-producing quality products for use within the country as well as worldwide. Fortunately, as the country's grip on industrial supremacy began to slip in the 1970s and early 1980s, knowledgeable people (including Kaplan, Johnson, and Goldratt, mentioned in Chapter 1) began to question the relevance of traditional cost accounting practices. They noted that, unlike financial and tax accounting, which serve to keep an organization in compliance with laws and regulations, *an organization's cost accounting system can actually make or break an otherwise sound business.*

The reason faulty cost information can have such a devastating impact on an organization can be seen from a listing of uses and users of information generated by the cost accounting system:

Use	User
Overall Inventory Valuation	Outsiders
Overall Cost of Goods Sold	Outsiders
Strategic Planning	Management
Capital Budgeting	Management
Operational Planning	Management
Operational Budgeting	Management
Product Cost Control	Management
Process Cost Control	Management
Product Pricing	Management
Decision Modeling	Management
Financial Analysis	Management

It is easy to see from this listing who ranks as the major user of cost information. Management uses cost information regularly in its day-to-day decision making. Outsiders care only that the organization's cost of goods sold and inventory valuation are correct.

Why is it, then, that most cost accounting systems are based upon laws, regulations, and pronouncements of tax and financial accounting authorities? One reason is that many accountants in industry have come from financial or public accounting backgrounds. They carry the outside reporting emphasis of their prior positions with them to their roles in industry. The possibility that something may be wrong with using financial reporting–oriented cost data in making management decisions simply never occurred to them.

Another reason is the misconception that maintaining two cost systems is too expensive and the benefits of having the second system cannot outweigh its additional expense. Because the tax and financial rules carry the weight of law, there is no option but to have a system that keeps the organization in compliance. With this system mandatory, the decision on a second system is easy if management believes such a system would be too costly. The day-to-day cost system was developed to support financial accounting. Throughout the development of accounting in this century, this practice has held until it evolved into an accepted law of nature: An organization's cost accounting system must support its financial accounting system. This, I believe, is Philosophical Error 1 in the establishment of most cost systems.

As I will show later in this book, using a cost system designed simply to comply with generally accepted accounting principles (GAAP) and tax rules can lead to disaster when used in day-to-day business operations. Tax and financial accounting rules are designed to fairly reflect results of operations and the financial position of the organization *as a whole*. Management, on the other hand, needs cost information to make a myriad of decisions on individual actions, parts, departments, and other subissues of the organization. It cannot depend on the generalities allowed by financial and tax accounting.

There *was* some truth to the contention that maintaining two systems was too expensive. *This is no longer true.* New methods, such as the one described in this book, and the advent of the personal computer make the development and maintenance of a second, management information–oriented cost system not only cost-effective, but mandatory, for an organization to be successful.

3

Impact of a Dysfunctional Cost System: Three Cases

Thus far, I have discussed the philosophical foundations of the smaller organization's approach to activity-based costing and have described how cost accounting has failed to keep pace with the changes in the world it is supposed to reflect. Although I have included a few examples of the problems a faulty cost system can cause, I doubt that I have convinced everyone that there truly are significant problems with traditional cost practices. To further explore the problems an inappropriate cost accounting system can cause, I present three hypothetical case studies.

The Tale of Two Nurseries

Several years ago, a homeowner needed some landscaping work at his home. He obtained quotes from two nurseries for the items he wished to purchase and work that needed to be performed. It is important to note that these two nurseries were identical except for their method of costing and pricing their services. The General Nursery used the standard industry practice of charging 50% of the product's sales price for its installation, whereas the ABC Nursery used an activity-based approach for determining the costs incurred and prices to charge for various installation activities.

Both organizations submitted quotes of $1,050 for the following products and services:

o Deliver and plant two 12-foot maple trees
o Deliver and install 150 feet of landscaping trim
o Deliver and spread 50 bags of landscaping stone
o Deliver and spread 30 bags of woodchips.

It would seem that it did not matter which nursery he selected for his landscaping needs.

Before making a final decision, however, he asked each nursery for a detailed breakdown of their quotes by product and service. The results of these detailed quotes are summarized as follows:

		General Nursery	ABC Nursery
2 — 12-ft maple trees	@ $100/ea	$ 200	$ 200
Planting	@ 50%	$ 100	
Planting	@ $100/hr		$ 250
150 — ft landscaping trim	@ $ 1/ft	$ 150	$ 150
Installation	@ 50%	$ 75	
Installation	@ $ 30/hr		$ 60
50 — bags landscape stone	@ $ 4/bg	$ 200	$ 200
Installation	@ 50%	$ 100	
Installation	@ $ .50/bg		$ 25
30 — bags woodchips	@ $ 5/bg	$ 150	$ 150
Installation	@ 50%	$ 75	
Installation	@ $ .50/bg		$ 15
Total quoted price		$1,050	$1,050

With great pride in himself for being such a shrewd businessman, he contracted with the General Nursery to deliver and plant the two maple trees and with the ABC Nursery for the balance of the order. Instead of paying $1,050 for the package, he paid only $900.

What impact did the split orders have on the nurseries? Using the activity-based approach of ABC Nursery—an approach that reflects the actual flow of costs in both nurseries—(remember, these nurseries are identical except for their methods of costing and pricing) I examine below the abc costs of these items.

		Line Item Cost	Product Cost
2 — 12-ft maple trees	@ $ 70/ea	$140	
Planting	@ $ 70/hr	$175	$315
150 — ft landscaping trim	@ $.70/ft	$105	
Installation	@ $ 20/hr	$ 40	$145
50 — bags landscape stone	@ $ 3/bg	$150	
Installation	@ $.30/bg	$ 15	$165
30 — bags woodchips	@ $ 4/bg	$120	
Installation	@ $.30/bg	$ 9	$129
Total estimated cost			$754

Planting the maple trees requires two specialized pieces of equipment (one for digging the hole and the other for placing the tree), as well as a three-person crew. The cost to either nursery for the crew's efforts runs $70 per hour. Because the combined time for planting both trees is $2^{1}/_{2}$ hours, the cost of planting the trees will run $175. Using the 50%-of-product-sales rule, General Nursery bids only $100 for the effort, whereas ABC Nursery wants $250.

Installing landscaping trim is much less capital intensive. It requires only a couple of laborers with a hand-held trenching device. Each hour of work by one of these crews costs either nursery about $20. Because it is estimated that two hours will be required to install the trim, the cost should run $40. Using their 50%-of-product-sales rule, General Nursery wants $75 for their effort, whereas ABC Nursery asks only $60.

In the cases of landscaping stone and woodchips, all that is required is to cut open the bags and spread the contents with a rake. Such an activity has almost no overhead and costs approximately $.30 per bag to accomplish. Total cost for both the landscaping stone and woodchips would then be $24. Again, using their 50%-of-product-sales rule, General Nursery wants $175 for this work, whereas ABC Nursery asks only $40.

The total cost to complete the entire order for either nursery would have been $754. Had either nursery received the entire order, its profit would have been $296 or 28.2%. Unfortunately for them, neither nursery received the entire order. Using the abc costs to determine each nursery's profit on the business it did receive generates the following results:

		General Nursery	ABC Nursery
2 — 12-ft maple trees	Sales	$ 300	
	Cost	$ 315	
150 — ft landscaping trim	Sales		$210
	Cost		$145
50 — bags landscape stone	Sales		$225
	Cost		$165
30 — bags woodchips	Sales		$165
	Cost		$129
Total sales		$ 300	$600
Total cost		$ 315	$439
Gross margin		$ (15)	$161
% Gross margin		(5.0)%	26.8%

By using an activity-based method of costing and, in turn, pricing its installation services, the ABC Nursery turned a substantial profit on the sales it did make, even though it did not obtain the entire contract. On the other hand, General Nursery received only the order for an item that its inappropriate quoting system severely underquoted. At the same time, General Nursery's system proposed outrageously high prices (e.g., installation of woodchips and landscaping stone) for items for which it could have earned a comfortable profit at considerably lower prices.

In the same manner, an inappropriate cost system can cause any organization to make pricing decisions that result in the winning of those orders its system inadvertently underprices (sometimes below its cost) while making it noncompetitive on the overpriced items that could have turned a profit at much lower prices.

Plantwide Rate

Plantwide Rate operates a manufacturing facility with two departments, A and B. It uses a plantwide overhead rate based on direct labor cost to charge the indirect costs of manufacturing to specific products. Recently, the departmental and total facility cost information for Plantwide looked as follows:

	($000)		
	Dept A	Dept B	Total
Overhead costs	$500	$500	$1,000
Direct labor costs	$238	$262	$ 500
Overhead rate			200%

As a consequence, all indirect costs were applied to products at 200% of the direct labor cost. At this point, there appears to be no major problem with using the plantwide rate because each department's rate, if calculated individually, would be plus or minus ten percentage points of that amount.

In attempting to improve performance, Plantwide's management decided to add computer-controlled equipment in Department A, effectively reducing its direct labor cost by $120,000 while adding $90,000 to its annual overhead. The result was the following revised cost information:

	($000)		
	Dept A	Dept B	Total
Overhead costs	$590	$500	$1,090
Direct labor costs	$118	$262	$ 380
Overhead rate			287%

This change raised the plantwide rate in use to 287% of direct labor cost.

It is interesting to look at two of Plantwide's products, one from either end of its manufacturing spectrum. Part Y is processed only in Department A and requires no Department B operations. Conversely, Part Z is processed only in Department B and requires no Department A operations. Prior to the installation of the computer-controlled equipment, the manufacturing costs of these two products was calculated:

	Part Y	Part Z
Direct labor	$23,800	$26,200
Overhead @ 200%	47,600	52,400
Total manufacturing cost	$71,400	$78,600

After installation of the new equipment, the calculation of manufacturing cost was revised:

	Part Y	Part Z
Direct labor	$ 11,800	$ 26,200
Overhead @ 287%	33,866	75,194
Total manufacturing cost	$ 45,666	$101,394
Part cost increase or (decrease)	$(25,734)	$ 22,794

How can this be? Overall savings from the investment in computer-controlled equipment was only $30,000 ($120,000 labor savings vs. $90,000 overhead increase). How is it that one product, Part Y, that uses only 10% of the department's resources ($11,800 of its $118,000 direct labor), receives 86% of the investment's benefit?

More amazingly, how is it that Part Z, which has absolutely nothing to do with the department in which the change took place, shows a cost 30% higher than before the improvement?

Absolutely nothing occurred that could affect the cost of manufacturing Part Z, yet its cost, according to the cost system, increased by $22,794.

These two parts from the opposite sides of the processing spectrum show the extreme impacts of having a plantwide rate at Plantwide Rate. In addition to these two parts, however, every other part manufactured in the facility that does not spend equal amounts of time in each department will have the same distortion, only to a lesser degree. Plantwide's management should not believe the product cost of any part it manufactures. Unfortunately, it probably makes daily decisions based on the assumption that those costs are accurate.

As a side note, Plantwide's method of applying indirect costs to products is *totally in accordance with GAAP* and would be accepted for both tax and financial reporting purposes.

One Big Press Corporation

Our final case is the One Big Press Corporation (OBPC). Both of the company's products, A and B, are processed using the company's one big press. Because it has only this one manufacturing operation, OBPC feels comfortable having a single, traditional overhead rate based on direct labor. Budgeted information for the coming year is:

	Hours	$/Hr	Annual $
Direct labor	6,000	$10	$ 60,000
Overhead costs			$300,000
Press operating hours	4,000		
Direct labor–based overhead rate			500%

Using direct labor as a basis for distributing overhead costs, the annual cost of producing OBPC's two products is determined as shown:

	Product A	Product B	Total
Press hours	2,000	2,000	4,000
Crew size	2	1	
Direct labor hours	4,000	2,000	6,000
Cost per labor hour	$ 10	$ 10	
Direct labor cost	$ 40,000	$ 20,000	$ 60,000
Overhead @ 500%	$200,000	$100,000	$300,000
Total production cost	$240,000	$120,000	$360,000

Intuition should indicate that something is wrong here. The only difference between these two products is that one requires a two-person crew and the other requires only one person. Should this manpower difference result in a $120,000 difference in the overhead cost necessary to manufacture the two products? Definitely not!

In an attempt to solve this problem, OBPC's management decided to change from direct labor as a basis for distributing overhead to a press hour basis. Using this basis, all conversion costs (direct labor and overhead) are included in an hourly rate for each hour the press is in operation. The revised budgeted information is:

	Hours	$/Hr	Annual $
Direct labor	6,000	$10	$ 60,000
Overhead costs			$300,000
Conversion costs			$360,000
Press operating hours	4,000		
Press hour–based overhead rate			$ 90

Using this new technique and revised rate, production cost by product can be restated:

	Product A	Product B	Total
Press hours	2,000	2,000	4,000
Cost per press hour	$ 90	$ 90	
Total production cost	$180,000	$180,000	$360,000

Intuition should indicate that this calculation provides a more equitable distribution of production costs. However, some doubts should remain. Because one product requires a two-person crew and the other only one person, it seems that there should be some difference in costs. The two amounts should not be identical.

It appears as if some costs are best distributed on labor and others on press hours. Unfortunately, OBPC believes that it can only use one basis for distributing the costs from a single cost center. The company seems to have imposed one of those artificial constraints mentioned earlier. However, there is no reason why a department cannot have two, independent rates for applying its costs.

Should OBPC choose to take this route, its new budgeted data would look like this:

	Hours	$/Hr	Annual $
Direct labor	6,000	$10	$ 60,000
Overhead costs			$300,000
Press operating hours	4,000		
Press hour–based overhead rate			$ 75

By charging labor directly to the products without attaching any manufacturing overhead cost, OBPC can correct the crew-size problem. By applying the nonlabor overhead to the products based on press hours, OBPC attaches these costs to the products that make the press operations necessary. The resulting new production cost by product is:

	Product A	Product B	Total
Press hours	2,000	2,000	4,000
Crew size	2	1	
Direct labor hours	4,000	2,000	6,000
Cost per labor hour	$ 10	$ 10	
Direct labor cost	$ 40,000	$ 20,000	$ 60,000
Overhead @ $75.00 per press hour	$150,000	$150,000	$300,000
Total production cost	$190,000	$170,000	$360,000

Based upon the set of facts presented, this last method would provide the results most compatible with intuition.

In this case, OBPC used three different methods, all in accordance with GAAP, all acceptable for valuing inventory and cost of goods sold, but all arriving at totally different answers. The results compare as follows:

	Product A	Product B	Total
Direct labor basis	$240,000	$120,000	$360,000
Press hour basis	$180,000	$180,000	$360,000
Two-rate basis	$190,000	$170,000	$360,000

Assuming for the time being that the two-rate basis most accurately reflects the actual cost of manufacturing these two products, what would have happened had management set the price of both products to earn a 20% gross margin using the direct labor basis costs? The following table shows what management would have thought it was doing:

	Product A	Product B
Sales	$300,000	$150,000
Cost w/direct labor basis	$240,000	$120,000
Gross margin	$ 60,000	$ 30,000
% Gross margin	20%	20%

In reality, management would have been quoting the business as follows:

	Product A	Product B
Sales	$300,000	$ 150,000
Cost w/two-rate basis	$190,000	$ 170,000
Gross margin	$110,000	$ (20,000)
% Gross margin	37%	(13)%

Under these circumstances, if the company were bidding to supply its products, it is likely that OBPC would receive the contract to produce Product B, but would be priced too high on Product A. Not only would OBPC lose $20,000 on Product B, but it would continue to incur any fixed costs that had been related to Product A. To top it all off, the company's accounting records would still show that Product B was profitable, because the cost of sales would be calculated as $120,000. (This situation is reminiscent of General Nursery, isn't it?)

Summary

These cases are admittedly oversimplified to make a particular point. The fact remains, however, that situations such as these exist in almost every organization that uses traditional methods of distributing indirect costs to products. The results in product pricing alone can be disastrous.

An equally great concern is that managers in these organizations often believe that costs actually behave the way their cost systems say they do. These managers make day-to-day decisions, whether consciously or subconsciously, based on erroneous cost assumptions. Whether used in evaluating performance, planning future operations, looking for cost reduction opportunities, or addressing any of a myriad of management concerns, the misleading information presented by defective cost systems can lead the intelligent manager to make totally inappropriate decisions.

4

Identifying the Problem
Cost System

How can an organization determine whether its cost system needs to be reviewed and possibly revised? There is no one simple answer to this question, but the following ten characteristics can be used as a guide. If an organization takes a traditional approach to cost accounting and has one or more of the ten characteristics noted, the probability is high that a review of current practices will reveal deficiencies.

   1. **Direct labor operations have been replaced with automated, tape, or computer-controlled equipment since the system was last revised.** As seen in the Plantwide Rate case in Chapter 3, adding equipment that can run without direct labor support can substantially distort the distribution of indirect costs if direct labor continues to be used as the allocation base.

   2. **Indirect costs are becoming a much larger percentage of total costs, or overhead rates have been increasing during recent years.** The trend in recent years is to replace repetitive labor operations with technology. Greater costs are incurred for the technology, but lower labor costs are required. The net result is that higher costs are being allocated on smaller bases.

At one time, it may have been true that indirect costs were actually related to the bases on which they are distributed. However, as the bases get smaller and/or the indirect expenses get larger, the validity of the assumed cause–effect relationship needs to be investigated and corrected if proven to be obsolete.

3. All overhead is applied to cost objectives on the basis of direct labor dollars or hours.   Direct labor remains the primary basis for charging indirect costs to individual products although it frequently has no relationship to the incurrence of those costs. As seen in the One Big Press Corporation case, direct labor can be a totally irrelevant way to distribute indirect costs. It can be the minor factor on which major mischarges of costs occur.

4. Only a few overhead application rates or perhaps only one plantwide rate is in use.   All operations are not created equal. Each has different cost behavior, and different factors influence that behavior. As seen in the Plantwide Rate case, failure to recognize the differences between the plant's various processes can lead to serious misallocations of costs.

5. The organization appears to be competitive on one end of its product line, but not on the other end.   Suppose for a moment that the reason Product A in the One Big Press Corporation case required a two-person crew was because of the part's large size. Product B, being smaller, required only a one-person crew. When prices were developed using the inappropriate direct labor basis for overhead cost application, the large-sized Product A would not have been competitively priced. Conversely, the smaller sized Product B would have been extremely competitive because its cost was substantially understated.

In the same manner, being competitive on certain types of products, but not on others manufactured in the same facility, can often be a sign that costs are being misassigned by the organization's cost system.

6. Operations exist that do not always require the same number of operators.   In the case of One Big Press Corporation, crew-size variability for the operation of its single press was the cause of a significant distortion in product cost under the company's traditional, direct labor–based costing system. The same problem existed even after switching to a press time basis. Such a problem could exist in any organization where heavy equipment, work cells, production lines, and the like are operated by work crews of varying sizes.

7. Many operations are set up, started, and can then run with little or no human intervention.   Many operations have significant cycle times during which only minimal attention is paid to them by the organization's employees. In most cases, it is during this "run time" that the majority of indirect expenses are being incurred. If the distribution of these costs is based not on the process' operation, but rather on its' setup and/or teardown (which would occur if the basis is direct labor), then a serious error in cost distribution will surely occur.

8. There are both "men using machines" and "machines using men" within the facility.   Within most facilities, there are some operations where employees are assisted by equipment in performing an activity over which the employee has control and other operations in which the employee simply acts as a material handler for the equipment, which really does the work. These two situations require different approaches to the distribution of costs. If only one method is used, mischarges will occur.

9. A disproportionate amount of cost is charged to "other" categories or general categories such as "other direct costs" or "supplies."   Organizations that pay little attention to basic categories of cost are unlikely to have a great deal of concern for the appropriateness of the overall design of their cost system. This is not a scientifically proven fact, but an observation that has proven true repeatedly.

10. Accounting personnel spend a great deal of time doing special studies to develop answers to fundamental questions.   If special studies must be performed to determine product/product line profitability, departmental operating costs, savings potential of various management actions, and so on, the cost system is not providing the day-to-day information that management could get from a well-designed cost system.

An organization that has any of the ten characteristics listed would do well to take a critical look at how its cost system is designed. Failure to do so could more than offset the advantages it might have in other areas of its operation. As the second item of the philosophical foundation given in Chapter 1 states, a great management accounting system will not itself make an organization great, but an inadequate and/or misleading system will keep one from becoming great or, worse yet, cause it to fail.

5

Activity-Based Costing

Activity-based costing has been developed as a solution to the problems inherent in using traditional cost accounting methods in a 1990s organization. Because the title is relatively new and its concepts are still evolving, varied definitions have been offered for activity-based costing. Nevertheless, all activity-based costing approaches share certain fundamentals:

> Activity-based costing is a cost accounting concept based on the premise that products require an organization to perform activities and that those activities require an organization to incur costs. In activity-based costing, systems are designed so that any costs that cannot be attributed directly to a product flow into the activities that make them necessary and that the cost of each activity then flows to the product(s) that make the activity necessary based on their respective consumption of that activity.

Product is used here in its broadest sense. It means any good or service that the organization offers for sale. This includes health care services, insurance, bank loans, auto parts, automobiles, consulting services, pizzas, gasoline, movies, hockey games, books on activity-based costing, or any other revenue-generating item. All of these products require that the organization providing them perform certain activities. These activities, in turn, consume resources.

Costs are either directly attributable to a product or attributable to an activity. The steel in an automobile fender is directly attributable to the fender. The salary of the fender plant's director of human resources is attributable to one or more of the plant's activities. In activity-based costing, all costs that cannot be charged directly to a product are charged to the activities that cause those costs to be incurred. The cost of each activity is then charged to the product(s) that make the activity necessary.

The discussion in this book of activity-based costing is from the perspective of a small or mid-sized organization. Thus, the definitions and concepts used here might not be the same as those being written about elsewhere. Most of the current literature is written by academics, consultants from large professional organizations, and financial professionals with large industrial and service firms. The theories and practices they promote are correct for and are usually practical in large organizations. However, the specifics are almost impossible to implement if an organization does not have the time or resources available to hire consultants, form multidisciplinary task forces, and embark on pilot projects. The definitions and concepts used in this chapter to describe activity-based costing are consistent with the approach to implementing abc at the small and mid-sized organization.

Activities

I have used the word *activities* repeatedly during the early chapters of this book, but I have not yet defined it. The ABC and abc definitions of activities are very similar, but not exactly the same.

In ABC, activities are usually defined as *processes or procedures that cause work.* For example, in an accounts payable department, activities might include collecting and filing receiving reports, purchase orders, and invoices; matching invoices, purchase orders, and receiving reports; auditing data on matched documents; following up audit exceptions; entering distribution data on invoices; assembling voucher packages; batching vouchers for data entry; keying information into a computer system; defacing processed documentation; and forwarding voucher documentation to the cash disbursements department. Together, these activities form an *activity center*.

In abc, activities are defined as *groups of related processes or procedures that together meet a particular work need of the organization*. Under this definition, the activities of the accounts payable department would most likely be accounts payable. Period. The large organization's activity center becomes the smaller firm's activity. The reason behind the different definitions is *materiality*. In a large organization, each process or procedure might represent a significant amount of time and cost. At the smaller organization, all the processes and procedures making up the accounts payable activity might not require the time or cost of only one of the processes or procedures considered an activity at the larger firm.

In developing abc at the small and mid-sized organization, the company must constantly keep in mind the third philosophical point: Accuracy is preferable to precision. The company should also recall its corollary: Precision does not imply accuracy. Dividing the organization into smaller and smaller pieces will not necessarily make the cost information more accurate.

The key in defining activities is to divide the organization's operations into its *relevant* activities. As the overall concepts and techniques of abc are better understood, this process becomes much easier.

Cost Objectives

Another important concept in understanding abc is that of *cost objectives*. A cost objective is *an end item for which the accumulation of costs is desired*. A final cost objective accumulates costs for transfer outside of the organization, whereas an interim cost objective accumulates costs for "recycling" within the organization.

Final cost objectives are products or services the firm provides to its customers. In a manufacturing setting, they can be such items as a finished product, a manufacturing process, a customer-owned tool, or an engineering service. The key characteristic of final cost objectives is that they are tangible or intangible assets whose ownership is eventually transferred *outside the organization*, with the objective's accumulated cost usually being matched against revenue.

Interim cost objectives are objectives whose costs are accumulated and then charged elsewhere *within the organization*. There are many examples of interim cost objectives:

o An organization builds a tool that it will own and use to manufacture products for several customers. The cost of this tool is accumulated as an interim cost objective and then capitalized in an asset account as "tooling." This cost is then recycled as tool amortization.

o The maintenance department is used to install a piece of capital equipment. The cost of this installation effort is collected in an interim cost objective and then capitalized as part of the capital asset's cost in a property, plant, and equipment account. This cost is then recycled as depreciation expense.

o Engineering performs a research and development project. The cost is accumulated as an interim cost objective to measure the cost of the research effort, but it is expensed as general and administrative expense on a monthly basis.

The recycling process that takes place with these interim cost objectives is discussed further in Chapter 7.

Cost Drivers

The definition of *cost driver* varies considerably between the ABC approach and the abc approach. In ABC, a cost driver is defined as *the "root cause" of a cost*. According to this definition, there can be scores of different cost drivers in a single facility, most with very narrow definitions. Some examples are:

o Lift-truck travel distance
o Number of material complaint notices
o Number of punches per die

o Material releases issued

o Engineering change notices by part.

As with the definition of activities, materiality plays a big role in the difference between ABC's and abc's definitions of cost driver. Under abc, a cost driver is *a factor used to measure how a cost is incurred and / or how best to charge the cost to activities or products.* Cost drivers are used to reflect the consumption of costs by activities and the consumption of activities by other activities and products. In practice, abc's cost drivers always indicate where to charge costs and often provide part of the formula for determining how much that cost should be. Some of the most common cost drivers used in developing abc systems are:

o The labor group: labor dollars, labor hours, direct labor dollars, direct labor hours, headcount

o The operating time group: cell time, line time, machine time, cycle time

o The throughput group: pieces, gallons, tankerloads, truckloads, tons, and so on

o The occupancy group: square footage, equipment location, equipment valuation

o Demand

o Surrogate cost drivers.

The labor group is the most appropriate cost driver either when some element of labor is determined to be the primary cause of an activity's costs or when changes in labor parallel the changes in the activity's actual cost driver. As a driver of the amount of cost, labor has many uses. Labor dollars often drive the amount of employer FICA and workers' compensation insurance. In some instances, labor hours drive the pension contribution. Direct labor hours (and sometimes dollars) can also drive the consumption of utilities. Headcount often drives health care costs.

As a means of determining where costs should be charged, the labor group also has many uses. Labor dollars or hours usually indicate where fringe benefit costs should be charged. In some cases, direct labor hours or dollars may prove to be the most effective means of charging activity costs to products. Even if another factor, such as machine operating time, is more appropriate, direct labor dollars or hours might still be an effective driver if there is a consistent one-person, one-machine relationship.

The operating time group is the most appropriate cost driver when the operation of individual pieces of equipment or several pieces of equipment organized into an operating group proves to be the primary cause of an activity's costs. As a driver of the amount of cost, operating time often has a direct bearing on the utilities, operating supplies, or indirect materials consumed. As a means of determining where cost should be charged, operating time is probably the most frequently used alternative to direct labor. Operating time drivers can be further divided into two subgroups: machine hour/cycle time and line/cell time. Chapter 8 covers these two subgroups in detail and discusses the situations in which each is most appropriate.

The throughput group is the most appropriate cost driver when units of throughput are determined to be the primary cause of an activity's costs. Although drivers in the first two groups often appear in traditional cost systems (although not always in the appropriate form or in the correct places), drivers in the throughput group are seldom used.

Accountants traditionally view costs as varying as labor or operating times vary. This assumption is not always accurate. The cost of operating a drill press might vary based on the amount of time it runs, but the drills themselves will more likely vary based on the number of holes drilled. When material, this fact must be taken into account in an activity-based system.

In many situations, throughput units provide the most appropriate cost driver. In a chemical company, for example, the entire production of a particular chemical might take place in one large batch. This batch, however, might be packaged in tankerloads, 55-gallon drums, and one-gallon cartons. Each packaging process can be established as a separate activity with the units of throughput (tankerloads, drums, and cartons) selected as drivers. Because the chemical was produced in a single batch, the production cost of each unit of chemical is the same. The cost difference results from the packaging. The arrangement described allows for cost differentials based solely on the differences in the cost of varied packaging.

The occupancy group is the most appropriate cost driver for distributing fixed costs based on the physical location of activities or assets. For example, building depreciation, real property taxes, exterior maintenance, or guard service can be distributed based on square footage occupied by each activity. Equipment depreciation, maintenance agreements, personal property taxes, or lease costs can be distributed based on the activity in which the asset is located.

Occupancy group drivers seldom serve as a basis for determining how much cost is to be incurred, but they are often appropriate for where-to distributions.

Demand is the most appropriate driver when the distribution of an activity's costs can be either to other activities or to cost objectives based on their "demand" for that activity's services.

Maintenance is one of the most common of the demand-driven activities. Maintenance costs should be distributed to those activities and other cost objectives that require its services. Only by using estimated or actual demand can an accurate distribution of these costs be obtained. Demand-based cost distributions are discussed in greater detail in Chapters 7 and 8. Like occupancy group drivers, demand seldom serves as a basis for determining how much cost is to be incurred, but it is often appropriate for where-to distributions.

Surrogate cost drivers are practical and readily available measures used to distribute costs to other activities or cost objectives when it is impractical to collect and maintain data relative to the activity's most theoretically correct cost driver. Selecting appropriate cost drivers for most activities is not difficult once the concept is understood. For some activities, however, either the cost driver is not very easy to measure or the activity involved is not material enough to warrant a unique cost driver. Production control, material handling, accounting, general management, and marketing often fall into this category.

Examples of surrogate drivers are material cost, total cost input, and conversion costs. Conversion costs, one of the most useful surrogate drivers in a small or mid-sized organization's abc system, are discussed in detail in Chapter 8.

Cost Centers

In discussing abc, cost centers are the lowest level of detail for which costs are accumulated and distributed. They can comprise a single activity or a group of activities. Keeping in mind the desire for accuracy, not precision, many activities can be grouped together to keep detail record keeping and data analysis to a minimum while gaining the greatest practical degree of accuracy. The process of combining activities into cost centers is described in Chapter 6.

Summary

With these four concepts—activities, cost objectives, cost drivers, and cost centers—an abc system can be described as one that (1) groups an organization's activities into cost centers; (2) accumulates costs not directly related to cost objectives in the cost centers using the appropriate cost drivers; and then (3) distributes the accumulated costs of each cost center to cost objectives or other cost centers, again using the appropriate cost drivers. The method of putting such a system together is described in the chapters that follow.

Part II

———

Developing an Activity-Based Cost System

6

Steps to Establishing an Activity-Based Cost System

Once an organization has established the need to improve the quality of its cost information system and determined that an activity-based approach is the most appropriate means of attaining that end, the company must take the necessary steps to put an effective abc system into place. These steps can be summarized as follows:

1. Identify and define relevant activities.
2. Organize activities by cost center.
3. Identify major elements of cost.
4. Determine relationships between activities and costs.
5. Identify cost drivers to assign costs to activities and activities to products.
6. Establish the cost flow pattern.
7. Select the appropriate tools for effecting the cost flow pattern.
8. Plan the cost accumulation model.
9. Gather the necessary data to drive the cost accumulation model.

10. Establish the cost accumulation model to simulate the organization's cost structure and flow and to develop costing rates.

In developing the abc system, an organization cannot simply go through these steps once and have its answer. Developing any system is an iterative process, and the abc system is no exception. By the time the tenth step is reached, information will have been gathered to change the system developer's mind about decisions made at earlier steps. Once those decisions are changed and their impact carried through to later steps, other information might require that the process be repeated again. This iterative process should not be looked at as wasted time; on the contrary, it is a process necessary to reach the most appropriate system design.

As a result of the process' iterative nature, discussion of the steps sometimes refers to information gathered from or decisions made at a later step. For example, in organizing activities by cost center (Step 2), mention will be made of activities having the same cost drivers (determined in Step 5) and similar overhead application rates (not known until Step 8). Sometimes the system developers' experience and intuition provide enough information so that Steps 5 and 8 merely confirm what they already know. In other cases, it may not be possible to finalize the Step 2 decision until drivers and rates for the individual activities have been established.

The balance of this chapter discusses the first five steps. Steps 6 through 9 are treated in Chapters 7 through 10, respectively, and Step 10 is covered thoroughly in Chapters 11 through 14.

Step 1. Identify and Define Relevant Activities

Activities in abc are usually considered activity centers in ABC. Where ABC would probably consider processing requisitions, soliciting quotations, evaluating quotations, negotiating long-term purchase agreements, placing purchase orders, issuing releases against blanket purchase orders, and performing vendor performance reviews to be individual activities that are part of an activity center known as Purchasing, abc treats the entire purchasing function as an activity.

When beginning to develop a list of activities, it is better to identify too many than too few. It is always possible to combine activities later if that proves to be the more appropriate move.

An organization's activities can be identified by reviewing organization charts and facility layouts, as well as by interviewing the organization's personnel to determine what it is they "do for a living." Without a great deal of effort, a system designer can develop a listing similar to the one provided below. Although each detailed action taking place within the facility need not appear, any function performed by an employee, a contractor, or a piece of equipment should fall into one of the activities identified by the organization.

Acid clean	Machine repair
Assembly	Machining
Building maintenance	Manufacturing engineering
CNC machine	Material handling
Coating	Packaging
Cost accounting	Paint
Cutoff	Plant management
Data processing	Polishing
Deburr	Production control
Design engineering	Program management
Die repair	Purchasing
Drilling	Quality assurance
Electrical repair	Receiving
Exterior maintenance	Sales administration
Extrusion	Shear
First aid	Shipping
General accounting	Shot blast
General management	Tool build
Guard service	Tool crib
Human resources	Tool refurbish
Industrial engineering	Tool repair
Inspection	Welding
Janitorial	X-ray
Laboratory	Zyglo

Step 2. Organize Activities by Cost Center

Once the activities have been identified and defined, they should be organized into a series of cost centers. The list that follows provides a suggested grouping of the activities listed above. A variety of factors need to be taken into account when making these combinations. Some are obvious, some not so obvious.

In all instances, the *materiality* of each activity should be kept in mind—not only its current level of materiality, but its future materiality based on the organization's plans. If the organization has only one welding station, it may be best to combine it with other related operations into an Assembly cost center. On the other hand, if the organization is planning to purchase more welding equipment in the future, it might be wise to leave Welding as a separate cost center.

Cost profile is another factor to consider. In its simplest sense, an activity's cost profile consists of its primary cost driver(s) and application rate(s). Two activities with direct labor as a driver and rates of $85 per hour and $92 per hour, respectively, might best be combined into one cost center with a rate of $88.50 even if no operating relationship exists between the two. On the other hand, a single piece of CNC equipment might be treated as a cost center if it is the only activity with machine hours as its cost driver.

If an identified activity has a unique cost profile, it is often preferable to leave it as a separate cost center even if it is otherwise immaterial. On the other hand, it may be advantageous to combine two unrelated activities into a cost center if their cost profiles are similar and there is no other need to keep them separate.

Major Activities	Cost Center Assignment
Cost accounting	Accounting/Info Systems
Data processing	Accounting/Info Systems
General accounting	Accounting/Info Systems
Assembly	Assembly
Acid clean	Cleaning
Shot blast	Cleaning
CNC machine	CNC Machine

Major Activities	Cost Center Assignment
Design engineering	Engineering
Industrial engineering	Engineering
Manufacturing engineering	Engineering
Extrusion	Extrusion
Deburr	Finishing
Polishing	Finishing
X-ray	Finishing
Paint	Finishing
Guard service	General Factory Overhead
Janitorial	General Factory Overhead
Plant management	General Factory Overhead
First aid	General/Administration
General management	General/Administration
Human resources	General/Administration
Program management	General/Administration
Drilling	Machining
Machining	Machining
Building maintenance	Maintenance
Electrical repair	Maintenance
Exterior maintenance	Maintenance
Machine repair	Maintenance
Material handling	Material Burden
Packaging	Material Burden
Receiving	Material Burden
Shipping	Material Burden
Production control	Material Management
Purchasing	Material Management
Coating	Material Prep
Cutoff	Material Prep
Shear	Material Prep
Inspection	Quality Control
Laboratory	Quality Control
Quality assurance	Quality Control
Zyglo	Quality Control
Sales administration	Sales
Die repair	Tool Room
Tool build	Tool Room

Major Activities	Cost Center Assignment
Tool crib	Tool Room
Tool refurbish	Tool Room
Tool repair	Tool Room
Welding	Welding

In our example, the activities cost accounting and general accounting were grouped with data processing into one cost center, Accounting/Information Systems. In this case, materiality made the difference. If one or all of these activities were material, it may have been more appropriate to treat each separately. This is especially true of Data Processing. If this function's cost is material and management's desire is to charge the user cost centers for its services, it would then be necessary to treat the activity as a separate service center, a concept discussed in greater detail in Chapter 7.

The collection into a cost center of deburr, polishing, X-ray, and paint is a curious combination of activities. In an operating sense, the activities have little to do with each other. From a cost system perspective, however, they have some common characteristics. In this case, all of the activities came toward the end of the production process, direct labor was identified as the driver for all of them, and the total cost of each activity was not material when viewed against the organization's overall costs. As a result, this group of seemingly unrelated activities made a logical cost center, and was given the title Finishing.

Similar types of characteristics were considered in all the other groupings in the example. Had the specifics of the situation been different, the activities could have been grouped differently.

Step 3. Identify Major Elements of Cost

Elements of cost can be viewed as the line items on a budget or as accounts included in the expense ledger. In this situation, only the indirect cost elements are considered. Direct materials, direct purchased parts, direct outside services, and similar direct costs are not included because they can be assigned directly to products without doing a cost flow analysis.

In most cases, it is necessary to identify more elements of cost than has been the practice in the organization's day-to-day accounting. This is necessary because two of the objectives are to forecast each cost's amount and to appropriately distribute each cost to cost centers. For example, the accounting records might contain an account titled Property Taxes. For purposes of abc, however, real property taxes and personal property taxes require different bases for distribution to cost centers. Real property taxes are often distributed on the basis of each cost center's square footage occupied, whereas personal property taxes might be distributed on the basis of the appraised value of fixed assets, or a combination of asset appraisal value and a factor to account for inventory investment.

Other areas where a breakout of cost elements from those used in day-to-day accounting is often required are:

○ Utility costs—Electric, gas, water, and so on, must often be treated separately if the consumption and distribution of these costs is to be handled correctly.

○ Supplies—Certain major supplies may be attributable to only a few cost centers and should be handled individually.

○ Fringe benefits—Some costs are driven by headcount, some by gross payroll, some by hours worked, and some by other bases.

The following is a listing of possible cost elements for the organization whose activities and cost centers were listed earlier:

Salary and wage cost elements
    Salaries
    Hourly wages
    Overtime premium
    Shift premium
    Vacation pay
    Holiday pay
    Paid breaks
Fringe benefit cost elements
    Group health insurance
    Workers' compensation insurance

State unemployment tax
Federal unemployment tax
Employer portion of FICA
Pension contribution
Disability insurance
Fixed cost elements
Building depreciation
Equipment depreciation
Leases and rentals
Real property taxes
Personal property taxes
Insurance
Variable operating cost elements
Utilities
Electricity
Gas
Water
Supplies
Argon
Drills and cutters
Chemicals
Other
Discretionary/budgeted cost elements
Travel/entertainment
Professional services
Legal and accounting
Telephone
Dues and subscriptions
Advertising/marketing.

Step 4. Determine Relationships among Activities and Costs

Once activities have been identified and organized into cost centers and the major elements of cost have been established, the relationships among activities and costs must be determined. This step consists primarily in determining which costs pertain to which cost centers. Using the cost centers and elements of cost listed earlier, a list of cost–cost center relationships would include items such as the following:

Cost	Cost Center(s)
Drills and cutters	CNC Machining Machining Material Prep (Cutoff/Shear) Tool Room
Chemicals	Cleaning (Acid Cleaning) Quality Control (Zyglo) Material Prep (Coating)
Electricity (power)	CNC Machine Extrusion Machining Material Prep (Cutoff/Shear) Welding

Step 5. Identify Cost Drivers to Assign Costs to Activities and Activities to Products

Once the general relationships have been determined in Step 4, the particular drivers that cause the costs to be incurred in specific cost centers need to be identified. In the case of building depreciation, the square footage occupied by each cost center might be used to distribute the amount of cost. For equipment, location or cost center "ownership" of the assets might be the basis. In the case of direct production cost centers (those that perform processes that change the product), the driver chosen to assign the cost center's cost to the product is usually, but not always, the same one that will be used to bring cost elements into the cost center.

For example, Step 4 shows that electricity consumed in the production process (vs. that used for temperature control and lighting) is attributable primarily to the following cost centers: CNC Machine, Extrusion, Machining, Material Prep (Cutoff/ Shear), and Welding.

Machining, Material Prep, and Welding are all cost centers in which an employee uses a single piece of equipment in processing the product. These are cost centers where "men are using machines." The driver for distributing costs from these cost centers will most likely remain the perenniel favorite—direct labor.

CNC Machining, on the other hand, has almost no direct labor involvement. It is a cost center where "machines are using men." A part is secured on the machine center's table, and the machine then runs, unattended, following commands from a computer program until the part is complete. The most likely driver for this cost center will be machine hours.

Neither direct labor nor machine hours seems to fit the cost center Extrusion. The extrusion process takes place in a manufacturing "cell," where several operations always take place before the part is extruded and other operations always take place after extruding. It is not a process completed in isolation, as is CNC Machining. As a result, *cell time*, a concept discussed more completely in Chapter 8, is the most likely driver.

With these drivers identified, one can see whether they would be appropriate for determining the consumption of electrical costs. Will the amount of direct labor affect the consumption of electricity in Machining, Material Prep, and Welding? Because there are one-to-one man-to-machine relationships in these cost centers and the incurrence of direct labor cost means the operation of the equipment, the answer is yes. Will the machine time affect the consumption of electricity in CNC Machining? Machine time indicates that the machine is operating, a condition that requires the consumption of electricity. As a result, the answer to this question would also be yes. Finally, does cell time affect the consumption of electricity in Extrusion? For the same reason as in the case of machine time, the answer is yes. The resulting cost center–driver combinations for the cost element electricity (power) can be summarized as follows:

Cost Center	Driver
CNC Machine	Machine hours
Extrusion	Cell time
Machining	Direct labor hours
Material Prep	Direct labor hours
Welding	Direct labor hours

Similar analyses should be performed for every major element of cost identified in Step 3.

It should be noted that the driver for costs included as discretionary/budgeted cost elements in the example is normally management's discretion. These costs are usually directly assignable to a particular cost center, often one that contains administrative or support activities. As a result, in-depth analyses of drivers for this category is not usually necessary.

Having established the cost centers, cost elements, and drivers that cause the cost elements to occur in the cost centers, the next step is to establish a logical cost flow for directing the costs, through the cost centers, to the cost objectives.

7

Establishing the Cost Flow Pattern

The sixth step in setting up an abc system is to establish an effective cost flow pattern. A well-designed cost flow pattern is critical to the effectiveness of any small or mid-sized organization's activity-based costing system. The technique described in this chapter for developing a sound cost flow pattern requires an understanding of several concepts and the acceptance of certain conventions.

Categories of Indirect Costs

All costs subject to the cost flow analysis (in this case, including all labor, whether considered direct or indirect, and other indirect costs) fall into one of three categories: salaries and wages, fringe benefits, or specific assignment costs.

Salaries and wages include all of the organization's gross payroll costs. These include all direct and indirect labor, salaries, overtime and shift premiums, bonuses, and time paid for not working, such as vacation pay, holiday pay, sick pay, and paid breaks.

Fringe benefits include all employee benefits not paid through payroll. These are sometimes referred to as purchased benefits to differentiate them from the time-paid-for-not-working benefits that are categorized as salaries and wages for cost flow purposes.

Fringe benefits include items such as health insurance, workers' compensation insurance, state and federal unemployment taxes, the employer portion of FICA, pension contributions, disability insurance, and employee assistance programs.

Specific assignment costs include all indirect operating costs not included as salaries and wages or fringe benefits. Their name is derived from the fact that each of these costs must be assigned to a specific cost center. Assignment to cost centers takes place through a variety of methods, depending of the type of cost element involved and its driver(s). Examples mentioned earlier include building depreciation and real property taxes assigned to cost centers based on square footage occupied, equipment depreciation distributed according to asset location, and personal property taxes assigned by equipment appraisal value.

Cost assignments for consumables (e.g., supplies, utilities) can be based on actual historical consumption statistics or best estimates. If utilities have not been distributed to cost centers through metered usage, data analysis and interviews can develop consumption estimates for cost center assignment using the driver identifications developed in Step 5. If supplies have not been charged to requisitioning cost centers, data analysis and interviews can again be used to provide a means of using driver information to estimate consumption and assign the costs to cost centers. The goal is to use the best information available to determine the proper amount for each cost element and to have that cost element distributed to the individual cost centers that make that cost element necessary.

One rule to remember is that 99 times out of 100, an imprecise estimate using some logical basis is better than a general distribution using an irrelevant, but available basis. For example, it is better to estimate in what proportions electricity is consumed than to distribute it on an irrelevant basis, such as square footage or direct labor.

Categories of Cost Centers

The first attempt at developing a cost flow pattern should divide cost centers into four categories: service centers, operations support activities, administrative support activities, and operating activities.

Service centers are businesses within the business. The services performed by these cost centers are usually performed for other cost centers, for parties outside of the organization, or for other specific projects on an as-needed basis. As a result, they could be (but not necessarily are) billed to user cost centers or objectives on a time-and-materials basis. Typical of this type of cost center are Maintenance, Tooling, Engineering, and CNC Programming. When its cost is substantial, Data Processing can also be considered in this category.

Maintenance does repair and maintenance work for specific pieces of equipment or particular cost centers, helps to install capital equipment, and performs other services for specific cost objectives. Tooling repairs and refurbishes specific tools for specific products and/or departments and it builds tools for internal use or for sale outside of the organization. Engineering works on specific engineering projects, bid and proposal work, and research and development projects, and it supports other organizational activities. CNC Programming develops and maintains programs for use in manufacturing specific tools and/or products, a function quite similar to tooling activities, except the tool is software.

For each of these cost centers, the key is that the majority of their services are performed for specific purposes based on demand for those services. Of the cost centers listed in Chapter 6, Engineering, Maintenance, and Tool Room would most likely be service centers.

Operations support activities are those cost centers whose activities support the direct operations activities, but whose services are not, like service centers, easily chargeable to specific products, services, or cost centers. Cost centers such as Purchasing, Production Control, Materials Management, Quality Assurance, General Factory Supervision, Shipping and Receiving, and Material Handling often are included in this category. All these activities support operations, but it is either impossible or impractical to measure the time and materials spent on specific activities. For example, when Production Control is preparing the production schedule, it is scheduling all products over the entire facility for a period of time. It might be possible, but not very practical, to charge that scheduling time to individual products or cost centers.

Some cost centers can be considered either operations support centers or operating centers (see discussion of operating activities later in this chapter). The key to deciding which they should be is often materiality and sometimes practicality. Receiving is a good example. Theoretically, the receiving function's costs should be assigned to items received and processed. This would include raw materials, purchased parts, supplies, work-in-process being returned from outside processors, and capital equipment. As a result, receiving could most properly be considered an operating center. Unfortunately, the characteristics of the items received vary so much that a straightforward, practical, and theoretically correct method of assigning costs to the items received is rarely found. In cases such as this, receiving should be treated as an operations support activity.

If, however, the cost of operating the receiving function is material and a practical, appropriate basis can be found for assigning cost directly to the product, it can be handled as an operating center. For example, in a major stamping facility, a large, mechanized receiving function may exist solely to receive and process steel coils. In such a case, it may be practical to charge the cost of receiving to each coil of steel based on pounds of steel received. If so, the receiving function should be treated as an operating activity.

Of the cost centers listed in Chapter 6, those most properly included as operations support activities are General Factory Overhead, Material Burden, Material Management, and Quality Control.

Administrative support activities are those involved in the overall management and administration of the organization. This category would normally include activities such as general management, accounting and finance, human resources, data processing, contract/sales administration, marketing, and sales.

Care must be taken if any of these activities are material. We have already mentioned that data processing could, under certain circumstances, be treated as a service center. Similarly, a large human resources department could be considered a special type of service center whose demand is measured by the location of employees throughout the organization. Likewise, if the sales effort is distributed unequally between the organization's product lines, it may be preferable to treat the sales function as an operating activity whose costs are charged only to the products it sells.

Of the cost centers in Chapter 6, those most likely to meet the criteria of administrative support activities are General/Administration, Accounting/Info Systems, and Sales.

Operating activities are made up of those non–service center activities directly processing the organization's products or providing its services. These usually include the organization's traditional direct departments, but often include other activities whose costs can be assigned directly to products or services. Sales was mentioned earlier, as was receiving. Shipping, packaging, contract administration, and quality control are other activities that could, under certain circumstances, be considered operating activities.

Cost centers from Chapter 6 that are most likely to be considered operating activities are Assembly, Cleaning, CNC Machine, Extrusion, Finishing, Machining, Material Prep, and Welding.

The Seven-Level Cost Flow-Down Diagram

Once costs and cost centers have been categorized, it is possible to begin designing the cost flow pattern. One helpful way to visualize the process is through the use of a cost flow-down diagram. For this diagram, the three cost categories and four cost center categories are set out as seven distinct levels, as shown in Exhibit 7.1. Also included on the diagram are the cost objectives (those end items for which the system is designed to accumulate costs), direct material, direct outside processing, and customers. The purpose of this cost flow diagram is twofold: to serve as a means of visualizing the cost flows as the system is under development and to serve as documentation of the final cost flow pattern when the system is completed.

Although it is advisable to begin the diagram with seven levels, it may be necessary to add levels as the system's design evolves. For example, if a company decides to treat the human resources activity as a high-level service center and distribute its costs based on headcount, a level can be added between current Levels III and IV to accommodate this change. Thus, human resources will

Exhibit 7.1   Cost Flow-Down Diagram/Step #1

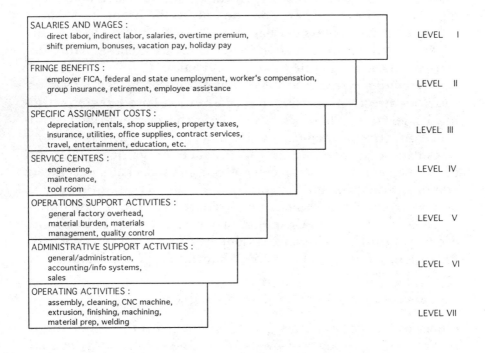

SALARIES AND WAGES :
   direct labor, indirect labor, salaries, overtime premium,
   shift premium, bonuses, vacation pay, holiday pay   LEVEL   I

FRINGE BENEFITS :
   employer FICA, federal and state unemployment, worker's compensation,
   group insurance, retirement, employee assistance   LEVEL   II

SPECIFIC ASSIGNMENT COSTS :
   depreciation, rentals, shop supplies, property taxes,
   insurance, utilities, office supplies, contract services,   LEVEL   III
   travel, entertainment, education, etc.

SERVICE CENTERS :
   engineering,
   maintenance,   LEVEL   IV
   tool room

OPERATIONS SUPPORT ACTIVITIES :
   general factory overhead,
   material burden, materials   LEVEL   V
   management, quality control

ADMINISTRATIVE SUPPORT ACTIVITIES :
   general/administration,
   accounting/info systems,   LEVEL   VI
   sales

OPERATING ACTIVITIES :
   assembly, cleaning, CNC machine,
   extrusion, finishing, machining,   LEVEL VII
   material prep, welding

COST OBJECTIVES

INTERNAL :
   capital project, expense project, tooling expense, prototype expense
EXTERNAL :
   finished production part, tool, prototype part

DIRECT MATERIALS :
   raw material cost,
   purchased parts,
   incoming freight

DIRECT OUTSIDE SERVICES :
   cost of service,
   outbound freight,
   incoming freight

CUSTOMER :

   cost of goods sold

be shown on the diagram above all activities having employees (headcounts), and its costs can visually "flow down" to the other activities.

It should be noted that the first three levels are the three cost categories. Only in these levels are costs incurred. Levels IV through VII represent the cost centers into which the organization's activities have been grouped (see Exhibit 7.2). From the first level down, costs are distributed down the diagram to the cost objectives. Sometimes this distribution is directly to the cost objective. At other times, costs flow down through interim levels until they reach a level at which they can be charged to the cost objective.

Once the components of the cost flow-down diagram have been established, the job of developing the cost flow begins. The first and simplest components to handle are the two direct categories: direct materials/purchased parts and direct outside services. As shown in Exhibit 7.3, these two components flow directly to the cost objective together with any incoming freight and, if it exists for outside services, any outgoing freight.

With this cost flow completed, the flow-down of direct and indirect costs can begin.

Level I—Salaries and Wages   Cost flow-down will be developed on a level-by-level basis. Level I costs, salaries and wages, can flow to any level where labor takes place. Another way to express the flow-down of salaries and wages is that they can flow to any level to which gross payroll can be charged in the payroll distribution.

The first such level is Level II, fringe benefits. When an employee is paid for not working, such as during holidays, vacations, illnesses, paid breaks, bereavement, and so forth, his or her gross pay becomes a fringe benefit. As a result, these Level I costs flow down to Level II. This flow can be seen by the first flow-down arrow on Exhibit 7.4.

The definition of Level III costs precludes the flow-down of any salaries and wages. Level III costs comprise non-payroll or non–fringe benefit indirect costs that can be charged directly to cost centers. For this reason, Exhibit 7.4 shows Level I costs bypassing Level III.

Levels IV through VII represent cost centers. Employees can work in an indirect capacity in any of these cost centers. As a

Exhibit 7.2   Cost Flow-Down Diagram/Costs vs. Activities

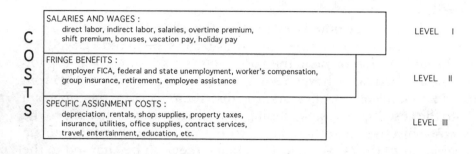

```
        SALARIES AND WAGES :
C           direct labor, indirect labor, salaries, overtime premium,        LEVEL    I
            shift premium, bonuses, vacation pay, holiday pay
O
S       FRINGE BENEFITS :
            employer FICA, federal and state unemployment, worker's compensation,
T           group insurance, retirement, employee assistance                 LEVEL    II
S
        SPECIFIC ASSIGNMENT COSTS :
            depreciation, rentals, shop supplies, property taxes,
            insurance, utilities, office supplies, contract services,         LEVEL  III
            travel, entertainment, education, etc.
```

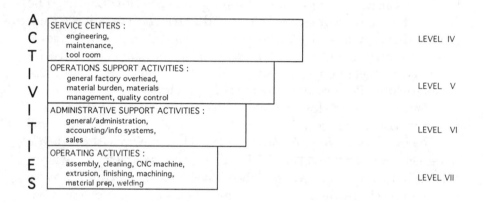

```
A
C       SERVICE CENTERS :
T           engineering,                                                      LEVEL  IV
            maintenance,
I           tool room
V
I       OPERATIONS SUPPORT ACTIVITIES :
            general factory overhead,
T           material burden, materials                                        LEVEL   V
I           management, quality control
E       ADMINISTRATIVE SUPPORT ACTIVITIES :
S           general/administration,
            accounting/info systems,                                          LEVEL  VI
            sales

        OPERATING ACTIVITIES :
            assembly, cleaning, CNC machine,
            extrusion, finishing, machining,                                  LEVEL VII
            material prep, welding
```

Exhibit 7.3   Cost Flow-Down Diagram/Step #2

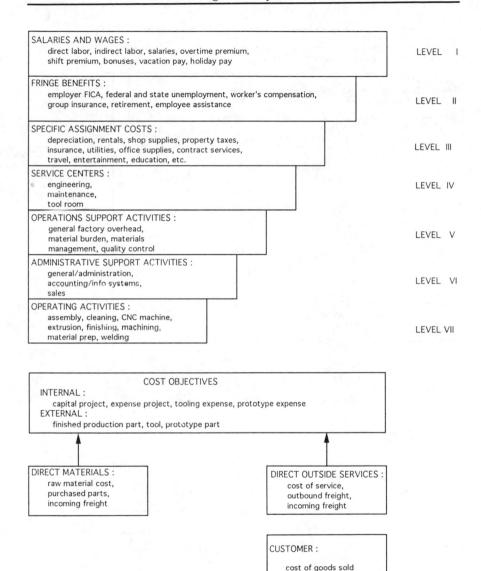

Exhibit 7.4   Cost Flow-Down Diagram/Step #3

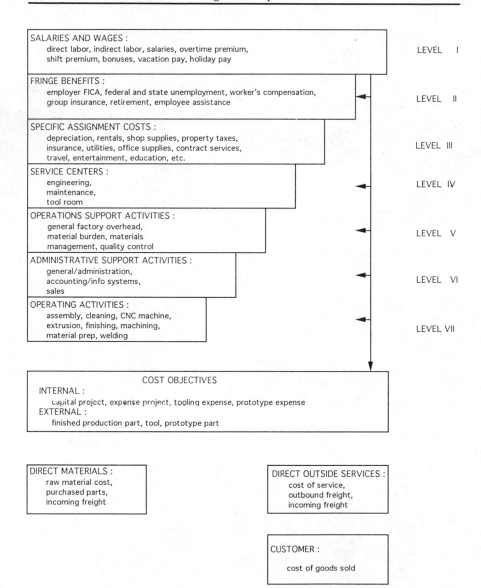

SALARIES AND WAGES :
    direct labor, indirect labor, salaries, overtime premium,
    shift premium, bonuses, vacation pay, holiday pay

LEVEL   I

FRINGE BENEFITS :
    employer FICA, federal and state unemployment, worker's compensation,
    group insurance, retirement, employee assistance

LEVEL   II

SPECIFIC ASSIGNMENT COSTS :
    depreciation, rentals, shop supplies, property taxes,
    insurance, utilities, office supplies, contract services,
    travel, entertainment, education, etc.

LEVEL III

SERVICE CENTERS :
    engineering,
    maintenance,
    tool room

LEVEL IV

OPERATIONS SUPPORT ACTIVITIES :
    general factory overhead,
    material burden, materials
    management, quality control

LEVEL V

ADMINISTRATIVE SUPPORT ACTIVITIES :
    general/administration,
    accounting/info systems,
    sales

LEVEL VI

OPERATING ACTIVITIES :
    assembly, cleaning, CNC machine,
    extrusion, finishing, machining,
    material prep, welding

LEVEL VII

COST OBJECTIVES
INTERNAL :
    capital project, expense project, tooling expense, prototype expense
EXTERNAL :
    finished production part, tool, prototype part

DIRECT MATERIALS :
    raw material cost,
    purchased parts,
    incoming freight

DIRECT OUTSIDE SERVICES :
    cost of service,
    outbound freight,
    incoming freight

CUSTOMER :

    cost of goods sold

result, Level I cost can flow to any of these levels, as shown in Exhibit 7.4.

Level I costs also can flow to the cost objective itself. If the wages are paid for activities defined in the system as direct labor, these costs should flow directly to the cost objective. This can be seen by the final arrow in Exhibit 7.4.

It should be noted that labor attributable to service center personnel is *usually* treated as indirect and flows to the service center itself even if, as is often the case, these employees are working directly on a cost objective. The flow-down of their costs to the cost objective then comes through the flow-down of their service center's costs. This is especially true in service centers such as Engineering and CNC Programming, in which a majority of the employees are salaried. Because the effective hourly rate of salaried employees varies with the number of hours they work, charging their efforts directly to cost objectives is impractical. As a result, they are charged as part of their service center's billing rate.

In cases where all work performed by the service center is done by hourly employees, some system designers prefer to charge their labor directly to the cost objective and use the service center as a traditional overhead pool that adds its cost to the employees' direct charge through an overhead cost per hour or a percentage of the direct labor cost.

Level II—Fringe Benefits   Fringe benefits follow employees. Wherever an employee's payroll cost goes, his or her fringe benefit cost should follow. As a result, the flow-down of Level II costs mirrors the flow-down of Level I costs from Level IV down to the final cost objective. This flow-down is shown in Exhibit 7.5.

In Exhibit 7.5, fringe benefits are shown flowing down directly to the cost objective. Another method is often used, however, in the flow-down of direct labor fringe benefits to the cost objective. Instead of a flow-down directly to the cost objective, this alternative calls for a flow-down of these benefits into the Level VII operating activity in which the direct labor is taking place. For example, the fringe benefits of an assembler, who is working directly on a cost objective (a product), can be included in the assembly department's cost center. In this manner, these direct labor fringe benefits are added to the operating activity's rate and reach the cost objective along with the other Level VII costs.

Exhibit 7.5   Cost Flow-Down Diagram/Step #4

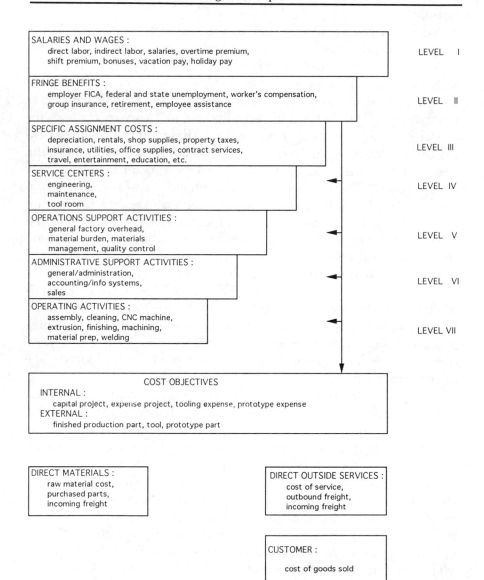

SALARIES AND WAGES :
   direct labor, indirect labor, salaries, overtime premium,
   shift premium, bonuses, vacation pay, holiday pay
                                                                    LEVEL   I

FRINGE BENEFITS :
   employer FICA, federal and state unemployment, worker's compensation,
   group insurance, retirement, employee assistance
                                                                    LEVEL   II

SPECIFIC ASSIGNMENT COSTS :
   depreciation, rentals, shop supplies, property taxes,
   insurance, utilities, office supplies, contract services,
   travel, entertainment, education, etc.
                                                                    LEVEL   III

SERVICE CENTERS :
   engineering,
   maintenance,
   tool room
                                                                    LEVEL   IV

OPERATIONS SUPPORT ACTIVITIES :
   general factory overhead,
   material burden, materials
   management, quality control
                                                                    LEVEL   V

ADMINISTRATIVE SUPPORT ACTIVITIES :
   general/administration,
   accounting/info systems,
   sales
                                                                    LEVEL   VI

OPERATING ACTIVITIES :
   assembly, cleaning, CNC machine,
   extrusion, finishing, machining,
   material prep, welding
                                                                    LEVEL VII

COST OBJECTIVES
INTERNAL :
   capital project, expense project, tooling expense, prototype expense
EXTERNAL :
   finished production part, tool, prototype part

DIRECT MATERIALS :
   raw material cost,
   purchased parts,
   incoming freight

DIRECT OUTSIDE SERVICES :
   cost of service,
   outbound freight,
   incoming freight

CUSTOMER :

   cost of goods sold

Level III—Specific Assignment Costs   Specific assignment costs, by definition, flow directly into the cost centers, which have been grouped into Levels IV through VII. These costs cannot be charged directly to the cost objective. If they could, they would be direct costs and not included in the flow-down of indirect costs. This flow-down is shown in Exhibit 7.6.

Level IV—Service Centers   As discussed earlier, service centers are "businesses within the business" that can charge their costs to the cost centers, customers, or projects that demand their services. As a result, Level V costs can flow down to any lower level or to the cost objective itself. This flow-down is shown in Exhibit 7.7.

One problem in the flow of service center costs that does not occur at other levels is that it is possible for service centers to demand each other's services. Maintenance may need to perform work in Engineering. Engineering may have to provide support for the Tool Room. Without a simple solution to this problem of transactions between service centers, the flow-down of costs could turn into a mathematical nightmare.

One solution would be to use simultaneous equations to calculate the impact of the service center cross-charges. A simpler solution would be to establish a flow-down hierarchy within the group of service centers so that costs could flow in only one direction.

In Exhibit 7.7, three cost centers are categorized as service centers: Engineering, Maintenance, and the Tool Room. To determine the hierarchy that will most effectively flow down costs through the service centers, the system designer must first estimate the annual hours that each service center would spend providing services for the others. These estimates can then be set into a matrix as follows:

	Charged To			
Charged From	Engineering	Maintenance	Tool Room	Total
Engineering	—	100	500	600
Maintenance	300	—	1,000	1,300
Tool Room	50	100	—	150
Total				2,050

Exhibit 7.6   Cost Flow-Down Diagram/Step #5

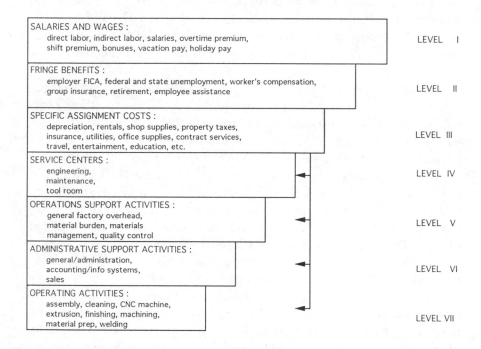

SALARIES AND WAGES :
    direct labor, indirect labor, salaries, overtime premium,
    shift premium, bonuses, vacation pay, holiday pay
        LEVEL   I

FRINGE BENEFITS :
    employer FICA, federal and state unemployment, worker's compensation,
    group insurance, retirement, employee assistance
        LEVEL   II

SPECIFIC ASSIGNMENT COSTS :
    depreciation, rentals, shop supplies, property taxes,
    insurance, utilities, office supplies, contract services,
    travel, entertainment, education, etc.
        LEVEL III

SERVICE CENTERS :
    engineering,
    maintenance,
    tool room
        LEVEL IV

OPERATIONS SUPPORT ACTIVITIES :
    general factory overhead,
    material burden, materials
    management, quality control
        LEVEL V

ADMINISTRATIVE SUPPORT ACTIVITIES :
    general/administration,
    accounting/info systems,
    sales
        LEVEL VI

OPERATING ACTIVITIES :
    assembly, cleaning, CNC machine,
    extrusion, finishing, machining,
    material prep, welding
        LEVEL VII

COST OBJECTIVES
INTERNAL :
    capital project, expense project, tooling expense, prototype expense
EXTERNAL :
    finished production part, tool, prototype part

DIRECT MATERIALS :
    raw material cost,
    purchased parts,
    incoming freight

DIRECT OUTSIDE SERVICES :
    cost of service,
    outbound freight,
    incoming freight

CUSTOMER :
    cost of goods sold

Exhibit 7.7   Cost Flow-Down Diagram/Step #6

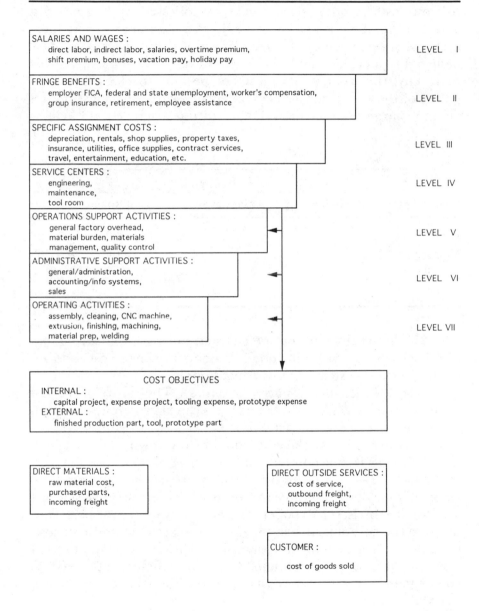

SALARIES AND WAGES :
  direct labor, indirect labor, salaries, overtime premium,
  shift premium, bonuses, vacation pay, holiday pay

LEVEL   I

FRINGE BENEFITS :
  employer FICA, federal and state unemployment, worker's compensation,
  group insurance, retirement, employee assistance

LEVEL   II

SPECIFIC ASSIGNMENT COSTS :
  depreciation, rentals, shop supplies, property taxes,
  insurance, utilities, office supplies, contract services,
  travel, entertainment, education, etc.

LEVEL   III

SERVICE CENTERS :
  engineering,
  maintenance,
  tool room

LEVEL   IV

OPERATIONS SUPPORT ACTIVITIES :
  general factory overhead,
  material burden, materials
  management, quality control

LEVEL   V

ADMINISTRATIVE SUPPORT ACTIVITIES :
  general/administration,
  accounting/info systems,
  sales

LEVEL   VI

OPERATING ACTIVITIES :
  assembly, cleaning, CNC machine,
  extrusion, finishing, machining,
  material prep, welding

LEVEL VII

COST OBJECTIVES
INTERNAL :
  capital project, expense project, tooling expense, prototype expense
EXTERNAL :
  finished production part, tool, prototype part

DIRECT MATERIALS :
  raw material cost,
  purchased parts,
  incoming freight

DIRECT OUTSIDE SERVICES :
  cost of service,
  outbound freight,
  incoming freight

CUSTOMER :

  cost of goods sold

The matrix makes it clear that Maintenance has the greatest need to flow costs to other service centers, followed by Engineering and then the Tool Room. As a result, the most appropriate hierarchy of service centers for cost flow-down purposes is Maintenance, Engineering, and the Tool Room. To implement this hierarchy, the Tool Room must not be able to charge costs to either of the other service centers and Engineering must not be able to charge Maintenance. The resulting matrix would look as follows:

	Charged To			
Charged From	Engineering	Maintenance	Tool Room	Total
Engineering	—	—	500	500
Maintenance	300	—	1,000	1,300
Tool Room	—	—	—	0
Total				1,800

The 250 hours that will not be charged out by Engineering and the Tool Room can be included as nonchargeable costs and included in their cost center's overhead pool.

Level V—Operations Support Activities   The nature of the cost centers at Level V are such that its costs can flow to only one level, the Level VII operating activities. Level V cost centers support Level VII activities, so the costs should flow down to those activities. This flow is shown in Exhibit 7.8.

Level VI—Administrative Support Activities   In some instances, it may be preferable to flow down administrative support activities to the Level VII operating activities where they can flow down to the cost objective in the operating activity's indirect costing rates. In the current situation, the decision was made to treat this level of costs as a traditional General/Administration (G&A) charge made directly to the cost objective. This treatment is shown in Exhibit 7.9.

Level VII—Operating Activities   Operating activity costs have only one place to go. By definition, operating activities work

Exhibit 7.8   Cost Flow-Down Diagram/Step #7

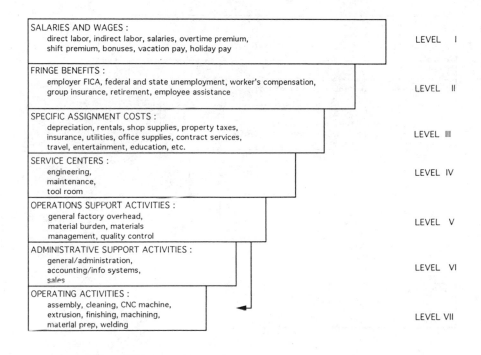

SALARIES AND WAGES :
    direct labor, indirect labor, salaries, overtime premium,
    shift premium, bonuses, vacation pay, holiday pay
         LEVEL   I

FRINGE BENEFITS :
    employer FICA, federal and state unemployment, worker's compensation,
    group insurance, retirement, employee assistance
         LEVEL   II

SPECIFIC ASSIGNMENT COSTS :
    depreciation, rentals, shop supplies, property taxes,
    insurance, utilities, office supplies, contract services,
    travel, entertainment, education, etc.
         LEVEL III

SERVICE CENTERS :
    engineering,
    maintenance,
    tool room
         LEVEL IV

OPERATIONS SUPPORT ACTIVITIES :
    general factory overhead,
    material burden, materials
    management, quality control
         LEVEL   V

ADMINISTRATIVE SUPPORT ACTIVITIES :
    general/administration,
    accounting/info systems,
    sales
         LEVEL VI

OPERATING ACTIVITIES :
    assembly, cleaning, CNC machine,
    extrusion, finishing, machining,
    material prep, welding
         LEVEL VII

COST OBJECTIVES
INTERNAL :
    capital project, expense project, tooling expense, prototype expense
EXTERNAL :
    finished production part, tool, prototype part

DIRECT MATERIALS :
    raw material cost,
    purchased parts,
    incoming freight

DIRECT OUTSIDE SERVICES :
    cost of service,
    outbound freight,
    incoming freight

CUSTOMER :
    cost of goods sold

Exhibit 7.9   Cost Flow-Down Diagram/Step #8

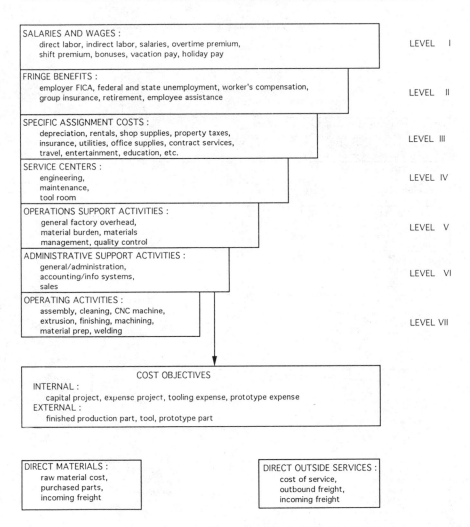

SALARIES AND WAGES :
    direct labor, indirect labor, salaries, overtime premium,
    shift premium, bonuses, vacation pay, holiday pay
       LEVEL   I

FRINGE BENEFITS :
    employer FICA, federal and state unemployment, worker's compensation,
    group insurance, retirement, employee assistance
       LEVEL   II

SPECIFIC ASSIGNMENT COSTS :
    depreciation, rentals, shop supplies, property taxes,
    insurance, utilities, office supplies, contract services,
    travel, entertainment, education, etc.
       LEVEL   III

SERVICE CENTERS :
    engineering,
    maintenance,
    tool room
       LEVEL   IV

OPERATIONS SUPPORT ACTIVITIES :
    general factory overhead,
    material burden, materials
    management, quality control
       LEVEL   V

ADMINISTRATIVE SUPPORT ACTIVITIES :
    general/administration,
    accounting/info systems,
    sales
       LEVEL   VI

OPERATING ACTIVITIES :
    assembly, cleaning, CNC machine,
    extrusion, finishing, machining,
    material prep, welding
       LEVEL   VII

COST OBJECTIVES
INTERNAL :
    capital project, expense project, tooling expense, prototype expense
EXTERNAL :
    finished production part, tool, prototype part

DIRECT MATERIALS :
    raw material cost,
    purchased parts,
    incoming freight

DIRECT OUTSIDE SERVICES :
    cost of service,
    outbound freight,
    incoming freight

CUSTOMER :

    cost of goods sold

directly on the products or services being provided by the organization. As a result, Level VII operating activity costs can be charged only to the cost objective. This situation is shown in Exhibit 7.10.

Disposition of Cost Objectives

Once all costs have been accumulated for a particular cost objective, something must be done with them. If the cost objective is a finished product, prototype part, engineering service, or tool for sale to the customer, the accumulated cost should be used to offset the revenues generated. This is shown by the arrow directing cost objectives to the customer in Exhibit 7.11.

If the cost objective is a capital project or expense project, the cost must be "recycled" through the flow-down process, either immediately or after a temporary respite on the balance sheet. This is demonstrated by the arrows flowing back up the flow-down diagram from the cost objectives in Exhibit 7.11. Examples of this recycling process include:

- o Engineering designs and Maintenance helps to build and install a capital asset. The costs of these service centers flow down to the cost objective (the capital asset) and are eventually put on the balance sheet as capital equipment. This asset is then depreciated back into the cost flow-down process as a specific assignment cost.
- o Maintenance repairs equipment used in the Tool Room. This cost is accumulated as a cost objective and is recycled back into the Tool Room as maintenance cost.
- o The Tool Room and several operating activities combine to develop a prototype product that is to be used for marketing a new product line. The prototype part is the cost objective for which the cost is accumulated and, upon its completion, the cost is recycled either by a direct flow to the Sales activity in Level VI or indirectly to Sales after being placed on the balance sheet and amortized.

Exhibit 7.10   Cost Flow-Down Diagram/Step #9

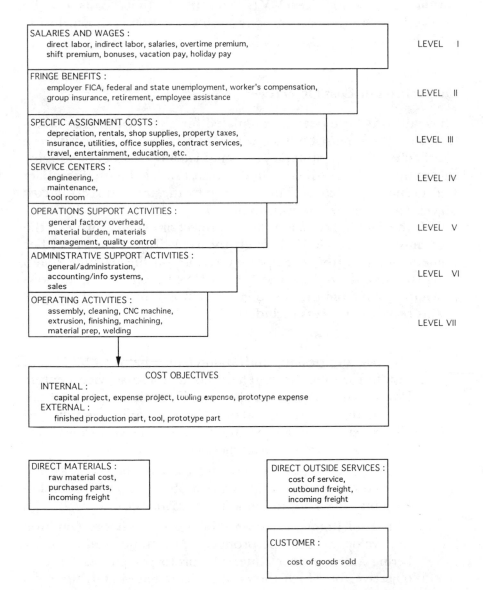

SALARIES AND WAGES :
  direct labor, indirect labor, salaries, overtime premium,
  shift premium, bonuses, vacation pay, holiday pay   LEVEL   I

FRINGE BENEFITS :
  employer FICA, federal and state unemployment, worker's compensation,
  group insurance, retirement, employee assistance   LEVEL   II

SPECIFIC ASSIGNMENT COSTS :
  depreciation, rentals, shop supplies, property taxes,
  insurance, utilities, office supplies, contract services,   LEVEL   III
  travel, entertainment, education, etc.

SERVICE CENTERS :
  engineering,
  maintenance,   LEVEL   IV
  tool room

OPERATIONS SUPPORT ACTIVITIES :
  general factory overhead,
  material burden, materials   LEVEL   V
  management, quality control

ADMINISTRATIVE SUPPORT ACTIVITIES :
  general/administration,
  accounting/info systems,   LEVEL   VI
  sales

OPERATING ACTIVITIES :
  assembly, cleaning, CNC machine,
  extrusion, finishing, machining,   LEVEL VII
  material prep, welding

COST OBJECTIVES
INTERNAL :
  capital project, expense project, tooling expense, prototype expense
EXTERNAL :
  finished production part, tool, prototype part

DIRECT MATERIALS :   DIRECT OUTSIDE SERVICES :
  raw material cost,   cost of service,
  purchased parts,   outbound freight,
  incoming freight   incoming freight

CUSTOMER :

  cost of goods sold

Exhibit 7.11   Cost Flow-Down Diagram/Step #10

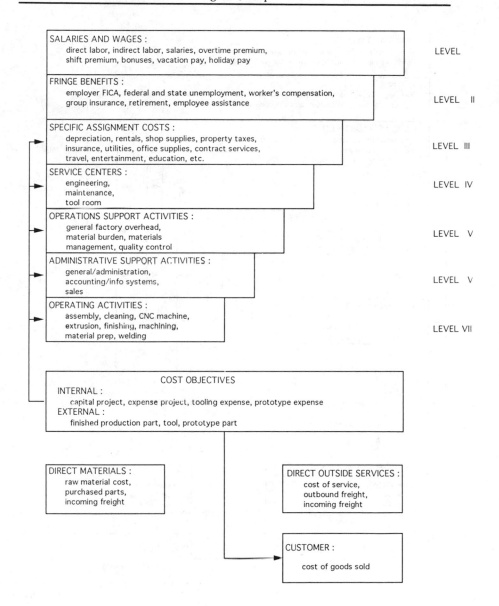

Exhibit 7.12   Cost Flow-Down Diagram/Total Cost Flow

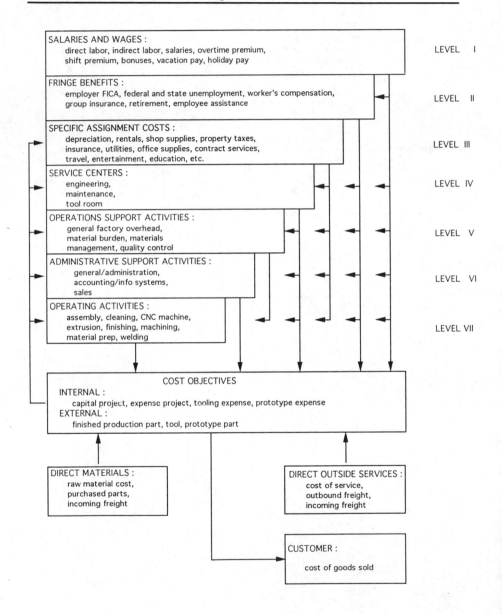

Overall Cost Flow Concept

The combination of each of these cost flows is presented as Exhibit 7.12. This complete cost flow-down diagram represents the organization's cost flow pattern. Once this pattern is established, the mechanics for implementing the concepts that went into the development of the pattern need to be developed. Before developing these system mechanics, however, the system designer must make sure that the right tools are available for putting together an effective system. Chapter 8 discusses a variety of tools that have proven effective in developing abc systems.

8

Tools for Implementing Activity-Based Costing

After developing a cost flow pattern, the system designer must reach into a "bag of tools" to select and assemble the suitable mechanics for implementing that pattern in an activity-based system. This selection process represents the seventh step in establishing an abc system. Before starting this task, the designer should make sure that as many tools (or options) as possible are available. This chapter presents a collection of tools that have proven useful in building a number of abc systems.

As noted in Chapter 1, the cost accumulation model is the key to abc. As a result, much of the explanation of the concepts and techniques is done in terms of their worksheet representation.

Conversion Costs

Chapter 5 discussed the concept of surrogate cost drivers. These are practical and readily available measures that are used to distribute costs to cost centers or cost objectives when it is impractical to collect and maintain data relative to the most theoretically correct cost driver. Keeping in mind the idea that accuracy is preferable to precision, these surrogate drivers should give the same general distribution of costs that the theoretically correct

79

driver would have provided, but the degree of precision is somewhat lower.

One of the most useful surrogate drivers is conversion cost. Roughly defined, conversion cost is all direct labor and indirect costs charged to a cost center through the point at which the cost center currently under consideration is to be distributed. If that definition seems confusing, read on; it should become clearer.

The number of purchase orders issued, material releases issued, lift-truck miles by product, production orders scheduled by product or by department, indirect material receipts, and shipments are all valid cost drivers that might be identified in an ABC system's development. Unfortunately, this is not information that most small or mid-sized organizations can afford to keep, or desire to maintain in great detail. This is especially true if the data must also be used for complex calculations of cost distribution. However, some characteristics shared by these drivers suggest one surrogate driver that can approximate all of them as a group.

The cost drivers listed above pertain primarily to the types of cost centers frequently included in the category operations support activities. These include activities such as purchasing, production scheduling, expediting, materials management, and material handling. The amount of effort each of these activities expends in support of the several operating activities usually varies with the *level of activity* in each. For example, if there is twice as much activity in the press department as there is in welding, it is likely that production scheduling spends more time planning production in press than in welding, that material handling spends more time moving material in press than in welding, that expediting spends more time following parts in press than in welding, and even that purchasing spends more time ordering/releasing indirect materials for press than for welding. If information were available that could serve as a measure of the level of activity, it could be used as a surrogate cost driver.

One such measure does exist, namely, conversion cost. Although not perfect, the level of materiality of cost centers involved, the ability of conversion costs to approximate the level of activity, and the ready availability of conversion cost information make it an ideal surrogate.

The worksheet in Exhibit 8.1 is an example of how conversion costs can be used in this capacity. Four cost centers are involved: Cost Center A, which is a production support activity, and Cost Centers B, C, and D, which are operating activities. Each cost center has incurred indirect labor costs, fixed overhead costs, and variable overhead costs. In addition, the operating activities have incurred direct labor costs. By the time Cost Center (Department) A is being distributed to the operating activities, all four cost centers have also received charges from Cost Centers (Departments) E and F. These would have been cost centers classified at levels above Cost Center A.

The cumulative cost in Cost Center A is $90,000. This cost is to be distributed to the three operating activities based on their levels of activity. Using conversion costs, Cost Center B has 44.4% of the activity (400,000/900,000), C has 33.3% (300,000/900,000), and D has 22.2% (200,000/900,000). The result is a distribution of $40,000 of Cost Center A's cost to Cost

Exhibit 8.1   Conversion Cost as a Surrogate Cost Driver

	Cost Center A	Cost Center B	Cost Center C	Cost Center D
Direct labor		150,000	50,000	100,000
Indirect labor	15,000	20,000	40,000	20,000
Fixed overhead	40,000	75,000	50,000	25,000
Variable overhead	20,000	95,000	100,000	10,000
Total specific assignment costs	75,000	190,000	190,000	55,000
Dept E distribution	5,000	35,000	25,000	20,000
Dept F distribution	10,000	25,000	35,000	25,000
Cumulative conversion costs	90,000	400,000	300,000	200,000
Conversion cost %		44.4%	33.3%	22.2%
Dept A distribution	(90,000)	40,000	30,000	20,000
Cumulative costs after distribution	0	440,000	330,000	220,000

Center B, \$30,000 to C, and \$20,000 to D. At the end of the process, no cost remains in Cost Center A—it has all been distributed to the operating activities based on an approximation of their levels of activity. This method may not be precise, but it is reasonably accurate.

Consumption Units

In developing an abc system, it is useful to divide the category of costs normally termed "variable" into two separate categories: variable costs that change automatically with a change in volume and those that change only if some action is taken by management.

For example, a change in production volume will not result in a change in labor costs unless action is taken to increase or decrease the labor force. Workers must be hired or laid off by management. They do not automatically report or volunteer to go home. However, once this action is taken, a change in fringe benefit costs will be automatic. On the other hand, a change in volume will result automatically in a change in operating supplies or power consumption. If there is less welding, less welding rod and argon will be consumed. If there are more machine hours in the machine centers, more electricity will be required.

In building the cost accumulation model, an attempt is made to vary those costs that would change automatically with changes in the activities that cause the costs to be incurred. This is done by using the appropriate cost drivers to "drive" the consumption of the resource involved.

To accomplish this, the system designer must establish a consumption unit for each element of cost classified as automatically variable. In some cases, a consumption unit can be an actual unit of measure, such as pounds, kilowatt hours, or thermal units. At other times, a "phantom" consumption unit must be devised. In the case of fringe benefits, drivers such as headcount, gross payroll, and hours worked are readily available and measurable. For the other major categories of automatically variable costs—major supplies and utilities—the driver is not easily converted into units of consumption.

The first difficulty comes when the cost driver for a particular element of cost is the same for all cost centers, but the amount that it affects each cost center varies. Office supplies are a common example of this situation. A driver frequently used to project the consumption of office supplies is headcount. If a company has many individuals working in a particular department, that department will usually experience greater consumption of office supplies than if it had fewer individuals. The problem arises in answering the question, "How much more consumption?" The use of *driver multipliers* to convert the cost drivers to consumption units is an effective way to answer this question.

For example, in Exhibit 8.2, General/Administration is selected as the cost center that represents the base consumption unit. This means that one General/Administration employee will consume one unit of office supplies. The cost of one consumption unit (budgeted or historical G/A office supply cost divided by headcount) is then determined. In the example, this unit cost is $500. This provides the base against which to compare all other cost centers.

Each cost center's consumption of office supplies can then be expressed in relation to G/A, the base unit. According to the example, each individual in Accounting, Engineering, and Production

Exhibit 8.2   Use of Consumption Units/Common Drivers with Different Impacts

	Driver Headcount	Driver Multiplier	Consumption Units[a]	Cost
General/Administration	8	1.0	8.0	4,000
Accounting	5	2.0	10.0	5,000
Data Processing	4	5.0	20.0	10,000
Engineering	8	2.0	16.0	8,000
Purchasing	3	1.5	4.5	2,250
Production Control	3	2.0	6.0	3,000
Maintenance	6	1.0	6.0	3,000
Tool Room	8	1.0	8.0	4,000
Prod Dept A	20	0.2	4.0	2,000
Prod Dept B	10	0.2	2.0	1,000
Prod Dept C	15	0.2	3.0	1,500
Prod Dept D	30	0.2	6.0	3,000
Total	120			46,750

[a] Cost per unit = $500.

Control requires twice as many office supplies as an individual in G/A, whereas individuals in Data Processing require five times as many; in Tool Room and Maintenance, the same amount; in Purchasing, 150% of the amount; and in all Production Departments, 20% of the base amount.

This information can be put into worksheet form, as in Exhibit 8.2. In this analysis, the headcount for each cost center is multiplied by the driver multiplier (the relationship of each cost center's consumption to the base's consumption) to arrive at the consumption units. The result is multiplied by the consumption unit cost to arrive at total office supply cost for each cost center. Any change in employee headcount causes a change in office supply consumption. The amount of the change depends on the department in which the headcount change occurs. If Engineering is reduced by two employees and two employees are added to Data Processing, there will be a net increase of $3,000 in office supply use (a reduction of $2,000 in Engineering and an increase of $5,000 in Data Processing), although total employment remains the same. This is the result of the driver multiplier.

The second difficulty occurs when a particular element of cost is driven by different cost drivers. This is often the case in determining variable utility costs. In most cases, variable utility costs are concentrated in the operating activities. This is especially true in manufacturing settings, where a variety of different cost drivers can exist. For example, one organization may have direct labor hours, cycle time, machine hours, and line time as drivers of its production activities. In these cases, the difficulty of having different impacts of the same driver is compounded by having multiple drivers for the same cost. Again, the use of driver multipliers can solve this problem.

Exhibit 8.3 shows such a situation. In this example, the manufacturing facility has four different drivers for its five production cost centers. The system designer's task is to develop a set of driver multipliers that will turn the drivers into the appropriate consumption units. If the cost element is electricity, the drivers can be converted into kilowatt hours (KWH). Water can be converted into gallons, and gas into hundreds of cubic feet. In the early stages of model development, the drivers might be converted into a phantom consumption unit that can be refined later.

Exhibit 8.3   Use of Consumption Units/Different Drivers with Different Impacts

Cost Center	Driver Type[a]	Driver Measure	Driver Multiplier	Consumption Units/KWH[b]	Cost
Press	DLHours	40,000	10.00	400,000	50,000
Fabricate	DLHours	80,000	2.50	200,000	25,000
Hot Form	CycTime	6,000	80.00	480,000	60,000
CNC Machine	MachHrs	8,000	15.00	120,000	15,000
Assembly	LinTime	4,000	12.00	48,000	6,000
Total				1,248,000	156,000

[a] DLHours = Direct labor hours
 CycTime = Cycle time
 MachHrs = Machine hours
 LinTime = Line Time
[b] Cost per KWH = $.125.

Because there are a variety of cost drivers, one cost center cannot be selected as a base, and then multipliers used to quantify consumption in relation to this base as was done when we had a common driver with different impacts. Instead, each cost center must be considered individually and an independent driver multiplier developed for each.

An analysis of the relationship between historical consumption and the volume of activity as measured by the various drivers enables the organization to arrive at driver multipliers that will change the drivers into an approximation of KWH consumed. This last sentence may imply this job is simple, but in most cases it is not. It is unusual for an organization to have the type of detailed driver and KWH consumption information necessary to make precise calculations of these multipliers. Keep in mind, however, that the goal is accuracy, not precision. By interviewing engineering and operating personnel and using other analytical techniques, reasonably accurate multipliers can be developed for the initial model. Although initial multipliers may contain a great many assumptions and estimates, they will be "reasoned-out" statistics and much preferable to arbitrary allocations. Subsequent experience and the accumulation of previously uncollected consumption information will make future refinement possible.

Once developed, these multipliers can be applied to the various cost drivers to develop the estimated KWH consumption. The kilowatt hours can then be extended by the unit cost to obtain variable electrical cost by cost center. Changes in the drivers will then result in the appropriate changes in the electrical costs depending on the cost center in which the changes took place. For example, a 500-hour increase in Hot Form will result in a $5,000 increase in electric cost (500 hours × 80.00 multiplier × $.125), whereas the same increase in CNC Machine will result in only a $938 increase (500 hours × 15.00 multiplier × $.125).

Labor-Based Cost Distribution

The most common and well-known method of distributing indirect costs is direct labor. This practice is only part of a larger concept that can be used for both the how-much and where-to aspects of cost accumulation. The larger concept is total labor-based cost distribution.

Exhibit 8.4 provides an example of both accumulating and distributing costs using a labor-based approach. The category of

Exhibit 8.4   Labor-Based Cost Distribution

Benefit	(Headcount) $/Employee	(Labor Dollars) % of Payroll	(Labor Hours) $/Hour	Driver	Benefit Cost
Health insurance	$4,200			100	420,000
Workers' compensation		5.00		2,200,000	110,000
State unemployment	380			100	38,000
Federal unemployment	60			100	6,000
Employer FICA		7.65		2,200,000	168,300
Pension			$0.15	208,000	31,200
Total purchased benefits					773,500
Vacation pay					84,600
Holiday pay					101,500
Total time-off benefits					186,100
Total fringe benefits					959,600
Base payroll hours					190,400
Fringe benefits per payroll hour					$ 5.040

costs in this case is fringe benefits. The organization in Exhibit 8.4 found three different measures of labor that serve as drivers for the incurrence of fringe benefit costs: headcount, labor dollars, and labor hours (the how-much aspect). One of these drivers, labor hours, was also found to be the most appropriate driver of fringe benefit cost distribution (the where-to aspect).

In developing the cost of fringe benefits, headcount is the preferred driver for costs that are basically the same for each employee, regardless of how much they earn. Labor dollars is preferred for benefits that depend on the level of earnings. Labor hours is best used for benefits based directly on hours worked, such as with many pension plans and supplemental unemployment benefit plans. In Exhibit 8.4, three of the benefits were deemed to be headcount driven: health insurance, state unemployment, and federal unemployment.

One issue to keep in mind when considering health insurance is whether the organization views insurance as *providing coverage* for the employee or *paying health care costs* for the employee. Self-insured organizations are often tempted to become more precise and charge the actual cost of benefits paid to the cost centers where the applicable employees work. Although this approach might be useful in gathering information for cost containment efforts, it is inappropriate for cost accumulation. For purposes of cost accumulation, a company should consider health insurance a payment for health care coverage, not the payment of health care costs for the employee. As a result, health insurance, as well as any similar coverage, should be treated as a cost per employee just as if it were an insurance premium. In the case at hand, health insurance is treated as a cost per employee and multiplied by the organization's headcount to arrive at the annual cost.

Initially, it might seem more logical to treat state and federal unemployment taxes as being driven by payroll dollars since they are calculated as a percentage of payroll. However, the maximum individual earnings on which the taxes are based is usually at a level low enough that all full-time employees exceed that level during the year. As a result, both of these elements of cost become a fixed amount for each employee as opposed to a fixed percentage of payroll cost. Their treatment in the cost accumulation process is, therefore, based on headcount.

Labor dollars is chosen as the driver for two of the cost elements in Exhibit 8.4: workers' compensation and employer FICA. Workers' compensation premiums are usually based on payroll dollars. As a result, the selection of this basis seems obvious. Like state and federal unemployment taxes, employer FICA is also a percentage of gross payroll, but unlike the other two, its maximum individual earnings basis is more than the gross pay of most employees. As a result, it can remain a labor dollars–driven cost element.

Some care must be taken in considering workers' compensation. If the activities taking place in the organization result in a group of widely varying workers' compensation rates, and the distribution of labor cost among those activities is such that the use of an average rate (e.g., the one used in Exhibit 8.4) would materially distort the distribution of the cost to the activities, an alternative treatment should be sought. One such alternative would be to handle workers' compensation as a specific assignment cost in a manner similar to that given to supplies in the discussion of driver multipliers (Exhibit 8.2).

In the example, it is assumed that the pension cost is based on labor hours. As a result, labor hours is the most appropriate driver for determining the organization's total pension cost.

Holiday and vacation pay would also have been driven by labor-related factors, but the analysis of this area is a subject in itself and is discussed fully in Chapter 11. For the time being, these categories are included in Exhibit 8.4 as given amounts.

In looking at the possible drivers for distributing fringe benefit costs, labor hours was chosen. Of the organization's purchased fringe benefit costs, $464,000 (60%) of them are driven by headcount and only $278,000 (36%) are driven by labor dollars. The balance of $31,000 (4%) are driven by labor hours. Although headcount is a practical means of distributing fringe benefit costs to cost centers, it is impractical for charging to the multitude of cost objectives. That leaves either labor dollars or hours.

In most instances, the selection of labor hours or labor dollars is one of individual preference. Both have good arguments for their use. If the circumstances of the specific organization do not give the advantage to one or the other, either will work effectively.

One final note is the difference between the labor hours used in calculating the pension cost and the labor hours used as a base for distributing fringe benefit costs. The 208,000 hours used for determining pension cost includes all hours for which the employee was compensated, including holiday and vacation hours. In distributing the costs, only hours actually worked receive fringe benefit charges, so holiday and vacation hours are excluded from the labor distribution bases.

Demand-Based Cost Distribution

As mentioned earlier, service centers are cost centers that are businesses within the business that can charge their costs to user activities on a time-and-materials basis. This type of procedure is termed demand-based cost distribution.

In demand-based cost distribution, the goal is to develop an hourly billing rate for the cost center's services and then charge user cost centers for these services as if they were customers. For example, if a CNC programming department has a calculated hourly rate of $30.00 and it spends 100 hours developing a program for machining Product A, $3,000 will be charged directly to that product. If, on the other hand, the department spends 50 hours performing general maintenance on programs already developed as a means of making the CNC equipment operate more effectively, $1,500 will be charged to the CNC Machine cost center as an indirect cost.

Exhibit 8.5 shows the development of the billing rate for a maintenance department and its distribution to user cost centers. Total employees as shown on the analysis include all employees assigned to the service center, including any full-time supervision and administrative support. To determine the number of hours that Maintenance can charge to other cost centers, nonbillable employees who perform supervision and administration must be eliminated from the calculation. Their costs are included in the rate to be charged by the employees directly involved in the maintenance efforts; they are not charged individually. In Exhibit 8.5, one employee was considered administrative support; thus, the seven total employees were reduced to six billable employees.

Exhibit 8.5   Demand-Based Cost Distribution

Billing Rate Calculation		
Total employees		7
Nonbillable employees		1
Net billable employees		6
Available hours per employee		1,908
Total available billable hours		11,448
% of available hours billable		90%
Billable hours		10,300
Departmental costs		$220,000
Billing rate per hour		$ 21.36
Cost Distribution	*Hours*	*Charge*
General/Admin	200	$ 4,272
Accounting/Info Systems	100	2,136
Data Processing	200	4,272
Engineering	100	2,136
Purchasing	50	1,068
Production Control	50	1,068
Tool Room	1,400	29,904
Press	4,200	89,712
Fabricate	500	10,680
Hot Form	800	17,088
CNC Machine	1,200	25,632
Assembly	900	19,224
Capital Projects	600	12,808
Total	10,300	$220,000

Next, the annual hours available for each employee are entered. By multiplying this amount by the number of employees, the total hours capable of being billed to other cost centers can be established. Maintenance workers do not, however, spend each of those hours working on something that can be charged out. They have administrative time, training time, time spent working on projects within the maintenance function itself, and other nonbillable hours. As a result, a percentage of total hours that can actually be billed to user cost centers is developed and used to reduce total available billable hours to an estimate of billable hours.

Total costs accumulated in Maintenance are then used to determine the maintenance cost per hour. These costs include all costs from Levels I through III. Total billable hours are divided into the total of these costs to establish the cost center's hourly billing rate.

An estimate of the hours necessary to support each of the other cost centers is then established, and those hours are used to distribute the cost of the Maintenance function using the calculated hourly rate. In addition to the cost centers, Maintenance can also perform work on capital projects. These costs must be capitalized as part of the assets being constructed or installed. As a result, the last category in Exhibit 8.5, Capital Projects, is established as a cost objective to collect these costs.

Similar analyses can be prepared for other service centers, such as Engineering, Tool Room, or CNC Programming. It must be remembered, however, that service centers cannot cross-charge each other. The sequencing of service centers described in the previous chapter must be followed to prevent mathematical difficulties.

Piece-Rate Cost Distribution

One general rule to follow in developing any cost system is to charge everything direct that can possibly be measured as direct. An area where this is often possible is that of indirect materials. Many of these materials are the type that do not vary with the passage of operating time. Instead, they vary with the number and type of products manufactured.

One example of this type of cost is coating material. In many forging or extruding operations, each part must be coated before it is processed. These coating materials are usually treated as indirect materials and included in the overhead costs of the cost center in which the coating activity takes place. Where the cost is material and the effort involved is within reason, it is preferable to treat these coating materials as if they were direct materials. Exhibit 8.6 shows the development of piece-rate cost distribution figures for one type of indirect material.

In this example, it was determined that a definite relationship existed between the surface area of a part and the amount of

Exhibit 8.6   Piece Rate Cost Distribution

	Surface Area (sq in)	Units Coating Material	Piece Rate
Part 0001	24.00	8.00	0.920
Part 0002	32.50	10.83	1.245
Part 0003	27.60	9.20	1.058
Part 0004	18.20	6.07	0.698
Part 0005	12.10	4.03	0.463
Part 0006	42.00	14.00	1.610
Part 0007	11.60	3.87	0.445
Part 0008	9.20	3.07	0.353
Part 0009	36.50	12.17	1.400
Part 0010	21.20	7.07	0.813
Part 0011	29.50	9.83	1.130

Area to units conversion factor   = $33^{1}/_{3}\%$
Cost per unit of coating material = $0.115.

coating material required to coat the part. For each three square inches of surface area, one unit of coating material is required. By establishing the surface area of each part, the cost of the coating material directly attributable to each part can be established. As a result of this analysis, coating materials can be treated as a direct cost, charged directly to the products on which they are used and excluded from the indirect cost accumulation process.

There are other instances when an engineered consumption can be used to convert indirect costs into direct costs. Perishable tools are a frequent candidate, especially when they contain industrial diamonds and are, therefore, not typical of the ordinary class of perishable tools. In such cases, the life of the tool can be established and a consumption rate per part developed. This information can then be used in a manner similar to the example of coating materials to turn this indirect cost into a direct material charge.

The use of piece-rate cost distribution is intended to enable the organization to charge the cost of high-dollar indirect materials directly to the products that use them. If used, the concept should be restricted to those materials that would not be fairly distributed if they were simply accumulated in a cost center and charged as part of the cost center's indirect cost rate. Keeping in mind the goal of accuracy, not precision, most organizations will have few, if any, indirect materials that require such treatment.

Machine Hour/Cycle Time Cost Distribution

Machine hour/cycle time cost distribution is a method of charging costs to cost objectives based on the amount of time the objective is processed on a particular piece of equipment. It is particularly useful in operating cost centers characterized by machines using men as opposed to men using machines.

In using this concept, an average hourly cost of operating all pieces of equipment in the cost center is established and then applied to all products produced on any one of those pieces of equipment. Some organizations calculate an hourly cost for each piece of equipment. This approach is not recommended. Equipment should be grouped into cost centers by appropriate characteristics and average rates established. At times, a cost center may contain only one piece of equipment due to its unique characteristics, but this should be the exception, not the rule.

As shown in the One Big Press Corporation case in Chapter 3, machine hour/cycle time rates do not have to be used as the only method of distributing costs from a cost center. They can be coupled with a labor-based rate to arrive at a more equitable distribution of costs. This idea is discussed further in the Production Manpower Pool section of this chapter.

Exhibit 8.7 shows the development of machine hour/cycle time rates for two cost centers: a hot forming activity and a CNC machining activity. In the first part of the analysis, the task is to determine the total number of hours available for use by each cost center in charging their costs to cost objectives. The initial step in this process is to determine the number of pieces of equipment included in each cost center. The annual hours per shift for each piece of equipment must then be established, as well as the number of shifts the cost center is expected to be manned and in operation. These three factors are multiplied to determine the total annual hours available within these cost centers.

However, this equipment will not run 100% of the time. Many manufacturers must maintain normal excess capacity and reduce total available hours to provide for setup, maintenance, and other

Exhibit 8.7   Machine Hour/Cycle Time Cost Distribution

	Hot Forming	CNC Machining
Pieces of equipment	10	4
Annual hours/machine/shift	1,750	1,750
Annual hours/shift	17,500	7,000
Shifts in operation	2.0	2.0
Annual hours available	35,000	14,000
Nonproduction hours		
Setup	1,750	700
Maintenance	1,750	700
Normal excess capacity	5,250	2,800
Other	1,750	700
Total	10,500	4,900
Annual production hours	24,500	9,100
Cost center costs	700,000	400,000
Machine/cycle rate per hour	28.57	43.96

nonproducing activities. These amounts are determined and used to reduce the annual hours available, and then to arrive at the annual production hours expected from each cost center.

The total cost accumulated in each cost center (which would include all costs from Levels I to III and all charges and distributions from Levels IV to VI) is divided by each cost center's annual production hours to arrive at the rates to be charged to cost objectives for any work performed in these cost centers.

One important characteristic of machine hour/cycle time cost distribution is that each piece of equipment charges costs to cost objectives individually. Each product receives a charge from each piece of equipment that processes it. This characteristic differentiates the machine hour/cycle time method from line/cell time cost distribution, discussed next.

Line/Cell Time Cost Distribution

Several pieces of equipment are sometimes arranged in such a manner that they are regularly used to perform the same series of operations, either on one product or on a group of similar products. Individual pieces of equipment are not used in isolation, but always in connection with the group as a whole. In such cases, line/cell time cost distribution is usually the best method of assigning costs to cost objectives.

This distribution is best even if all of the equipment is not used on all products. For example, a manufacturing line is established for producing Products A and B. This line is made up of Machines 1 through 4, which are used in a specified sequence. If Product A is produced by using Machines 1 through 4 in sequence, but Product B is produced without using Machine 3, the cell/line time concept nevertheless applies to both products. By grouping the machines together to be used as a continuous process, the organization has dedicated those resources to all products that go through the line or cell. As a result, all products being produced by the line must bear the cost of the entire line.

The cell/line concept develops an hourly cost for using one resource—the cell or line—instead of a cost for each piece of equipment on that line or in that cell. That rate is then applied to each product produced by the line based on the product's hourly production rate.

For example, Exhibit 8.8 shows the calculation of the hourly cost of a finishing line. Although this calculation is for a single line or cell, not multiple pieces of equipment, the calculation mirrors that in Exhibit 8.7 for machine/cycle time activities. The organization can finish 100 units of Product X per hour, 150 units of Product Y per hour, and 75 units of Product Z per hour. Regardless of whether X, Y, and Z use all individual operations available, each product has the entire line or cell dedicated to its manufacture while it is being processed through the line or cell. As a result, finishing costs for the three products are calculated as follows:

Product X: $142.86/100 per hour = $1.4286 per unit.
Product Y: $142.86/150 per hour = $0.9524 per unit.
Product Z: $142.86/75 per hour   = $1.9048 per unit.

Care must be taken in using the line/cell concept. In some cells, variable costs may be so great that two rates would be

Exhibit 8.8   Line/Cell Time Cost Distribution

Annual hours/shift	1,750
Shifts in operation	2.0
Annual hours available	3,500
Nonproduction hours	
Setup	175
Maintenance	175
Normal excess capacity	525
Other	175
Total	1,050
Annual production hours	2,450
Cost center costs	350,000
Line/cell cost per hour	142.86

appropriate: one line/cell rate to cover the dedication of the entire line to the product's manufacture, and a second machine hour rate to cover the variable costs driven by the operation of each piece of equipment in the cell or line.

It is important to note the difference between machine/cycle time cost distribution and line/cell time cost distribution. These similar, but not identical, concepts both have places in the development of an effective cost system.

Production Manpower Pool

A concept already touched on several times in this text is the production manpower pool. This concept is especially useful in connection with the use of machine/cycle time rates and line/cell time rates.

The case of the One Big Press Corporation (Chapter 3) showed the benefits of having direct labor treated as a separate cost element in calculating the cost of items produced on the big press. What would be the case if OBPC had five big presses or even 100 big presses? Varying crew sizes could be used on any of the organization's presses, compounding the problem reflected in the OBPC case many times.

Similarly, a cell or line, such as the finishing line from the previous section, could also have a varying crew-size problem. If certain parts of the cell or line are not used, it probably is unnecessary to have an employee stationed at the unused operations. Thus, a procedure is needed to account for this condition.

The use of a production manpower pool is a convenient solution to this problem. Exhibit 8.9 shows how such a pool would operate. This organization has many presses that have been grouped into three cost centers based on their size and other operating characteristics. All personnel-related costs applicable to employees working as press operators have been ⸱cumulated in a cost center titled Press Manpower. Costs involved in the ownership and operation of the presses have been accumulated in the cost center for the applicable presses.

In the Press Manpower cost center, the personnel-related costs include fringe benefit costs, indirect labor worked by these primarily direct personnel, and overtime and shift premiums. It

Exhibit 8.9   Production Manpower Pool

	Press Manpower	Small Press Group	Mid-Sized Press Group	Large Press Group
Fringe benefits	50,000			
Indirect labor	75,000			
Overtime/shift premiums	20,000			
Fixed costs		75,000	50,000	100,000
Variable costs		100,000	125,000	225,000
Specific assignment costs	145,000	175,000	175,000	325,000
Distribution A	35,000			
Distribution B		25,000	15,000	45,000
Distribution C		10,000	20,000	30,000
Total costs	180,000	210,000	210,000	400,000
Direct labor dollars	240,000			
Annual press hours		7,000	3,500	5,000
Indirect cost application rate	75% of direct labor	30.00 per press hour	60.00 per press hour	80.00 per press hour

also includes distributions from other cost centers. Distribution A can be seen as General Factory Overhead distributed on the basis of headcount.

Each of the three press cost centers accumulates the appropriate specific assignment costs, as well as distributions from other cost centers. In the example, Distributions B and C could be viewed as coming from cost centers such as Maintenance and Engineering, or the various production support activities.

Once these costs have been accumulated by cost center, they can be divided by the appropriate cost drivers (direct labor dollars for Production Manpower and press hours for the three press cost centers) to determine the individual indirect cost distribution rates. The result is one rate for any direct labor personnel involved in the operation of any press and separate rates for the presses themselves.

With these cost concepts packed into a bag of tools, the system designer can move forward and begin planning the organization's cost accumulation model.

9

Planning the Cost Accumulation Model

Now that the system designer has the ability to design a cost flow pattern and a variety of tools with which to put that pattern into effect, he or she can select the tools for implementation and incorporate them into a model that will simulate the flow of costs within the organization.

To demonstrate this process, I use the case of Costa Manufacturing Company, a $9 million manufacturer that currently uses traditional cost accounting practices. In the current year, Costa expects to incur $4,051,855 of net indirect costs. These are distributed among Costa's three current cost centers, as shown in Exhibit 9.1.

Costa's direct labor costs are expected to be $1,103,450. The recaptured costs represent labor and other indirect costs that are capitalized as tooling, machinery and equipment, or engineering projects for which Costa is reimbursed by its customers.

In applying these costs to products, Costa's current system uses the following bases:

Manufacturing overhead: % of direct labor dollars

Engineering overhead: % of manufacturing conversion cost input

General/Admin: % of total conversion cost input

Exhibit 9.1

	General/ Admin	Engineering Overhead	Manufacturing Overhead	Total
Salaries	500,000	280,000	360,000	1,140,000
Indirect labor		154,896	551,172	706,068
Fringe benefits	159,386	152,822	793,777	1,105,985
Overtime and shift premiums		4,000	101,900	105,900
Depreciation	9,000	13,000	358,000	380,000
Maintenance materials	488	488	92,877	93,853
Leases and rentals	3,800	3,000	500	7,300
Insurance	443	443	24,122	25,008
Property taxes	1,754	3,154	50,096	55,004
Utilities	580	1,130	190,460	192,170
Supplies	10,000	16,000	324,550	350,550
Recaptured costs		(171,952)	(254,031)	(425,983)
Other	250,000	54,000	12,000	316,000
Total indirect costs	935,451	510,981	2,605,423	4,051,855

The resulting indirect cost application rates are calculated as follows:

Manufacturing overhead: $2,605,423/$1,103,450 = 236.1%

Engineering overhead: $510,981/$3,708,873 = 13.8%

General/Admin: $935,451/$4,219,854 = 22.2%

Knowing that it needed a better understanding of the cost of its processes and products, Costa embarked on a project to develop an activity-based costing system. After completing the first six steps of the project, the company had developed a cost flow pattern as shown in Exhibit 9.2.

One unusual feature included by Costa was the establishment of an Outside Processing cost center in Level VIII. The company believes that the $400,000 of direct outside processing services incurred during the year are no different from internal operating activities; they merely happen to be performed outside the facility. These operations need to be scheduled, shipping and receiving activities are required, and quality assurance personnel need to

Exhibit 9.2   Cost Flow-Down Diagram/Costa Manufacturing Company

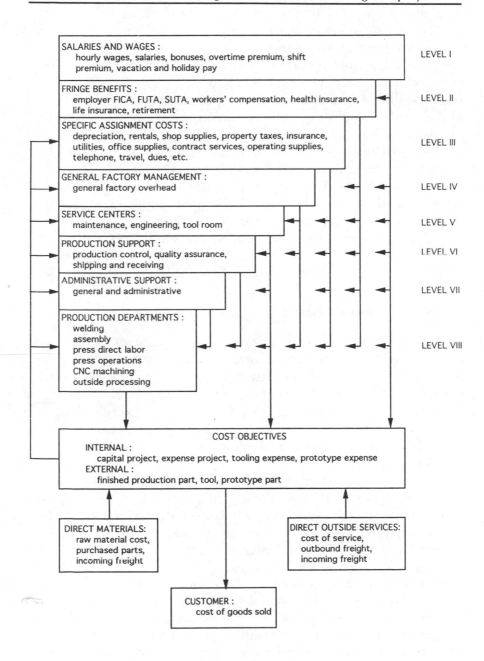

SALARIES AND WAGES :
  hourly wages, salaries, bonuses, overtime premium, shift
  premium, vacation and holiday pay — LEVEL I

FRINGE BENEFITS :
  employer FICA, FUTA, SUTA, workers' compensation, health insurance,
  life insurance, retirement — LEVEL II

SPECIFIC ASSIGNMENT COSTS :
  depreciation, rentals, shop supplies, property taxes, insurance,
  utilities, office supplies, contract services, operating supplies,
  telephone, travel, dues, etc. — LEVEL III

GENERAL FACTORY MANAGEMENT :
  general factory overhead — LEVEL IV

SERVICE CENTERS :
  maintenance, engineering, tool room — LEVEL V

PRODUCTION SUPPORT :
  production control, quality assurance,
  shipping and receiving — LEVEL VI

ADMINISTRATIVE SUPPORT :
  general and administrative — LEVEL VII

PRODUCTION DEPARTMENTS :
  welding
  assembly
  press direct labor
  press operations
  CNC machining
  outside processing — LEVEL VIII

COST OBJECTIVES
  INTERNAL :
    capital project, expense project, tooling expense, prototype expense
  EXTERNAL :
    finished production part, tool, prototype part

DIRECT MATERIALS:
  raw material cost,
  purchased parts,
  incoming freight

DIRECT OUTSIDE SERVICES:
  cost of service,
  outbound freight,
  incoming freight

CUSTOMER :
  cost of goods sold

actively participate. As a result, the system was designed to collect a portion of these production support activity costs in a Level VIII cost center and apply them to those products with operations taking place at outside processors.

Costa also split its press activities into a Press Direct Labor cost pool and a Press Operations cost pool because different parts required different crew sizes. As noted earlier, the establishment of a separate manpower pool is an effective solution to the varying crew-size problem.

A third point to note is that Costa added to its cost flow diagram an eighth level, General Factory Overhead. This level was added at Level IV (pushing other levels down one) to make it possible to distribute the cost of the plant superintendent and general foremen to all factory-related activities.

After reviewing the possible mechanics of implementing this cost flow concept, Costa arrived at the distribution bases summarized in Exhibit 9.3. These bases are discussed below.

Costa's Distribution Bases

Level I—Salaries and Wages   Because salaries and wages come directly from the labor distribution, there is no cost center in which the costs are accumulated. The costs are charged directly to cost objectives or cost centers as they are incurred.

Level II—Fringe Benefits   Fringe benefits are accumulated in two cost centers, one for hourly fringe benefits and one for salary fringe benefits. In both cases, the costs are distributed on straight-time labor dollars.

Labor dollars were chosen over labor hours for simplicity. Measuring labor hours for salaried employees would involve the accumulation of data not currently collected. Because Costa believes that the difference between the two methods would be immaterial, it selected the simpler one.

Costs are collected in two cost centers for two reasons. First, there is a difference in benefits for these two categories of employees. To charge these costs to the appropriate employees, separate cost centers are required. Second, because salaried employees' compensation levels are generally higher than those for hourly workers, an all-employee rate would distribute a disproportionate

Exhibit 9.3   Cost Flow Summary/Costa Manufacturing Company

Level	Cost Centers	Distribution Basis
I	Not applicable[a]	Labor distribution
II	Hourly fringe benefits	Straight-time labor dollars
	Salary fringe benefits	Straight-time labor dollars
III	Not applicable[a]	Various direct methods such as square footage, equipment location, other consumption basis
IV	General Factory Overhead	Factory headcount
V	Tool Room	Estimated demand
	Maintenance	Estimated demand
	Engineering	Estimated demand
VI	Shipping and Receiving	Conversion costs thru V^b
	Production Control	Conversion costs thru V^b
	Quality Assurance	Conversion costs thru V^b
VII	General/Administration	Conversion costs thru VI
VIII	Assembly	Direct labor dollars
	Welding	Direct labor dollars
	Press Direct Labor	Direct labor dollars
	Press Operations	Machine hours
	CNC Machine	Machine hours
	Outside processing	% of processing cost

[a] Labor costs charged directly to cost centers or cost objectives; specific assignment costs charged directly to cost centers.

[b] Outside processing cost included as conversion cost and direct press labor excluded for Level VI distributions.

percentage to the salaried group of those fringe costs that are the same for all employees.

Finally, Costa elected to charge fringe benefits relating to direct labor to the cost center in which the direct labor takes place, not to the cost objective itself. In this manner, the fringe rate becomes part of the production cost center's direct labor–based overhead rate.

Level III—Specific Assignment Costs   Costa charges specific assignment costs directly to cost centers as incurred or accrued. As a result, no cost center is required to accumulate the costs for subsequent distribution.

As noted previously, these costs are charged to cost centers using a variety of drivers depending on the nature of the cost. The common factor in distributing each specific assignment cost is that each is charged in the most practical way to the cost center(s) that make it necessary.

Level IV—General Factory Overhead   A General Factory Overhead cost center was established by Costa to accumulate the costs required for the general supervision of the manufacturing facility (vis-à-vis the management of the entire manufacturing organization). This cost center is to be distributed to factory cost centers, including the Tool Room, on the basis of employee headcount.

Level V—Service Centers   The Tool Room, Maintenance, and Engineering are categorized as service centers. The costs of these activities are distributed to other cost centers and cost objectives based on demand. Costa's analysis resulted in a sequencing of these service centers for cross-charging of Maintenance, then Engineering, and finally the Tool Room.

Level VI—Production Support Activities   Costa established Shipping and Receiving, Production Control, and Quality Assurance cost centers to accumulate the costs of the production support activities. Each of these cost centers is distributed to the Level VIII production activities on the basis of the production activities' conversion costs through Level V distributions. For the purpose of this distribution, Outside Processing cost is considered a conversion cost, but Press Direct Labor is not. Press Direct Labor was excluded because Costa's management decided the press operation was more appropriate for that activity, and including both Direct Labor and Press Operations in the conversion cost would skew the Level VI costs too heavily to press activities.

Level VII—General/Administration   All general and administrative costs are accumulated in a single cost center and distributed to Level VIII cost centers on the basis of conversion costs through Level VI. For the purpose of this distribution, Outside Processing cost is not considered a conversion cost.

Level VIII—Production Activities   The facility's in-house production activities are combined into five cost centers: Assembly, Welding, Press Direct Labor, Press Operations, and CNC

Machining. As noted earlier, Costa also included Outside Processing as a production activity as a means of applying production support costs to products with operations taking place at outside processors.

Three of the cost centers—Assembly, Welding, and Press Direct Labor—retain a direct labor dollar basis for distributing their costs to cost objectives. Press Operations and CNC Machining use a machine hour basis for cost distribution, and Outside Processing distributes its costs as a percentage of outside processing cost.

It should be kept in mind that these are the decisions made by Costa's management. They do not necessarily represent the only correct cost flow concept, or even the best one. The design of a cost flow concept and the selection of methods for its implementation is an art, not a science. As a result, there is always room for debate as to whether the best solution was the one selected.

Laying Out the Model

Before personal computers and spreadsheet software were developed, an organization could take a cost flow pattern, such as that developed by Costa, and calculate its annual indirect cost rates using several pads of multicolumn "green sheets," a dozen pencils, extra erasers, a long straightedge, and several rolls of adding machine tape. This series of green sheets was, in effect, a model of the cost system. Once completed, anyone suggesting that changes be made was sure to see a fall in his or her popularity. The clerical effort and risk of errors involved in making any significant (or even minor) changes made this process a once-a-year project.

In laying out one of these green sheet models, a series of worksheets, such as the following schedules, might have been developed.

- o *Schedule 1: Personnel and Gross Pay Information*—On this schedule, headcounts and straight-time gross pay by cost center would be summarized.

- o *Schedule 2: Overtime Premium*—This schedule would take the estimates of overtime by cost center and, using data from Schedule 1, calculate the additional straight-time labor that would be incurred as well as the overtime premium costs that would be paid.

○ *Schedule 3: Shift Premium*—The distribution of each cost center's employees between shifts would be determined and used along with Schedule 1's gross pay information to calculate shift premium costs.

○ *Schedule 4: Direct Working Indirect*—Because personnel classified as direct labor do not normally work 100% of the time on direct activities, provision must be made for the time they spend on indirect activities. The cost of this portion of their activities must be included as indirect labor. The percentages of total time spent on indirect activities by direct labor personnel would be used, together with total direct labor costs developed in Schedules 1 and 2, to determine the amount of this direct-working-indirect cost.

○ *Schedule 5: Vacation, Holiday, and Sick Pay*—Average vacation hours, holiday hours, and other paid-while-not-working benefit hours would be used together with gross pay information from earlier schedules to determine the costs of these fringe benefits, as well as the amount of labor cost that would remain to be charged as direct or indirect labor.

○ *Schedule 6: Fringe Benefit Rate Calculations*—Fringe benefit information developed in Schedule 5, together with costs determined for other fringe benefits, would be gathered and summarized. The totals would be divided by the labor hours or dollars from earlier schedules to determine fringe benefit rates.

○ *Schedule 7: Square Footage Distribution*—A schedule would be prepared determining the percentage distribution of the facility's square footage between cost centers.

○ *Schedule 8: Depreciation Expense*—Equipment depreciation expense would be summarized by cost center from lapse schedules, and building depreciation would be multiplied by the various square footage percentages from Schedule 7 to distribute it among the cost centers. Other distribution information relating to capital assets (e.g., original cost or appraised value) would also be included.

o *Schedule 9: Leases and Rentals*—A schedule would be prepared summarizing all lease and rental costs by cost center.

o *Schedule 10: Other Fixed Allocations*—Other costs needing to be distributed on the basis of square footage or any other basis that might have been included on Schedules 7 or 8 would be determined and distributed according to the appropriate percentages.

o *Schedule 11: Utilities*—Utility costs would be determined by cost center.

o *Schedule 12: Supplies*—The cost of major supplies would be determined by cost center.

o *Schedule 13: Budgeted Expenses*—All other budgeted costs would be determined by cost center.

At this point, a schedule is needed on which this information can be accumulated and summarized. I refer to this worksheet as Schedule 20. All of the costs determined by Schedules 1 through 13 would be carried forward to this schedule. The information accumulated on Schedule 20 is used for calculations on the schedules discussed below.

o *Schedule 14: General Factory Overhead Distribution*—Total general factory overhead costs would be taken from Schedule 20 and their distribution determined from the headcount information on Schedule 1. The resulting distribution would be carried to Schedule 20, where it would appear as a credit to general factory overhead and as charges to the applicable cost centers.

o *Schedule 15: Service Centers Distributions*—The total cost of Maintenance (the first-sequence service center) would be taken from Schedule 20 and distributed to other cost centers (including other service centers) and cost objectives based on an estimate of their demand. The result would be carried forward to Schedule 20, where it would appear as a credit to Maintenance and as charges to the appropriate cost centers and objectives. This process would then be repeated twice, for Engineering and for the Tool Room.

o *Schedule 16: Direct Materials and Outside Services* —A schedule would be prepared summarizing the direct material purchases for the year, as well as the direct outside processing costs and tooling purchased from outside sources. These amounts would be used to update Schedule 20.

o *Schedule 17: Production Support Distribution* —The total costs of the production support cost centers, the cumulative conversion costs of the production activities, and direct outside processing costs would be taken from Schedule 20. The latter two items would be used to distribute the total costs of the production support cost centers. The results would be carried forward to Schedule 20, where credits would appear in all production support cost centers and charges made to the appropriate production cost centers.

o *Schedule 18: Administrative Support Distribution* —The total general and administrative costs and the updated cumulative conversion costs of production cost centers would be taken from Schedule 20, and the administrative costs distributed on the basis of the updated conversion costs. The results would again be carried to Schedule 20, where a credit would appear in General/Administration and charges made to the appropriate production support activities.

o *Schedule 19: Machine Time Information* —A schedule would be developed to calculate the machine hours available for those cost centers whose costs are distributed on a machine hour basis. This data would be carried forward to Schedule 20.

o *Schedule 20: Departmental Cost Accumulation* —By the time Schedules 1 through 19 are completed, Schedule 20 contains all accumulated and distributed costs, as well as the three bases necessary for calculating indirect cost rates: direct labor dollars, machine hours, and direct outside processing costs. Once these calculations have been completed, the green sheet model is done.

In developing this green sheet model, three schedules were included whose sole purpose was to introduce indirect cost allocation bases into the model:

Schedule   7: Square Footage Distribution
Schedule 16: Direct Materials and Outside Services
Schedule 19: Machine Time Information

The balance of the schedules might very well be organized as follows:

Level I — Salaries and Wages
   Schedule 1: Personnel and Gross Pay Information
   Schedule 2: Overtime Premium
   Schedule 3: Shift Premium
   Schedule 4: Direct Working Indirect
Level II — Fringe Benefits
   Schedule 5: Vacation, Holiday, and Sick Pay
   Schedule 6: Fringe Benefit Rate Calculations
Level III — Specific Assignment Costs
   Schedule 8: Depreciation Expense
   Schedule 9: Leases and Rentals
   Schedule 10: Other Fixed Allocations
   Schedule 11: Utilities
   Schedule 12: Supplies
   Schedule 13: Budgeted Expenses
Level IV — General Factory Overhead
   Schedule 14: General Factory Overhead Distribution
Level V — Service Centers
   Schedule 15: Service Centers Distributions
Level VI — Production Support Activities
   Schedule 17: Production Support Distribution
Level VII — General / Administration
   Schedule 18: Administrative Support Distribution
Level VIII — Production Activities
   Schedule 20: Departmental Cost Accumulation

If a model simulating the cost flow pattern and its implementation mechanics can be developed using a series of green sheets,

Exhibit 9.4   Cost Accumulation Model Layout/Costa Manufacturing Company

A81 PR-1	T81 AL-1	
Personnel & Gross Pay	General Factory Overhead	
A161 PR-2	**T161 AL-2**	
Overtime Information	Service Center Billings	
A241 PR-3	**T241 AL-3**	
Shift Premium	Production Support Activity Distribution	
A321 PR-4	**T321 AL-4**	
Direct Working Indirect	Administrative Support Activity Distribution	
A401 FB-1	**T401 AL-5**	
Vacation, Holiday & Sick Pay	Direct Material & Outside Processing	
A481 FB-2	**T481 AL-6**	
Fringe Rate Calculations	Machine Time Information	
A561 SA-1	**T561** **DC-1**	
Square Footage Information	Departmental Cost Accumulation	
A641 SA-2	**T641** **DC-2**	
Depreciation Expense	Indirect Cost Rate Calculations	
A721 SA-3	**T721** **DC-3**	
Leases and Rentals	Rate/Cost Reconciliation	
A801 SA-4		
Other Fixed Allocations		
A881 SA-5		
Utilities		
A961 SA-6		
Supplies		
A1041 SA-7		
Budgeted Expenses		

it is possible not only to build one using standard spreadsheet software, but to develop one with interactive schedules and automatically variable costs that will change as their cost drivers are changed. Such a model would be more than merely a means of calculating annual indirect costing rates following the activity-based design of the system. It could be a valuable tool for use in planning, budgeting and forecasting, capital expenditure decisions, long-term pricing, process value analysis, and a variety of other decision support situations. The personal computer/ spreadsheet software model could be developed by laying out the schedules used in the green sheet model as one, much larger worksheet with each schedule being one section of this *cost accumulation model.*

Exhibit 9.4 shows the layout of the cost accumulation model developed by Costa Manufacturing to simulate its activity-based costing system. The notations in the upper left-hand corner of each section indicate the upper left-hand spreadsheet cell reference of the schedule in the cost accumulation model. The specific schedule reference numbers (e.g., Schedule PR–1, SA–6, DC–1) are located in the upper right-hand corner of each section. Note that the schedules in the left-hand column of the diagram represent Levels I to III in Costa's cost flow pattern, and those on the right represent Levels IV through VIII.

The system designer is now ready to begin gathering the information that will be necessary to drive the cost accumulation model once it has actually been built.

10

Data Gathering

In gathering the information necessary to drive the cost accumulation model, the system designer must continue to keep in mind that the goal is accuracy, not precision. To this point, the process has involved concepts, not statistical data. Where it may be easy to keep the desire for precision under control during the conceptual stages, the tendency is to revert back to the comfort of precision when confronted with hard, cold, statistical data. For abc to be cost-effective, this tendency must be kept under control.

Advantage should be taken of any good historical data that are available. Where none are available, however, interviews with and estimates by appropriate and knowledgeable employees are effective substitutes. When the information is material, mechanisms can be established for gathering the necessary data for use in later model updates.

By the time this step in the process is reached, the organization has a cost flow concept based on cause–effect relationships. Estimated distributions along this new cost flow will be vastly superior to distributions measured precisely using the organization's previous inappropriate drivers along its former cost flows. Even with these estimates, tremendous improvements will be made in cost accuracy, providing the estimates are developed by working with individuals knowledgeable about the information being sought. The data required for Levels I, II, III, and V are described in the following sections.

Level I—Salaries and Wages

In developing the worksheet schedules necessary to introduce Level I cost information into the cost accumulation model, the following data are needed:

- By *category* (salary, hourly direct, hourly indirect) and by *cost center:*
  1. Headcount
  2. Gross, straight-time payroll cost
  3. Percentage of overtime worked
- By *category* (salary, hourly) and by *cost center:*
  4. Headcount by shift
  5. Overtime premium formula
  6. Shift premium formula
- By *cost center* only:
  7. Percentage of time spent on indirect activities by employees categorized as direct
- By *category* (hourly) only:
  8. Average paid-for-not-working benefit hours (such benefits for salaried employees are not usually broken out for cost accounting purposes).

It is usually advisable to accumulate and summarize detailed salary and wage information before entering it into the cost accumulation model. The model and its data must be accessible to many employees and some outsiders; however, salary and wage information is usually confidential. These conflicting needs can be reconciled by the aggregation of salary and wage data in a separate worksheet accessible only to authorized personnel.

Items 1 and 2, headcount and gross, straight-time payroll cost, can be derived, without too much difficulty, from personnel and payroll records. Even if new cost centers have been added, it is rarely difficult to determine in which cost centers employees are working and then calculate their annual, straight-time compensation for inclusion in that cost center.

Items 3 and 4, percentage of overtime worked and the head-count distribution by shift, can be more difficult to determine. If these premiums were not previously summarized by employee or cost center, it may be necessary to interview the appropriate personnel to determine each cost center's normal shift and overtime levels.

Items 5 and 6, overtime and shift premium formulas, are usually straightforward and available from union contracts, policy statements, and the like.

Obtaining accurate information on Item 7, indirect activities of direct employees, may prove to be the most difficult of the Level I items. Unless the existing system collects labor information at an extraordinary level of detail, management's estimates may be the best possible for the initial model.

The difficulties of collecting data on the indirect activities of direct labor personnel are compounded by the fact that, in earlier steps, the organization has most likely redefined "direct labor." As a result, any historical data that have not been broken down in sufficient detail will not be adequate in developing these percentages.

In collecting information relative to Item 8, paid-for-not-working benefit hours, most errors occur in overlooking benefits, not in collecting inaccurate information. Average vacation hours can usually be determined from data available in personnel records. Average holiday hours is even simpler to determine. It may take a little more analysis to develop an average for paid sick days, but the raw data are usually available. Paid breaks can be determined from union contracts or the organization's policy statements.

Level II—Fringe Benefits

To introduce Level II cost information into the cost accumulation model, the following data are needed by *category* (salary, hourly):

9. Identification of each purchased fringe benefit
10. Identification of the driver of each purchased fringe benefit's cost

11. The cost factor for using drivers to determine each fringe benefit's cost to the organization.

For Item 9, purchased fringe benefits can be identified by reviewing union contracts, policy statements, and expense ledgers, and by interviewing appropriate management or staff personnel. The nature of each benefit will suggest its most appropriate driver (Item 10), whereas examination of tax returns, invoices, annual insurance reports or audits, and the like, will provide the cost factors needed to apply to the driver to estimate each benefit's total cost (Item 11).

Level III—Specific Assignment Costs

There are two categories into which specific assignment costs are divided while building a cost accumulation model. The first category consists of fixed costs and those variable costs that *do not vary automatically* with changes in the level of operation. These include items such as depreciation charges, leases and rentals, property taxes, some types of insurance, budgeted expenses, and certain (fixed) elements of utilities. The second category consists of those variable costs that *do vary automatically* with changes in the level of operation. These include items such as variable utility costs and supplies.

In developing the worksheet schedules necessary to introduce into the model the first category of Level III cost information, the following data are needed by *cost center:*

12. Required nonexpense data to be used for cost distribution purposes
13. Depreciation and other non-working capital–related expenses
14. Lease and rental costs
15. Budgeted expenses
16. Fixed utility cost.

Item 12 would include nonexpense distribution–basis information, such as building square footage, original capital asset cost and/or accumulated depreciation, capital asset replacement cost, and any other data required to provide any necessary fixed distribution basis.

The building square footage can be calculated from a reasonably accurate plant layout diagram. Remember, the goal is accuracy, not precision. Aisles can be included with the adjoining cost centers. Locker rooms, cafeterias, and other general areas can be categorized as General/Administration, General Factory Overhead, Fringe Benefits, or whatever classification would most closely match the organization's cost flow concept. Expense information relating to capital assets (Item 13) can be taken from fixed asset records and recent capital asset appraisals. Other nonworking capital–related expense data can be obtained from amortization schedules or other appropriate records.

Items 14 and 15, lease, rental, and other budgeted expenses, can be determined by reviewing expense listings, lease agreements, or profit plans and budgets.

Fixed utility cost, Item 16, is not as easily determined as the other costs in this category. For most small and mid-sized organizations, utility costs are recorded in total or by type (e.g., electric, gas, water). Fixed and variable elements are not separated. As a result, input from plant engineers or other knowledgeable individuals is required. Whether determined through sophisticated calculations or informed intuition, that portion of utilities that remains fixed over the "relevant range" of operating levels can and should be segregated from the total utility costs.

In the case of Costa Manufacturing, this fixed utility component represents the electricity needed to light the facility, operate office equipment, and control climate. At a higher level of sophistication, a separate fixed demand-charge component of the electricity cost for operating the factory equipment could be identified for special treatment. In either case, if the fixed portion of utility costs is deemed to be material, an approximation of that amount is preferable to totally ignoring the fact that it exists.

The information necessary to develop worksheet schedules for the second category of Level III costs, those that vary with operating levels, requires considerable statistical analysis. The major costs falling into this category are the variable utility costs and operating supplies.

In building the model, one goal is to have variable utility costs vary along with their drivers. To show how the information can be developed to attain this goal, I describe how it was accomplished at Costa Manufacturing.

During the Costa project, the system designer learned that $182,000 of electricity cost was incurred during the previous year. Of this total, engineering personnel estimated that $30,000 was the fixed portion discussed earlier. This left $152,000 of electricity cost that needed to be related somehow to the facility's operation.

Interviews with plant and engineering personnel indicated that most of the electricity consumption takes place in Welding, Assembly, Press Operations, and CNC Machining. Engineering's analysis estimated the following distribution of electricity consumption: 16% Welding, 13% Assembly, 51% Press Operations, and 20% CNC Machining. The problem is how to turn this information into a means of calculating this variable electric cost at various levels of operations.

The answer comes in the form of a tool discussed in Chapter 8, namely, consumption units. In Chapter 9, the drivers were selected for measuring activity and distributing costs in all of Costa's cost centers, including the four mentioned above. Direct labor dollars was identified as the driver of Assembly and Welding and machine hours as the driver for Press Operations and CNC Machining. Because there are two different drivers, the situation is similar to that shown in Exhibit 8.3, where a single element of cost is driven by more than one type of driver.

The task for this cost, as well as for later automatically variable costs, is to do the following by *cost center* and *variable cost element:*

17. Select a consumption unit.
18. Determine the cost per consumption unit.
19. Select the appropriate cost driver for charging the cost element into the cost center.
20. Estimate the amount of the period's cost driver (direct labor dollars or machine hours in the case of variable electricity costs).

Exhibit 10.1 Variable Electricity Cost Analysis/Costa Manufacturing Company

Cost Center	Driver	% Distribution	Variable Electric Cost	Assumed Cost per Unit	Driver Estimate	Calculated Driver Multiplier
Welding	DLDollars	16.00	24,320	150	320,000	0.0005
Assembly	DLDollars	13.00	19,760	150	260,000	0.0005
Press Operations	MHours	51.00	77,520	150	25,900	0.0200
CNC Machine	MHours	20.00	30,400	150	10,150	0.0200
		100.00	152,000			
Estimated fixed electric cost			30,000			
Total electric cost			182,000			

21. Use Items 17 through 20, together with the data already gathered, to calculate the driver multipliers that will be needed for the model to calculate the automatically variable costs.

The consumption unit selected by Costa for electricity consumption (Item 17) is 1,000 KWH. The average cost per 1,000 KWH hours during the previous year (Item 18) was $150. The following information was developed by production control for the year (Items 19 and 20): Welding $320,000 direct labor, Assembly $260,000 direct labor, Press Operations 25,900 machine hours, and CNC Machining 10,150 machine hours. With this information, Costa was then able to calculate the appropriate driver multipliers (Item 21), as shown in Exhibit 10.1.

In Exhibit 10.1, the $152,000 variable utility cost was distributed among the four applicable operating cost centers using the percentages noted earlier. These costs were then divided by the cost per consumption unit ($150), and the resulting amount was divided by the driver estimate. The result is a series of driver multipliers that can be used in the cost accumulation model to calculate variable electricity costs. For example, with a multiplier of .0005, $400,000 of direct labor in Welding will generate a variable electricity cost of $30,000 ($400,000 \times .0005 \times 150). If direct labor fell to $250,000, only $18,750 of variable electricity cost would be generated ($250,000 \times .0005 \times 150).

Variable supplies present a similar problem. The operating supply costs at Costa are broken down approximately as follows:

Argon	$ 96,000
Drawing compounds	77,000
Drills and cutters	51,600
Other variable supplies	125,000

Argon is used exclusively in Welding, drawing compounds in Press Operations, and drills and cutters in CNC Machining. Discussions with plant and administrative management resulted in an estimated distribution of the other variable supplies as follows:

General/Administration	8.0%
General Factory	3.2%
Engineering	12.8%
Maintenance	4.8%
Tool Room	8.0%
Production Control	3.2%
Quality Control	4.0%
Shipping and Receiving	1.6%
Welding	25.6%
Assembly	0.0%
Press Operations	20.8%
CNC Machining	8.0%

In developing a set of driver multipliers to be used in calculating the amount of the variable supply costs, separate driver multipliers must be calculated for each major supply category and a separate set for the other category. Exhibit 10.2 shows the calculation of multipliers for the three major supply categories. For each category, an average cost per consumption unit was established and used, along with the driver information already estimated for use in determining variable electric cost, to arrive at the cost center's driver multiplier.

Using Welding as an example, the $96,000 cost of argon was divided by the $320,000 cost of direct labor, and the result was divided by the $6.00 average unit cost to arrive at the multiplier of .05. Using this driver multiplier, argon costs can be projected based on direct labor dollars incurred in Welding. For example, an increase in direct labor to $400,000 will result in argon costs of $120,000 ($400,000 × .05 × $6.00). A decrease of direct labor to $250,000 will result in a reduction of argon costs to $75,000 ($250,000 × .05 × $6.00).

The calculation of driver multipliers for other variable supplies, shown in Exhibit 10.3, encompasses more than merely the operating cost centers. This calculation also includes the Levels IV through VII cost centers. Discussions with management indicate that the most appropriate driver of supplies in these cost centers is headcount. As a result, estimated headcount in each cost center is included as the driver estimate.

Exhibit 10.2 Major Variable Supplies Analysis/Costa Manufacturing Company

Cost Center	Driver	Driver Estimate	Argon	Drawing Compounds	Drills & Cutters	Average Cost per Unit	Calculated Driver Multiplier
Welding	DLDollars	320,000	96,000			6.000	0.05
Assembly	DLDollars	260,000					
Press Operations	MHours	25,900		77,000		3.000	1.00
CNC Machining	MHours	10,150			51,600	5.556	0.90

Exhibit 10.3 Other Variable Supplies Analysis/Costa Manufacturing Company

Cost Center	Driver	Driver Estimate	% Distribution	Other Variable Supplies	Assumed Cost per Unit	Calculated Driver Multiplier
General/Admin	Headcount	10	8.00	10,000	1.00	1,000
General Factory	Headcount	4	3.20	4,000	1.00	1,000
Engineering	Headcount	16	12.80	16,000	1.00	1,000
Maintenance	Headcount	6	4.80	6,000	1.00	1,000
Tool Room	Headcount	10	8.00	10,000	1.00	1,000
Prod Control	Headcount	4	3.20	4,000	1.00	1,000
Quality Control	Headcount	5	4.00	5,000	1.00	1,000
Ship & Receiving	Headcount	2	1.60	2,000	1.00	1,000
Welding	DLDollars	320,000	25.60	32,000	1.00	0.100
Assembly	DLDollars	260,000	0.00	0	1.00	0.000
Press Operations	MHours	25,900	20.80	26,000	1.00	1.000
CNC Machine	MHours	10,150	8.00	10,000	1.00	1.000
			100.00	125,000		

After distributing the other variable supplies cost of $125,000 according to the percentages established earlier and setting the assumed cost per unit at $1.00 (remember that this is a phantom consumption unit—there is no real unit of measure), the same series of calculations is performed as in Exhibits 10.1 and 10.2 to arrive at the driver multipliers for the calculation of other variable supplies.

Level V—Service Centers

Service centers are designed so that their costs can be charged out as needed on a time-and-materials basis. As a result, hours of demand by other cost centers and cost objectives must be established for the distribution of each service center's accumulated cost. To accomplish this, it is necessary to determine the following by *service center* and in some cases (as we will see in Engineering) by *subcategories* within the service centers:

22. Potential billable hours per employee
23. Anticipated percentage of potential hours that will actually be billable
24. Percentage of total billable hours demanded by each of the other cost centers and cost objectives.

The first service center to be considered is Engineering. During preliminary discussions with Costa's director of engineering, the system designer learned that there was no such thing as an "average" engineer whose activities could be analyzed to establish the demand for the department's services. Engineers were divided into four categories; four industrial engineers, two welding engineers, five process engineers, and four product engineers. The director of engineering believed that it was possible to develop separate demand information for the services of the "average" industrial engineer, welding engineer, process engineer, and product engineer.

Interviews were conducted with engineering personnel, and the results were combined with other data to develop the analysis presented in Exhibit 10.4. Average annual hours available were

Exhibit 10.4 Engineering Demand Analysis/Costa Manufacturing Company

	Industrial Engineers (4)		Welding Engineers (2)		Process Engineers (5)		Product Engineers (4)		Total Engineers (15)
	%	Hours	%	Hours	%	Hours	%	Hours	Hours
General Administration	11.2	747	15.0	499	50.0	4,156	50.0	3,325	8,727
General Factory Overhead		0		0		0		0	0
Engineering		—		—		—		—	—
Maintenance		0		0		0		0	0
Tool Room		0		0		0		0	0
Production Control		0		0		0		0	0
Quality Assurance		0		0		0		0	0
Shipping and Receiving		0		0		0		0	0
Welding	13.8	915	85.0	2,825		0		0	3,740
Assembly		0		0	15.0	1,247		0	1,247
Direct Press Labor		0		0		0		0	0
Press Operations	25.0	1,662		0	10.0	832		0	2,494
CNC Machine	25.0	1,662		0	10.0	832		0	2,494
Other direct costs		0		0		0	18.8	1,247	1,247
Tooling projects		0		0	5.0	416	31.2	2,078	2,494
Capital projects	25.0	1,663		0	10.0	831		0	2,494
Total	100.0	6,649	100.0	3,324	100.0	8,314	100.0	6,650	24,937

Potential billable hours per employee: 2,078.
Anticipated billing percentage: 80%.
Planned billable hours per employee: 1,662.

derived from historical payroll and personnel records (Item 22). The amount of available time spent working on projects for other cost centers or cost objectives was established (Item 23). Finally, the percentage of demand for each of the engineering subcategories also was established (Item 24).

The potential billable hours per employee of 2,078 (Item 22) were reduced to 1,662 planned billable hours using the 80% anticipated billing percentage (Item 23). For each category of engineer, the 1,662 hours was multiplied by the number of engineers in that category, and that amount was multiplied by each cost center's demand percentage (Item 24) to establish the number of hours of engineering time demanded by each cost center. By combining the resulting hours for each category of engineer, total demand (in hours) for the entire Engineering cost center's services was established.

The next service center to be addressed was Maintenance. Unlike Engineering, Maintenance had only one general category of worker, so the percentage of demand for its services was more easily determined through interviews with plant management and the maintenance supervisor. These interviews, together with a review of payroll and personnel data, showed that Items 22 and 23 for Maintenance were the same as those for Engineering. An analysis similar to that done for Engineering created an estimated demand, in hours, for the Maintenance cost center's services. This is shown in Exhibit 10.5.

An analysis of Maintenance requires some information not needed in developing data for Engineering. This involves the additional purchased maintenance costs that usually accompany the performance of maintenance work by Maintenance employees. These purchased maintenance costs are described in more detail in Chapter 13. To establish this cost element in the model, the following must be determined by *cost center:*

> 25. The percentage of relationship between Maintenance cost center charges and the additional purchased maintenance cost required.

To establish these percentages, projected purchased maintenance costs by cost center are estimated through analysis of

Exhibit 10.5   Maintenance Demand Analysis/Costa Manufacturing Company

	Maintenance Personnel (6)		Est. Cost @ $25.00 per Hour	Purchased Maintenance Cost Percentages	
	%	Hours	Est $	Est $	% $
General/Administration	2.0	200	5,000	500	10.0
General Factory Overhead		0	0		
Engineering	2.0	200	5,000	500	10.0
Maintenance	—	0	0		
Tool Room	4.0	399	9,975	1,000	10.0
Production Control	4.0	399	9,975	1,000	10.0
Quality Assurance	4.0	399	9,975	1,000	10.0
Shipping and Receiving	4.0	399	9,975	1,000	10.0
Welding	10.0	998	24,950	5,000	20.0
Assembly	10.0	997	24,925	5,000	20.0
Direct Press Labor		0			
Press Operations	25.0	2,494	62,350	60,000	100.0
CNC Machine	15.0	1,496	37,400	20,000	50.0
Other direct costs	10.0	997	24,925		
Tooling projects		0	0		
Capital projects	10.0	997	24,925		
	100.0	9,975	249,375	95,000	

Potential billable hours per employee: 2,078.
Anticipated billing percentage: 80%.
Planned billable hours per employee: 1,662

historical data and discussions with Maintenance personnel. A provisional Maintenance hourly billing rate (in Costa's case, $25) is chosen to convert demand hours to dollars. The percentage of relationship between these Maintenance billings and the purchased maintenance costs is then calculated. This calculation is also shown in Exhibit 10.5.

The final service center requiring data collection is the Tool Room. Investigation again showed data for Items 22 and 23 to be the same as for Engineering. Interviews with Tool Room personnel indicated that the percentages of distribution of the Tool Room's services were as follows:

Welding	5.0
Assembly	5.0
Press Operations	21.4
CNC Machining	8.6
Other direct costs	5.0
Tooling projects	55.0

By using the same procedures as with Engineering and Maintenance, the demand, in hours, of Tool Room's services can be estimated as shown in Exhibit 10.6.

Exhibit 10.6   Tool Room Demand Analysis/Costa Manufacturing Company

	Tool Room Personnel (10)	
	%	Hours
General/Administration	—	0
General Factory Overhead	—	0
Engineering	—	0
Maintenance	—	0
Tool Room	—	0
Production Control	—	0
Quality Assurance	—	0
Shipping and Receiving	—	0
Welding	5.0	831
Assembly	5.0	831
Direct Press Labor		0
Press Operations	21.4	3,563
CNC Machine	8.6	1,425
Other direct costs	5.0	831
Tooling projects	55.0	9,144
Capital projects		0
	100.0	16,625

Potential billable hours per employee: 2,078.
Anticipated billing percentage: 80%.
Planned billable hours per employee: 1,662.

Data for Other Levels

Data required for Level IV, VI, VII, and VIII worksheet schedules is either collected as part of other levels' data needs or derived from data collected elsewhere in the model. However, a few other data items remain to be gathered:

26. Annual direct material cost
27. Annual direct outside service costs
28. Annual tooling material purchases.

To provide for variability in the machine hours generated by Press Operations and CNC Machining, the following must be established by *machine hour–driven cost center:*

29. The number of pieces of equipment whose cost is to be distributed on a machine hour basis
30. The percentage of estimated downtime by cause.

With the collection of these data, it is now possible to move forward and create a cost accumulation model to simulate the flow of costs throughout the organization.

11

Building the Cost
Accumulation Model:
Salaries, Wages, and
Fringe Benefits

The cost accumulation model is easiest to follow if it is given the form of a computerized set of green sheets. The temptation may arise occasionally to use the software to "shortcut" the calculations and derive the answer without providing a clear visual depiction of the flow of information and reasoning. These temptations should be resisted. Using shortcuts can turn the model into a "black box" that is fully understood only by the model builder and the few individuals who regularly use the model. By retaining the green sheet format, the model becomes a much more effective tool for other members of management to visualize the flow of costs and change the way they think about costs.

In describing the model, I proceed through each schedule in sequence. I do not provide details about coding the worksheets, because each model builder most likely has techniques with which he or she is most comfortable. The combination of the narrative description of each schedule's calculations and the copies of Costa Manufacturing's schedules should provide the model builder with the necessary information as to how each schedule works and how it fits together with the model as a whole. Keep in mind, however, that no mathematical process more difficult than addition, subtraction, multiplication, and division should be necessary.

For each schedule, I describe where the data came from and how the data is processed by the model. I use diagrams to show each schedule's placement within the entire model, the other schedules that provide it with input, and the schedules to which it sends output. Finally, I provide Costa's completed copy of the applicable schedule. Information that must be newly entered on each schedule (not calculated or carried forward from another schedule) is italicized in the narrative and boxed on the schedule from Costa's model.

The centerpiece of the model is Schedule DC–1: Departmental Cost Accumulation (Chapter 14). This is the equivalent of Schedule 20 of the Chapter 9 green sheets on which the costs of all cost centers are accumulated. I specifically state the interaction of each schedule with Schedule DC–1.

Six schedules are involved in this section of the model regarding salaries, wages, and fringe benefits. The first four relate to payroll information and are referenced as PR schedules. The last two pertain to fringe benefits and are known as FB schedules.

Schedule PR–1: Personnel & Gross Payroll Information

Schedule PR–1 (Exhibits 11.1 and 11.2) is used to *enter both salary and hourly headcounts and annual gross straight-time pay for all but one of Costa's Level IV through Level VIII cost centers.* The exception is Outside Processing in Level VIII. This cost center receives only production support cost center distributions and, thus, does not appear in the model until that point is reached.

This schedule's listing of cost center titles and their grouping for subtotal purposes is repeated on most schedules in the model. Because this is the first schedule to be created, the model builder should enter these captions on this schedule and then use the appropriate function (if the software allows) to automatically copy them to the other schedules on which they appear. In this manner, it is much easier to change cost center titles when necessary.

Because Costa does not pay overtime to salaried personnel, salary cost by cost center goes directly to Schedule DC–1: Departmental Cost Accumulation.

Schedule PR–2: Overtime Information

Schedule PR–2 (Exhibits 11.3 and 11.4) is used to determine the additional straight-time direct and indirect labor to be incurred due to overtime as well as the overtime premium cost.

To accomplish this, direct and indirect headcounts by cost center are brought forward from Schedule PR–1. *The percentage of overtime expected to be worked by direct and indirect labor in each cost center is entered.* Using these percentages, the headcount information, and a standard 2,080-hour straight-time year, the additional hours to be worked in each cost center are calculated.

From the information on Schedule PR–1, the average hourly wage for each cost center is calculated and extended by the overtime hours to determine the additional straight-time wages to be paid for these overtime hours.

The premium percentage for overtime worked is entered and multiplied by each cost center's straight-time overtime wages to determine the overtime premium cost expected for each cost center.

Finally, the average overtime hours per hourly employee is calculated from the total headcount and total additional hours already included on the schedule.

Overtime premium costs go directly to Schedule DC–1: Departmental Cost Accumulation.

Schedule PR–3: Shift Premium

Schedule PR–3 (Exhibits 11.5 and 11.6) is used to determine the amount of shift premium paid for each cost center.

Total headcount by cost center is brought forward from Schedule PR–1. *The numbers of employees working on second and third shifts are entered.* The model then calculates the number of employees working on each cost center's first shift by subtracting shift-two and shift-three employees from the total headcount.

Exhibit 11.1   Schedule PR—1 Information

PURPOSE: To provide for the input and summarization of basic personnel and gross pay information.

MANUAL INPUT: Headcount and gross annual straight-time pay by cost center for both salary and hourly employees

INPUT FROM: No other schedules

OUTPUT TO:

Schedule PR—2	Schedule FB—1	Schedule DC—1
Schedule PR—3	Schedule FB—2	Schedule SA—6
Schedule PR—4	Schedule AL—2	Schedule AL—1

LEVEL: I—Salaries and Wages

A81 PR-1	T81 AL-1
Personnel & Gross Pay	General Factory Overhead
A161 PR-2	T161 AL-2
Overtime Information	Service Center Billings
A241 PR-3	T241 AL-3
Shift Premium	Production Support Activity Distribution
A321 PR-4	T321 AL-4
Direct Working Indirect	Administrative Support Activity Distribution
A401 FB-1	T401 AL-5
Vacation, Holiday & Sick Pay	Direct Material & Outside Processing
A481 FB-2	T481 AL-6
Fringe Rate Calculations	Machine Time Information
A561 SA-1	T561 DC-1
Square Footage Information	Departmental Cost Accumulation
A641 SA-2	T641 DC-2
Depreciation Expense	Indirect Cost Rate Calculations
A721 SA-3	T721 DC-3
Leases and Rentals	Rate/Cost Reconciliation
A801 SA-4	
Other Fixed Allocations	
A881 SA-5	
Utilities	
A961 SA-6	
Supplies	
A1041 SA-7	
Budgeted Expenses	

Exhibit 11.2   Schedule PR—1

| | HEADCOUNT | | | | GROSS PAYROLL | | | |
| | | HOURLY | | | | HOURLY | | |
	SALARY	DIRECT	INDIRECT	TOTAL	SALARY	DIRECT	INDIRECT	TOTAL
General & Administrative	10.0	0.0	0.0	10.0	500,000	0	0	500,000
General Factory Overhead	4.0	0.0	0.0	4.0	120,000	0	0	120,000
Engineering	8.0	0.0	8.0	16.0	280,000	0	160,000	440,000
Maintenance	2.0	0.0	4.0	6.0	72,000	0	88,000	160,000
Tool Room	0.0	0.0	10.0	10.0	0	0	196,000	196,000
Production Control	2.0	0.0	2.0	4.0	72,000	0	36,000	108,000
Quality Assurance	2.0	0.0	3.0	5.0	96,000	0	100,000	196,000
Shipping & Receiving	0.0	0.0	2.0	2.0	0	0	32,000	32,000
TOTAL STAFF & INDIRECT	28.0	0.0	29.0	57.0	1,140,000	0	612,000	1,752,000
Welding	0.0	16.0	0.0	16.0	0	352,000	0	352,000
Assembly	0.0	16.0	0.0	16.0	0	288,000	0	288,000
Direct Press Labor	0.0	24.0	0.0	24.0	0	480,000	0	480,000
Press Operations	0.0	0.0	0.0	0.0	0	0	0	0
CNC Machining	0.0	0.0	4.0	4.0	0	0	80,000	80,000
TOTAL PRODUCTION	0.0	56.0	4.0	60.0	0	1,120,000	80,000	1,200,000
TOTAL	28.0	56.0	33.0	117.0	1,140,000	1,120,000	692,000	2,952,000

Exhibit 11.3   Schedule PR—2 Information

PURPOSE: To determine the overtime hours worked and the additional straight-time wages and overtime premium cost incurred by cost center

MANUAL INPUT: Percentage of direct and indirect labor overtime required by cost center

Percentage of average overtime premium

INPUT FROM: Schedule PR—1

OUTPUT TO:

Schedule PR—4   Schedule FB—1   Schedule DC—1

LEVEL: I—Salaries and Wages

A81 PR-1	T81 AL-1
Personnel & Gross Pay	General Factory Overhead
A161 PR-2	T161 AL-2
Overtime Information	Service Center Billings
A241 PR-3	T241 AL-3
Shift Premium	Production Support Activity Distribution
A321 PR-4	T321 AL-4
Direct Working Indirect	Administrative Support Activity Distribution
A401 FB-1	T401 AL-5
Vacation, Holiday & Sick Pay	Direct Material & Outside Processing
A481 FB-2	T481 AL-6
Fringe Rate Calculations	Machine Time Information
A561 SA-1	T561 DC-1
Square Footage Information	Departmental Cost Accumulation
A641 SA-2	T641 DC-2
Depreciation Expense	Indirect Cost Rate Calculations
A721 SA-3	T721 DC-3
Leases and Rentals	Rate/Cost Reconciliation
A801 SA-4	
Other Fixed Allocations	
A881 SA-5	
Utilities	
A961 SA-6	
Supplies	
A1041 SA-7	
Budgeted Expenses	

Exhibit 11.4 Schedule PR—2

	HEADCOUNT			OVERTIME PERCENTAGE			AVERAGE	ADDITIONAL LABOR		OVERTIME	
	DIRECT	INDIRECT	TOTAL	DIRECT	INDIRECT	ADDL HOURS	WAGE/HOUR	DIRECT	INDIRECT	PCT	PREMIUM
General & Administrative	0.0	0.0	0.0	0%	0%	0	0.00	0	0	50%	0
General Factory Overhead	0.0	0.0	0.0	0%	0%	0	0.00	0	0	50%	0
Engineering	0.0	8.0	8.0	0%	5%	832	9.62	0	8,000	50%	4,000
Maintenance	0.0	4.0	4.0	0%	5%	416	10.58	0	4,400	50%	2,200
Tool Room	0.0	10.0	10.0	0%	5%	1,040	9.42	0	9,800	50%	4,900
Production Control	0.0	2.0	2.0	0%	5%	208	8.65	0	1,800	50%	900
Quality Assurance	0.0	3.0	3.0	0%	5%	312	16.03	0	5,000	50%	2,500
Shipping & Receiving	0.0	2.0	2.0	0%	5%	208	7.69	0	1,600	50%	800
TOTAL STAFF & INDIRECT	0.0	29.0	29.0			3,016		0	30,600		15,300
Welding	16.0	0.0	16.0	10%	10%	3,328	10.58	35,200	0	50%	17,600
Assembly	16.0	0.0	16.0	10%	10%	3,328	8.65	28,800	0	50%	14,400
Direct Press Labor	24.0	0.0	24.0	10%	10%	4,992	9.62	48,000	0	50%	24,000
Press Operations	0.0	0.0	0.0	10%	0%	0	0.00	0	0	50%	0
CNC Machining	0.0	4.0	4.0		10%	832	9.62	0	8,000	50%	4,000
TOTAL PRODUCTION	56.0	4.0	60.0			12,480		112,000	8,000		60,000
TOTAL	56.0	33.0	89.0			15,496		112,000	38,600		75,300

AVERAGE OVERTIME HOURS
PER HOURLY EMPLOYEE 174.1

137

Exhibit 11.5   Schedule PR—3 Information

PURPOSE: To determine the premium paid for work performed on second and third shifts

MANUAL INPUT: Headcount of personnel working in each cost center on second and third shifts

Percentage of average shift premium

INPUT FROM: Schedule PR—1

OUTPUT TO:

Schedule FB—1   Schedule DC—1

LEVEL: I—Salaries and Wages

A81 PR-1 Personnel & Gross Pay	**T81** AL-1 General Factory Overhead		
A161 PR-2 Overtime Information	**T161** AL-2 Service Center Billings		
A241 PR-3 Shift Premium	**T241** AL-3 Production Support Activity Distribution		
A321 PR-4 Direct Working Indirect	**T321** AL-4 Administrative Support Activity Distribution		
A401 FB-1 Vacation, Holiday & Sick Pay	**T401** AL-5 Direct Material & Outside Processing		
A481 FB-2 Fringe Rate Calculations	**T481** AL-6 Machine Time Information		
A561 SA-1 Square Footage Information	**T561** DC-1 Departmental Cost Accumulation		
A641 SA-2 Depreciation Expense	**T641** DC-2 Indirect Cost Rate Calculations		
A721 SA-3 Leases and Rentals	**T721** DC-3 Rate/Cost Reconciliation		
A801 SA-4 Other Fixed Allocations			
A881 SA-5 Utilities			
A961 SA-6 Supplies			
A1041 SA-7 Budgeted Expenses			

Exhibit 11.6   Schedule PR—3

	EMPLOYEES	1st	2nd	3rd	AVG DEPT WAGES	SHIFT PREMIUM [5.0%]
General & Administrative	10.0	10.0			27,500	0
General Factory Overhead	4.0	4.0			26,700	0
Engineering	16.0	16.0			19,600	0
Maintenance	6.0	4.0	2.0		27,000	2,700
Tool Room	10.0	10.0	0.0		39,200	0
Production Control	4.0	4.0	0.0		16,000	0
Quality Assurance	5.0	3.0	2.0			3,900
Shipping & Receiving	2.0	2.0	0.0			0
TOTAL STAFF & INDIRECT	57.0	53.0	4.0	0.0		6,600
Welding	16.0	10.0	6.0		22,000	6,600
Assembly	16.0	10.0	6.0		18,000	5,400
Direct Press Labor	24.0	14.0	10.0		20,000	10,000
Press Operations	0.0	0.0			0	0
CNC Machining	4.0	2.0	2.0		20,000	2,000
TOTAL PRODUCTION	60.0	36.0	24.0	0.0		24,000
TOTAL	117.0	89.0	28.0	0.0		30,600

Schedule PR–1 information is also used to calculate average annual cost center wages. *The shift premium rate is entered.* These two items are then used to calculate the amount of each cost center's shift premium.

Shift premium costs go directly to Schedule DC–1: Departmental Cost Accumulation.

Schedule PR–4: Direct Working Indirect

Schedule PR–4 (Exhibits 11.7 and 11.8) separates the cost of direct labor personnel into the time they are actually performing direct labor activities and the time they are acting as indirect labor.

Straight-time direct labor cost for a 2,080-hour year is brought forward from Schedule PR–1. Straight-time direct labor overtime cost is brought forward from Schedule PR–2. These combine to become the total straight-time wages paid to direct labor personnel.

Wages paid to hourly employees are not only for time worked. A certain portion is paid during vacations, holidays, sick days, and the like. The percentage of such paid-but-not-working time for hourly employees is calculated on Schedule FB–1. This calculation is not dependent on any data being calculated in Schedule PR–4. As a result, the percentage of wages paid for work being performed (chargeable time) can be brought forward from Schedule FB–1.

This chargeable direct labor percentage is multiplied by the total straight-time wages paid to employees to calculate the total chargeable wages paid to direct labor personnel.

The percentage of direct employees' time spent on indirect activities is entered for each applicable cost center. This percentage is then used to separate direct labor personnel's chargeable wages into direct and indirect categories.

Indirect labor costs attributable to direct labor personnel go directly to Schedule DC–1: Departmental Cost Accumulation.

Schedule FB–1: Vacation, Holiday, and Sick Pay

Schedule FB–1 (Exhibits 11.9 and 11.10) is used to calculate the cost of vacation and holiday pay for hourly employees and to determine the percentage of hourly time paid that workers are actually performing direct or indirect activities.

Straight-time direct and indirect hourly wages for a 2,080-hour year are brought forward from Schedule PR–1. Using direct and indirect headcounts from the same schedule, the total hours worked in a 2,080-hour year are calculated for each category. Overtime hours and overtime cost at straight time are both brought forward from Schedule PR–2. The totals of these labor dollars and hours serve as a base for subsequent calculations.

Average overtime hours per employee is brought forward from Schedule PR–2 and added to a standard year's 2,080 hours to arrive at the average employee's annual hours. *Average vacation and holiday hours are entered.* Costa does not pay for sick time, so sick hours are excluded from the calculations. Percentages of total annual hours are calculated for both vacation and holiday hours. These percentages are then applied to the total straight-time labor dollars to determine the annual cost of each of these two benefits.

The two calculated percentages are subtracted from 100% to determine the percentage of paid time that hourly employees are performing direct or indirect activities. This is the percentage that was used on Schedule PR–4 in the calculation of chargeable direct labor dollars.

Shift premium costs are brought forward from Schedule PR–3 for use in reconciling gross payroll dollars.

Vacation and holiday pay costs go directly to Schedule DC–1: Departmental Cost Accumulation.

Schedule FB–2: Fringe Benefit Rate Calculation

Schedule FB–2 (Exhibits 11.11 and 11.12) is used to calculate the costs of the various purchased fringe benefits for both salaried and hourly personnel and to develop a fringe benefit rate for both categories of employees.

The cost of each fringe benefit, either as a percentage of gross payroll or cost per employee, is entered. Gross hourly payroll is brought forward from Schedule FB–1. Gross salaries and both hourly and salary headcounts are brought forward from Schedule PR–1.

The appropriate multiplier—either headcount or gross payroll dollars—is multiplied by the cost factor to determine annual

Exhibit 11.7   Schedule PR—4 Information

PURPOSE: To establish the amount of direct labor personnel's time and cost that will actually be indirect labor

MANUAL INPUT: Percentage of direct labor time actually spent on indirect activities by cost center

INPUT FROM:

Schedule PR—1   Schedule PR—2   Schedule FB—1

OUTPUT TO:

Schedule SA—5   Schedule DC—1   Schedule DC—2
Schedule SA—6

LEVEL: I—Salaries and Wages

A81 PR-1 Personnel & Gross Pay	T81 AL-1 General Factory Overhead
A161 PR-2 Overtime Information	T161 AL-2 Service Center Billings
A241 PR-3 Shift Premium	T241 AL-3 Production Support Activity Distribution
A321 PR-4 Direct Working Indirect	T321 AL-4 Administrative Support Activity Distribution
A401 FB-1 Vacation, Holiday & Sick Pay	T401 AL-5 Direct Material & Outside Processing
A481 FB-2 Fringe Rate Calculations	T481 AL-6 Machine Time Information
A561 SA-1 Square Footage Information	T561 DC-1 Departmental Cost Accumulation
A641 SA-2 Depreciation Expense	T641 DC-2 Indirect Cost Rate Calculations
A721 SA-3 Leases and Rentals	T721 DC-3 Rate/Cost Reconciliation
A801 SA-4 Other Fixed Allocations	
A881 SA-5 Utilities	
A961 SA-6 Supplies	
A1041 SA-7 Budgeted Expenses	

Exhibit 11.8 Schedule PR—4

	S/T DIRECT LABOR	OVERTIME DIRECT LABOR	TOTAL DIRECT	CHARGABLE DIRECT %	CHARGABLE DIRECT	% TIME INDIRECT ACTIVITIES	DIRECT WORKING INDIRECT	NET DIRECT LABOR
Welding	352,000	35,200	387,200	92.2%	356,998	10%	35,700	321,298
Assembly	288,000	28,800	316,800	92.2%	292,090	10%	29,209	262,881
Direct Press Labor	480,000	48,000	528,000	92.2%	486,816	10%	48,682	438,134
Press Operations	0	0	0	92.2%	0	N/A	0	0
CNC Machining	0	0	0	92.2%	0	N/A	0	0
TOTAL	1,120,000	112,000	1,232,000				113,590	1,022,314

Exhibit 11.9   Schedule FB—1 Information

PURPOSE: To determine the amount paid to hourly employees for time not worked and establish the percentage of paid time actually worked

MANUAL INPUT: Average vacation, holiday, and sick pay hours

INPUT FROM:

Schedule PR—1	Schedule PR—2	Schedule PR—3

OUTPUT TO:

Schedule PR—4	Schedule AL—2	Schedule DC—1
Schedule FB—2	Schedule AL—6	

LEVEL: II—Fringe Benefits

A81 PR-1 Personnel & Gross Pay	T81 AL-1 General Factory Overhead
A161 PR-2 Overtime Information	T161 AL-2 Service Center Billings
A241 PR-3 Shift Premium	T241 AL-3 Production Support Activity Distribution
A321 PR-4 Direct Working Indirect	T321 AL-4 Administrative Support Activity Distribution
A401 FB-1 Vacation, Holiday & Sick Pay	T401 AL-5 Direct Material & Outside Processing
A481 FB-2 Fringe Rate Calculations	T481 AL-6 Machine Time Information
A561 SA-1 Square Footage Information	T561 DC-1 Departmental Cost Accumulation
A641 SA-2 Depreciation Expense	T641 DC-2 Indirect Cost Rate Calculations
A721 SA-3 Leases and Rentals	T721 DC-3 Rate/Cost Reconciliation
A801 SA-4 Other Fixed Allocations	
A881 SA-5 Utilities	
A961 SA-6 Supplies	
A1041 SA-7 Budgeted Expenses	

Exhibit 11.10   Schedule FB—1

	% HOURLY LABOR $	$ / LABOR HOUR
"FRINGE BASE" HOURLY WAGES:		
Hourly Wages/Hours - Direct	1,120,000	116,480
Hourly Wages/Hours - Indirect	692,000	68,640
Hourly Wages/Hours - Overtime	150,600	15,496
TOTAL "FRINGE BASE" HOURLY WAGES	1,962,600	200,616
VACATION:		
Base hours per annum	2,254	
Average vacation hours	80	
Hourly vacation cost	3.5% 68,691	3.5% 7,022
HOLIDAY:		
Base hours per annum	2,254	
Average paid holiday hours	96	
Hourly holiday pay cost	4.3% 84,392	4.3% 8,626
SICK PAY:		
Base hours per annum	2,254	
Average allowable sick pay hours	0	
Hourly sick pay cost	0.0% 0	0.0% 0
PERCENTAGE TIME NOT WORKED BENEFITS:		
Time not worked benefits	7.8% 153,083	7.8% 15,648
PERCENTAGE TIME NOT WORKED - UNPAID		
Hourly gross reduction due to sick time	0.0% 0	0.0% 0
PERCENTAGE NET WAGES FOR DISTRIBUTION:		
Hourly wages/hours distribution base	92.2% 1,809,517	92.2% 184,968
"NON-FRINGE" HOURLY WAGES:		
Hourly Wages - Overtime Premium	75,300	
Hourly Wages - Shift Premium	30,600	
GROSS HOURLY WAGES FOR TIME WORKED	1,915,417	
GROSS HOURLY WAGES FOR TIME NOT WORKED	153,083	
GROSS HOURLY WAGES	2,068,500	
RECONCILIATION:		
"Fringe Base" Hourly Wages per above	1,962,600	
Overtime Premium	75,300	
Shift Premium	30,600	
Less: unpaid sick days	0	
GROSS HOURLY WAGES	2,068,500	

Exhibit 11.11   Schedule FB—2 Information

PURPOSE: To determine the annual cost of each purchased fringe benefit and to establish separate fringe benefit rates for hourly and salary personnel

MANUAL INPUT: The percentage of payroll or cost per employee for each hourly and salary fringe benefit

INPUT FROM:

Schedule PR—1   Schedule FB—1

OUTPUT TO: Schedule DC—1

LEVEL: II—Fringe Benefits

A81 PR-1 Personnel & Gross Pay	T81 AL-1 General Factory Overhead	
A161 PR-2 Overtime Information	T161 AL-2 Service Center Billings	
A241 PR-3 Shift Premium	T241 AL-3 Production Support Activity Distribution	
A321 PR-4 Direct Working Indirect	T321 AL-4 Administrative Support Activity Distribution	
A401 FB-1 Vacation, Holiday and Sick Pay	T401 AL-5 Direct Material and Outside Processing	
A481 FB-2 Fringe Rate Calculations	T481 AL-6 Machine Time Information	
A561 SA-1 Square Footage Information	T561 Departmental Cost Accumulation	DC-1
A641 SA-2 Depreciation Expense	T641 Indirect Cost Rate Calculations	DC-2
A721 SA-3 Leases and Rentals	T721 DC-3 Rate/Cost Reconciliation	
A801 SA-4 Other Fixed Allocations		
A881 SA-5 Utilities		
A961 SA-6 Supplies		
A1041 SA-7 Budgeted Expenses		

Exhibit 11.12 Schedule FB—2

	HOURLY				SALARY			
BENEFIT	% OF PAYROLL	ANNUAL COST/EMP	MULTIPLIER	BENEFIT COST	% OF PAYROLL	ANNUAL COST/EMP	MULTIPLIER	BENEFIT COST
Group health insurance		3,073	89	273,500		3,154	28	88,300
Workers' compensation	4.29%		2,068.500	88,700	0.17%		1,140.000	1,900
State unemployment		380	89	33,800		380	28	10,600
Federal unemployment		60	89	5,300		60	28	1,700
Employer portion FICA	7.65%		2,068.500	158,200	7.65%		1,140.000	87,200
401(k) contribution		0	89	0		0	28	0
Group life insurance		70	89	6,200		95	28	2,700
Long/short term disability		0	89	0		0	28	0
Pension/profit sharing	0.00%		2,068.500	0	15.00%		1,140.000	171,000
Other benefit(s)		267	89	23,800		0	28	0
TOTAL PURCHASED BENEFITS				589,500				363,400
Vacation pay				68,691				N/A
Holiday pay				84,392				N/A
Sick pay				0				N/A
TOTAL TIME-OFF BENEFITS				153,083				0
TOTAL BENEFITS				742,583				363,400
BASE HOURLY PAYROLL DOLLARS				1,809,517				1,140,000
HOURLY FRINGE RATE PER LABOR DOLLAR				41.04%				31.88%
BASE HOURLY LABOR HOURS				184,968		2,080	28	58,240
HOURLY FRINGE RATE PER LABOR HOUR				4.015				6.240

147

cost for each benefit. Hourly vacation and holiday pay is brought forward from Schedule FB–1 and added to the total of hourly personnel's other benefits.

For hourly personnel, base hourly payroll dollars and hours are brought forward from Schedule FB–1 and used to calculate hourly fringe benefit rates as a percentage of straight-time dollars and as a cost per hour.

Salaried personnel's total benefits are divided by the total salary payroll cost brought forward from Schedule PR–1 to arrive at a fringe rate percentage of salary dollars. Headcounts are also brought forward from Schedule PR–1 and multiplied by the standard 2,080-hour year to arrive at total hours to calculate the salary fringe benefit rate as a cost per hour. Purchased fringe benefit costs go directly to Schedule DC–1: Departmental Cost Accumulation.

12

Building the Cost
Accumulation Model:
Specific Assignment Costs

In Chapter 11, the payroll and fringe benefit sections of the model were developed, thus completing the mechanics of implementing Levels I and II. This chapter discusses Level III, the specific assignment costs. Seven schedules are involved in this section of the model. These are called the SA schedules.

Schedule SA–1: Square Footage Allocation Percentages

Schedule SA–1 (Exhibits 12.1 and 12.2) is used to enter square footage information into the model. This information is used to assign a variety of occupancy-related costs to the cost centers. If other fixed allocation bases were to be used, they could also be included in this section of the model.

Square footage by cost center information is entered into the model. The model then calculates each cost center's percentage of the total square footage. In some instances, Costa assigns costs on the basis of manufacturing square footage only. As a result, the model also identifies square footage pertaining to manufacturing cost centers and calculates each cost center's percentage of total manufacturing square footage.

149

Exhibit 12.1   Schedule SA—1 Information

PURPOSE: To provide square footage distribution percentages for later cost assignment calculations

MANUAL INPUT: Square footage occupied by each cost center

INPUT FROM: No other schedules

OUTPUT TO:

Schedule SA—2   Schedule SA—4   Schedule SA—5

LEVEL: None—data input only

A81 PR-1 Personnel & Gross Pay	T81 AL-1 General Factory Overhead
A161 PR-2 Overtime Information	T161 AL-2 Service Center Billings
A241 PR-3 Shift Premium	T241 AL-3 Production Support Activity Distribution
A321 PR-4 Direct Working Indirect	T321 AL-4 Administrative Support Activity Distribution
A401 FB-1 Vacation, Holiday & Sick Pay	T401 AL-5 Direct Material & Outside Processing
A481 FB-2 Fringe Rate Calculations	T481 AL-6 Machine Time Information
A561 SA-1 Square Footage Information	T561 DC-1 Departmental Cost Accumulation
A641 SA-2 Depreciation Expense	T641 DC-2 Indirect Cost Rate Calculations
A721 SA-3 Leases and Rentals	T721 DC-3 Rate/Cost Reconciliation
A801 SA-4 Other Fixed Allocations	
A881 SA-5 Utilities	
A961 SA-6 Supplies	
A1041 SA-7 Budgeted Expenses	

Exhibit 12.2   Schedule SA—1

	TOTAL FACILITY		MANUFACTURING ONLY	
TOTAL SQUARE FOOTAGE	50,000	100.0%	44,000	100.0%
General & Administrative	2,000	4.0%		
General Factory Overhead	1,000	2.0%	1,000	2.3%
Engineering	4,000	8.0%		
Maintenance	3,000	6.0%	3,000	6.8%
Tool Room	4,000	8.0%	4,000	9.1%
Production Control	1,000	2.0%	1,000	2.3%
Quality Assurance	2,000	4.0%	2,000	4.5%
Shipping & Receiving	2,000	4.0%	2,000	4.5%
TOTAL STAFF & INDIRECT	19,000	38.0%	13,000	29.5%
Welding	5,000	10.0%	5,000	11.4%
Assembly	8,000	16.0%	8,000	18.2%
Direct Press Labor	0	0.0%	0	0.0%
Press Operations	10,000	20.0%	10,000	22.7%
CNC Machining	8,000	16.0%	8,000	18.2%
TOTAL PRODUCTION	31,000	62.0%	31,000	70.5%

Schedule SA–2: Depreciation Expense

Schedule SA–2 (Exhibits 12.3 and 12.4) is used to input depreciation expense and original equipment cost information into the model, as well as to distribute the building depreciation to cost centers.

Building depreciation is entered in total. Equipment depreciation and the original cost basis of the assets are entered by cost center. Using square footage percentages from Schedule SA–1, the model distributes the building's depreciation expense to the cost centers.

Original asset cost information is used for future cost assignments. To accomplish this, the percentage of the total asset cost applicable to each cost center is calculated.

Building and equipment depreciation expenses go directly to Schedule DC–1: Departmental Cost Accumulation.

Schedule SA–3: Leases and Rentals

Schedule SA–3 (Exhibits 12.5 and 12.6) is used to enter lease and rental information into the model.

Exhibit 12.3　　Schedule SA—2 Information

PURPOSE:　To provide depreciation expense information, distribute building depreciation and provide asset cost data for subsequent cost assignment

MANUAL INPUT:　Total building depreciation
Equipment depreciation expense and original cost by cost center

INPUT FROM:　Schedule SA—1

OUTPUT TO:　Schedule SA—4　　　　Schedule DC—1

LEVEL:　III—Specific Assignment Costs

A81　　　　　　PR-1 Personnel & Gross Pay	T81　　　　　　　AL-1 General Factory Overhead	
A161　　　　　　PR-2 Overtime Information	T161　　　　　　AL-2 Service Center Billings	
A241　　　　　　PR-3 Shift Premium	T241　　　　　　AL-3 Production Support Activity Distribution	
A321　　　　　　PR-4 Direct Working Indirect	T321　　　　　　AL-4 Administrative Support Activity Distribution	
A401　　　　　　FB-1 Vacation, Holiday & Sick Pay	T401　　　　　　AL-5 Direct Material & Outside Processing	
A481　　　　　　FB-2 Fringe Rate Calculations	T481　　　　　　AL-6 Machine Time Information	
A561　　　　　　SA-1 Square Footage Information	T561 Departmental Cost Accumulation	DC-1
A641　　　　　　SA-2 Depreciation Expense	T641 Indirect Cost Rate Calculations	DC-2
A721　　　　　　SA-3 Leases and Rentals	T721　　　　　　DC-3 Rate/Cost Reconciliation	
A801　　　　　　SA-4 Other Fixed Allocations		
A881　　　　　　SA-5 Utilities		
A961　　　　　　SA-6 Supplies		
A1041　　　　　SA-7 Budgeted Expenses		

Exhibit 12.4 Schedule SA—2

	BUILDING DEPRECIATION		EQUIPMENT DEPRECIATION	EQUIPMENT/ ORIGINAL COST BEGINNING OF YEAR $	
TOTAL EXPENSE	100.0%	100,000	280,000	1,980,000	100.0%
General & Administrative	4.0%	4,000	5,000	35,000	1.8%
General Factory Overhead	2.0%	2,000	5,000	35,000	1.8%
Engineering	8.0%	8,000	5,000	35,000	1.8%
Maintenance	6.0%	6,000	5,000	35,000	1.8%
Tool Room	8.0%	8,000	10,000	70,000	3.5%
Production Control	2.0%	2,000	10,000	70,000	3.5%
Quality Assurance	4.0%	4,000	10,000	70,000	3.5%
Shipping & Receiving	4.0%	4,000	10,000	70,000	3.5%
TOTAL STAFF & INDIRECT	38.0%	38,000	60,000	420,000	21.2%
Welding	10.0%	10,000	50,000	400,000	20.2%
Assembly	16.0%	16,000	20,000	160,000	8.1%
Direct Press Labor	0.0%	0	0	0	0.0%
Press Operations	20.0%	20,000	75,000	500,000	25.3%
CNC Machining	16.0%	16,000	75,000	500,000	25.3%
TOTAL PRODUCTION	62.0%	62,000	220,000	1,560,000	78.8%

Exhibit 12.5   Schedule SA—3 Information

PURPOSE: To enter costs relating to leases and rentals

MANUAL INPUT: Annual lease or rental costs by cost center

INPUT FROM: No other schedule

OUTPUT TO: Schedule DC—1

LEVEL: III—Specific Assignment Costs

A81 — PR-1 Personnel & Gross Pay	T81 — AL-1 General Factory Overhead	
A161 — PR-2 Overtime Information	T161 — AL-2 Service Center Billings	
A241 — PR-3 Shift Premium	T241 — AL-3 Production Support Activity Distribution	
A321 — PR-4 Direct Working Indirect	T321 — AL-4 Administrative Support Activity Distribution	
A401 — FB-1 Vacation, Holiday & Sick Pay	T401 — AL-5 Direct Material & Outside Processing	
A481 — FB-2 Fringe Rate Calculations	T481 — AL-6 Machine Time Information	
A561 — SA-1 Square Footage Information	T561 — Departmental Cost Accumulation	DC-1
A641 — SA-2 Depreciation Expense	T641 — Indirect Cost Rate Calculations	DC-2
A721 — SA-3 Leases and Rentals	T721 — DC-3 Rate/Cost Reconciliation	
A801 — SA-4 Other Fixed Allocations		
A881 — SA-5 Utilities		
A961 — SA-6 Supplies		
A1041 — SA-7 Budgeted Expenses		

Exhibit 12.6 Schedule SA—3

	TOTAL	COPIERS	FAX MACHINE	LEASE C (DESCRIBE)	LEASE D (DESCRIBE)	LEASE E (DESCRIBE)
TOTAL EXPENSE	7,300	6,500	800	0	0	0
General & Administrative	3,800	3,000	800			
General Factory Overhead	0					
Engineering	3,000	3,000				
Maintenance	0					
Tool Room	0					
Production Control	0					
Quality Assurance	0					
Shipping & Receiving	500	500				
TOTAL STAFF & INDIRECT	7,300	6,500	800	0	0	0
Welding	0					
Assembly	0					
Direct Press Labor	0					
Press Operations	0					
CNC Machining	0					
TOTAL PRODUCTION	0	0	0	0	0	0

155

Rental and lease costs by major type are entered by cost center. The model totals these lease costs for each cost center.

Lease and rental costs in total go directly to Schedule DC–1: Departmental Cost Accumulation.

Schedule SA–4: Other Fixed Allocations

Schedule SA–4 (Exhibits 12.7 and 12.8) assigns costs to cost centers based on fixed allocation bases that have already been entered into the model.

Two fixed allocation bases were brought forward into Schedule SA–4. Square footage distribution percentages were brought forward from Schedule SA–1 and original asset cost distribution percentages from Schedule SA–2.

Costa's real property taxes are assigned to cost centers on the basis of square footage occupied. *Total real property taxes are entered in the "total" section of the square footage section of the schedule.* They are then assigned to cost centers by the model using the appropriate percentages.

Personal property taxes and property insurance are assigned on the basis of original asset costs. *Total personal property taxes and property insurance are entered in the "total" section of the original cost section of the schedule.* They are then assigned to cost centers by the model using the appropriate percentages.

Real and personal property taxes and property insurance go directly to Schedule DC–1: Departmental Cost Accumulation.

Schedule SA–5: Utilities

Schedule SA–5 (Exhibits 12.9 and 12.10) is used to estimate the dollar amount and distribution of utility costs for each cost center. At Costa, the primary utility cost is electricity. Other utilities amount to about $10,000 annually and are treated as an annual fixed cost.

There are two components to the cost of electricity: a fixed amount that covers heating and cooling costs as well as basic service and availability charges for production cost centers, and a significant portion that varies with the level of activity in the production cost centers.

Square footage occupied was selected by Costa as the driver for staff and indirect cost centers. Utility costs in these cost centers pay for the "creature comforts." For determining variable electric costs, Costa selected direct labor dollars as the driver for Assembly and Welding, and machine hours for Press Operations and CNC Machining. No utility costs are charged to Direct Press Labor; utilities applicable to the presses are included in the Press Operations cost center. For determining the assignment of other utility costs, all cost centers use square footage occupied.

Square footage drivers are brought forward from Schedule SA–1, direct labor dollar drivers from Schedule PR–4, and machine hour drivers from Schedule AL–6 (a schedule discussed in Chapter 13).

In developing Schedule SA–5, the driver multiplier concept is used. *These driver multipliers are developed and entered into the schedule.* They are then used to convert the drivers into electrical consumption units (the concept of consumption units was discussed in Chapter 8). Percentages are developed to determine the percentage of total consumption units pertaining to each cost center.

The fixed electricity charge and a cost per electrical consumption unit are entered into the model. The model assigns the fixed electricity charge based on the assignment percentages. The unit consumption cost is multiplied by the consumption units in the production cost centers to establish the variable electricity cost.

The total fixed cost of other utilities is entered into the model. This is assigned on the basis of square footage occupied by the various cost centers.

The electricity and other utility costs go directly to Schedule DC–1: Departmental Cost Accumulation.

Schedule SA–6: Supplies

Schedule SA–6 (Exhibits 12.11 and 12.12) is used to determine the amount and distribution of supply costs. Major operating supplies are handled individually. The remaining supplies are handled as a group.

The driver selected for staff and indirect cost centers is headcount, which is brought forward from Schedule PR–1. Production cost center cost drivers are the same as for electricity

158   Developing an Activity-Based Cost System

Exhibit 12.7   Schedule SA—4 Information

PURPOSE: To assign other fixed costs to cost centers

MANUAL INPUT: Total annual amounts of other fixed costs

INPUT FROM: Schedule SA—1   Schedule SA—2

OUTPUT TO: Schedule DC—1

LEVEL: III—Specific Assignment Costs

A81 PR-1 Personnel & Gross Pay	T81 AL-1 General Factory Overhead
A161 PR-2 Overtime Information	T161 AL-2 Service Center Billings
A241 PR-3 Shift Premium	T241 AL-3 Production Support Activity Distribution
A321 PR-4 Direct Working Indirect	T321 AL-4 Administrative Support Activity Distribution
A401 FB-1 Vacation, Holiday & Sick Pay	T401 AL-5 Direct Material & Outside Processing
A481 FB-2 Fringe Rate Calculations	T481 AL-6 Machine Time Information
A561 SA-1 Square Footage Information	T561 DC-1 Departmental Cost Accumulation
A641 SA-2 Depreciation Expense	T641 DC-2 Indirect Cost Rate Calculations
A721 SA-3 Leases and Rentals	T721 DC-3 Rate/Cost Reconciliation
A801 SA-4 Other Fixed Allocations	
A881 SA-5 Utilities	
A961 SA-6 Supplies	
A1041 SA-7 Budgeted Expenses	

Exhibit 12.8 Schedule SA—4

	SQUARE FOOTAGE ALLOCATIONS			ORIGINAL COST ALLOCATIONS		
	ALLOC	REAL PROPERTY TAXES	OTHER	ALLOC	PERSONAL PROPERTY TAXES	PROPERTY INSURANCE
TOTAL TAX	100.0%	35,000	0	100.0%	20,000	25,000
General & Administrative	4.0%	1,400	0	1.8%	354	443
General Factory Overhead	2.0%	700	0	1.8%	354	443
Engineering	8.0%	2,800	0	1.8%	354	443
Maintenance	6.0%	2,100	0	1.8%	354	443
Tool Room	8.0%	2,800	0	3.5%	708	885
Production Control	2.0%	700	0	3.5%	708	885
Quality Assurance	4.0%	1,400	0	3.5%	708	885
Shipping & Receiving	4.0%	1,400	0	3.5%	708	885
TOTAL STAFF & INDIRECT	38.0%	13,300	0	21.2%	4,248	5,312
Welding	10.0%	3,500	0	20.2%	4,040	5,050
Assembly	16.0%	5,600	0	8.1%	1,616	2,020
Direct Press Labor	0.0%	0	0	0.0%	0	0
Press Operations	20.0%	7,000	0	25.3%	5,050	6,313
CNC Machining	16.0%	5,600	0	25.3%	5,050	6,313
TOTAL PRODUCTION	62.0%	21,700	0	78.8%	15,756	19,696
		35,000	0		20,004	25,008

Exhibit 12.9   Schedule SA—5 Information

PURPOSE: To determine the amount and distribution of utility costs

MANUAL INPUT: Total amounts of fixed utility costs
Driver multipliers
Unit cost of variable electricity consumption units

INPUT FROM:
Schedule PR—4   Schedule SA—1   Schedule AL—6

OUTPUT TO: Schedule DC—1

LEVEL: III—Specific Assignment Costs

A81 PR-1	T81 AL-1
Personnel & Gross Pay	General Factory Overhead
A161 PR-2	T161 AL-2
Overtime Information	Service Center Billings
A241 PR-3	T241 AL-3
Shift Premium	Production Support Activity Distribution
A321 PR-4	T321 AL-4
Direct Working Indirect	Administrative Support Activity Distribution
A401 FB-1	T401 AL-5
Vacation, Holiday & Sick Pay	Direct Material & Outside Processing
A481 FB-2	T481 AL-6
Fringe Rate Calculations	Machine Time Information
A561 SA-1	T561 DC-1
Square Footage Information	Departmental Cost Accumulation
A641 SA-2	T641 DC-2
Depreciation Expense	Indirect Cost Rate Calculations
A721 SA-3	T721 DC-3
Leases and Rentals	Rate/Cost Reconciliation
A801 SA-4	
Other Fixed Allocations	
A881 SA-5	
Utilities	
A961 SA-6	
Supplies	
A1041 SA-7	
Budgeted Expenses	

Exhibit 12.10 Schedule SA—5

	DRIVER MULTIPLIER	DRIVER	CONS UNITS	ELECTRIC FIXED %	ELECTRIC FIXED $	ELECTRIC VARIABLE $/UNIT	ELECTRIC VARIABLE $	ELECTRIC TOTAL $	OTHER UTILITIES ALLOC	OTHER UTILITIES $
TOTAL			1,073	100.1%	30,000	1.50	152,140	182,140	100.0%	10,000
General & Administr	0.0015	4,000	6	0.6%	180			180	4.0%	400
General Factory Ove	0.0015	2,000	3	0.3%	90			90	2.0%	200
Engineering	0.0015	8,000	12	1.1%	330			330	8.0%	800
Maintenance	0.0015	6,000	9	0.9%	270			270	6.0%	600
Tool Room	0.0015	8,000	12	1.1%	330			330	8.0%	800
Production Control	0.0015	2,000	3	0.3%	90			90	2.0%	200
Quality Assurance	0.0015	4,000	6	0.6%	180			180	4.0%	400
Shipping & Receivin	0.0015	4,000	6	0.6%	180			180	4.0%	400
TOTAL STAFF & INDIRECT				5.5%	1,650			1,650	38.0%	3,800
Welding	0.0005	321,298	161	15.0%	4,500	150	24,097	28,597	10.0%	1,000
Assembly	0.0005	262,881	131	12.3%	3,690	150	19,716	23,406	16.0%	1,600
Direct Press Labor / Press Operations	0.0200	25,792	516	48.1%	14,430	150	77,376	91,806	20.0%	2,000
CNC Machining	0.0200	10,317	206	19.2%	5,760	150	30,951	36,711	16.0%	1,600
TOTAL PRODUCTION				94.6%	28,380		152,140	180,520	62.0%	6,200
				100.1%	30,030		152,140	182,170	100.0%	10,000

161

Exhibit 12.11   Schedule SA—6 Information

PURPOSE: To determine the amount and distribution of supply costs

MANUAL INPUT: Driver multipliers

Unit cost of variable supply consumption units

INPUT FROM:

| Schedule PR—1 | Schedule PR—4 | Schedule AL—6 |

OUTPUT TO: Schedule DC—1

LEVEL: III—Specific Assignment Costs

A81 **PR-1** Personnel & Gross Pay	T81 **AL-1** General Factory Overhead
A161 **PR-2** Overtime Information	T161 **AL-2** Service Center Billings
A241 **PR-3** Shift Premium	T241 **AL-3** Production Support Activity Distribution
A321 **PR-4** Direct Working Indirect	T321 **AL-4** Administrative Support Activity Distribution
A401 **FB-1** Vacation, Holiday & Sick Pay	T401 **AL-5** Direct Material & Outside Processing
A481 **FB-2** Fringe Rate Calculations	T481 **AL-6** Machine Time Information
A561 **SA-1** Square Footage Information	T561 **DC-1** Departmental Cost Accumulation
A641 **SA-2** Depreciation Expense	T641 **DC-2** Indirect Cost Rate Calculations
A721 **SA-3** Leases and Rentals	T721 **DC-3** Rate/Cost Reconciliation
A801 **SA-4** Other Fixed Allocations	
A881 **SA-5** Utilities	
A961 **SA-6** Supplies	
A1041 **SA-7** Budgeted Expenses	

Exhibit 12.12 Schedule SA—6

	DRIVER	MULTIPLIER	ARGON $/UNIT	ARGON $	DRAWING COMPOUNDS $/UNIT	DRAWING COMPOUNDS $	DRILLS & CUTTERS $/UNIT	DRILLS & CUTTERS $	OTHER SUPPLIES MULTIPLIER	OTHER SUPPLIES CONS UNIT	@	OTHER SUPPLIES $
TOTAL			6.000	96,389	3.000	77,376	5.556	51,585			1.000	125,200
General & Administr	10	1000								10,000		10,000
General Factory Ove	4	1000								4,000		4,000
Engineering	16	1000								16,000		16,000
Maintenance	6	1000								6,000		6,000
Tool Room	10	1000								10,000		10,000
Production Control	4	1000								4,000		4,000
Quality Assurance	5	1000								5,000		5,000
Shipping & Receivin	2	1000								2,000		2,000
Welding	321,298	0.05	6.000	96,389					0.100	32,130		32,100
Assembly	262,881											
Direct Press Labor												
Press Operations	25,792	1.00			3.000	77,376			1.000	25,792		25,800
CNC Machining	10,317	0.90					5.556	51,585	1.000	10,317		10,300

163

Exhibit 12.13   Schedule SA—7 Information

PURPOSE: To enter budgeted and discretionary expense and income items into the model

MANUAL INPUT: Estimated expenses and income by type and cost center

INPUT FROM: No other schedules

OUTPUT TO: Schedule DC—1

LEVEL: III—Specific Assignment Costs

A81 PR-1 Personnel & Gross Pay	T81 AL-1 General Factory Overhead
A161 PR-2 Overtime Information	T161 AL-2 Service Center Billings
A241 PR-3 Shift Premium	T241 AL-3 Production Support Activity Distribution
A321 PR-4 Direct Working Indirect	T321 AL-4 Administrative Support Activity Distribution
A401 FB-1 Vacation, Holiday & Sick Pay	T401 AL-5 Direct Material & Outside Processing
A481 FB-2 Fringe Rate Calculations	T481 AL-6 Machine Time Information
A561 SA-1 Square Footage Information	T561 DC-1 Departmental Cost Accumulation
A641 SA-2 Depreciation Expense	T641 DC-2 Indirect Cost Rate Calculations
A721 SA-3 Leases and Rentals	T721 DC-3 Rate/Cost Reconciliation
A801 SA-4 Other Fixed Allocations	
A881 SA-5 Utilities	
A961 SA-6 Supplies	
A1041 SA-7 Budgeted Expenses	

Exhibit 12.14 Schedule SA—7

	TOTAL	TRAVEL	PROF SERVICES	TELEPHONE	GENERAL INSURANCE	MARKETING EXPENSE	TRAINING/ SEMINARS	OTHER	SCRAP SALES	OTHER INCOME
TOTAL	316,000	90,000	90,000	44,000	60,000	25,000	10,000	42,000	(35,000)	(10,000)
General & Administrative	250,000	50,000	80,000	15,000	60,000	25,000	5,000	25,000		(10,000)
General Factory Overhead	2,000			2,000						
Engineering	54,000	25,000	10,000	10,000			5,000	4,000		
Maintenance	3,000			3,000						
Tool Room	4,000			4,000						
Production Control	10,000	5,000		4,000				1,000		
Quality Assurance	26,000	10,000		4,000				12,000		
Shipping & Receiving	2,000			2,000						
TOTAL STAFF & INDIRECT	351,000	90,000	90,000	44,000	60,000	25,000	10,000	42,000	0	(10,000)
Welding	0									
Assembly	0									
Direct Press Labor	(25,000)								(25,000)	
Press Operations	(10,000)								(10,000)	
CNC Machining										
TOTAL PRODUCTION	(35,000)	0	0	0	0	0	0	0	(35,000)	0

165

on Schedule SA–5. Direct labor dollars are brought forward from Schedule PR–4 and machine hours from Schedule AL–6 (Chapter 13).

Driver multipliers and consumption unit costs for the four categories of supplies are determined and entered into the model. Separate multipliers are used for operating supplies and other supplies in the production cost centers.

The model calculates the consumption units and multiplies those units by their cost per unit to determine the amount and distribution of supply costs for each cost center.

The cost of each of the three operating supply categories and the other supplies go directly to Schedule DC–1: Departmental Cost Accumulation.

Schedule SA–7: Budgeted Expenses

Schedule SA–7 (Exhibits 12.13 and 12.14) provides for the entry of budgeted or discretionary expenses and other income into the model. Most of these expenses are classified as variable, but they are not automatically variable, as is the case with utilities and supplies. Management has more control over these costs than does the level of operations. As a result, they are not treated as variable by the model.

Estimated costs and other income items by type and cost center are entered into the model. The model summarizes the input and calculates totals by cost center.

Budgeted expenses go directly to Schedule DC–1: Departmental Cost Accumulation.

13

Building the Cost Accumulation Model: Service Centers/ General Factory Overhead/ Production and Administrative Support Activities

At this point in the development of the model, all but one element of the Costa Manufacturing's labor and indirect costs (Levels I, II, and III) have been entered. That one element, purchased maintenance costs, could be included as a specific assignment cost (SA) schedule, but it is much easier to visualize the cost and its relationship to its driver if it is included in this section of the model.

The task now is to begin the cost flow-down involving Levels IV through VIII. When this task is completed, all costs will have been accumulated and distributed to the cost centers that will ultimately charge them to a cost objective.

The schedules in this part of the model might be best described as the cost allocation schedules. Thus, they are identified as AL schedules.

167

Schedule AL–1: General Factory Overhead

Schedule AL–1 (Exhibits 13.1 and 13.2) is used to make the distribution of the General Factory Overhead cost pool to the appropriate cost centers. The driver selected for this distribution was factory headcount.

General Factory Overhead costs have been accumulated on Schedule DC–1: Departmental Cost Accumulation. The total costs of this cost center are brought forward from Schedule DC–1 to Schedule AL–1. From Schedule PR–1, the headcounts for the factory cost centers are brought forward. At Costa, the factory cost centers are defined as all production cost centers, as well as the Tool Room, Production Control, Quality Assurance, and Shipping and Receiving.

The model calculates the percentage that the headcount in each cost center represents of the total factory headcount, and then uses those percentages to distribute the total cost from General Factory Overhead.

The results of this distribution are posted by the model to Schedule DC–1: Departmental Cost Accumulation, where the appropriate amount is added to each cost center and the total subtracted from General Factory Overhead. This distribution has no impact on total costs and should result in no cost remaining in General Factory Overhead.

Schedule AL–2: Service Centers

Schedule AL–2 (Exhibits 13.3 and 13.4) is used to distribute the cost of Costa's service centers to the cost centers and cost objectives that demand their services. The schedule also calculates purchased maintenance costs and the distribution of those costs.

Headcounts for each service center are brought forward from Schedule PR–1. *The number of nonbillable employees from each service center is entered.* Included in this category are management, administrative, and clerical employees whose services support the service center, but who do not actually perform the services for the cost centers. These employees might include a secretary, administrator, clerk, and vice president.

The model calculates the number of employees whose time can be billed. The average base hours, including overtime hours and average annual holiday and vacation hours, are brought forward from Schedule FB–1. The holiday and vacation hours are subtracted from the base hours to arrive at billable hours per employee. The model then multiplies these hours by the number of billable employees to arrive at the total available billable hours.

The percentage of available hours that each service center anticipates being able to charge to other cost centers and cost objectives is entered. It is unlikely that all available hours are spent on chargeable activities. Time is spent on training, meetings, and internal activities, and there is time when there simply is no demand. The Tool Room and Engineering also have activities that cannot be charged to other service centers within Level V due to the hierarchy established within the level. The percentage entered is used by the model to calculate the planned billable hours for the period.

Each service center's total cost is accumulated on Schedule DC–1: Departmental Cost Accumulation. The development of the hierarchy within the service center level eliminates any problem that may have arisen from service center cross-charges. By precluding Engineering from charging Maintenance and the Tool Room from charging either Maintenance or Engineering, the total cost of each service center can be brought forward from Schedule DC–1. These amounts, along with each cost center's planned billable hours, are used to develop hourly billing rates.

The estimated number of hours of service provided by each service center to each cost center or cost objective is entered. The model then extends these hours by the service centers' hourly rates to calculate the amounts to charge each other cost center or objective. These amounts go directly to Schedule DC–1: Departmental Cost Accumulation.

In Maintenance, the model requires one additional step. The cost of purchased maintenance must be established by cost center. These are outside costs directly involved in specific repairs, not incidental costs that support the overall maintenance effort. The cost of these materials depends primarily on two factors: the general nature of repairs in each cost center and the amount of maintenance effort that takes place in each center. For example,

Exhibit 13.1   Schedule AL—1 Information

PURPOSE: To distribute general factory overhead costs to the various cost centers based on factory headcount

MANUAL INPUT: None

INPUT FROM:
Schedule DC—1   Schedule PR—1

OUTPUT TO: Schedule DC—1

LEVEL: IV—General   Factory Overhead

A81 PR-1	T81 AL-1
Personnel & Gross Pay	General Factory Overhead
A161 PR-2	T161 AL-2
Overtime Information	Service Center Billings
A241 PR-3	T241 AL-3
Shift Premium	Production Support Activity Distribution
A321 PR-4	T321 AL-4
Direct Working Indirect	Administrative Support Activity Distribution
A401 FB-1	T401 AL-5
Vacation, Holiday and Sick Pay	Direct Material and Outside Processing
A481 FB-2	T481 AL-6
Fringe Rate Calculations	Machine Time Information
A561 SA-1	T561 DC-1
Square Footage Information	Departmental Cost Accumulation
A641 SA-2	T641 DC-2
Depreciation Expense	Indirect Cost Rate Calculations
A721 SA-3	T721 DC-3
Leases and Rentals	Rate/Cost Reconciliation
A801 SA-4	
Other Fixed Allocations	
A881 SA-5	
Utilities	
A961 SA-6	
Supplies	
A1041 SA-7	
Budgeted Expenses	

Exhibit 13.2 Schedule AL—1

	HEADCOUNT	%	COST TO ALLOCATE
Total cost to allocate	81.0	100.0%	173,040
General & Administrative	10.0	12.3%	21,364
General Factory Overhead	4.0	4.9%	8,545
Engineering	5.0	6.2%	10,682
Maintenance	2.0	2.5%	4,272
Tool Room			
Production Control			
Quality Assurance			
Shipping & Receiving			
TOTAL STAFF & INDIRECT	21.0	25.9%	44,862
Welding	16.0	19.8%	34,181
Assembly	16.0	19.8%	34,181
Direct Press Labor	24.0	29.6%	51,272
Press Operations	0.0	0.0%	0
CNC Machining	4.0	4.9%	8,545
TOTAL PRODUCTION	60.0	74.1%	128,179
TOTAL	81.0	100.0%	173,041

171

Exhibit 13.3   Schedule AL—2 Information

PURPOSE: To determine the cost of purchased maintenance, calculate service center billing rates, and distribute the cost of service centers to other cost centers and cost objectives

MANUAL INPUT: Headcounts for non-billable employees

Anticipated billing percentages

Purchased maintenance cost percentages

Hours billable to cost centers and cost objectives

INPUT FROM:
Schedule PR—1   Schedule FB—1   Schedule DC—1

OUTPUT TO: Schedule DC—1

LEVEL: V—Service Centers

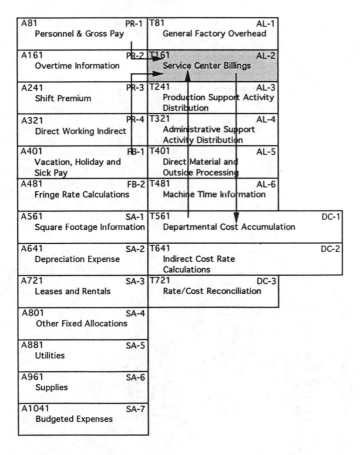

| A81   PR-1 | T81   AL-1 |
| Personnel & Gross Pay | General Factory Overhead |

| A161   PR-2 | T161   AL-2 |
| Overtime Information | Service Center Billings |

| A241   PR-3 | T241   AL-3 |
| Shift Premium | Production Support Activity Distribution |

| A321   PR-4 | T321   AL-4 |
| Direct Working Indirect | Administrative Support Activity Distribution |

| A401   FB-1 | T401   AL-5 |
| Vacation, Holiday and Sick Pay | Direct Material and Outside Processing |

| A481   FB-2 | T481   AL-6 |
| Fringe Rate Calculations | Machine Time Information |

| A561   SA-1 | T561   DC-1 |
| Square Footage Information | Departmental Cost Accumulation |

| A641   SA-2 | T641   DC-2 |
| Depreciation Expense | Indirect Cost Rate Calculations |

| A721   SA-3 | T721   DC-3 |
| Leases and Rentals | Rate/Cost Reconciliation |

| A801   SA-4 |
| Other Fixed Allocations |

| A881   SA-5 |
| Utilities |

| A961   SA-6 |
| Supplies |

| A1041   SA-7 |
| Budgeted Expenses |

Exhibit 13.4 Schedule AL—2

	ENGINEERING		MAINTENANCE		PURCHASED MAINTENANCE COSTS		TOOL ROOM	

BILLING RATE DETERMINATION:

	ENGINEERING	MAINTENANCE	TOOL ROOM
Total employees	16	6	10
Non-billable employee(s)	1	0	0
Billable employees	15	6	10
Billable hours/employee	2,078	2,078	2,078
Available billable hours	31,172	12,469	20,781
Anticipated billing percentage	80%	80%	80%
TOTAL PLANNED BILLABLE HOURS	24,937	9,975	16,625
TOTAL COST CENTER EXPENSES	687,808	243,773	342,129
BILLING RATE	27.58	24.44	20.58

	ENGINEERING		MAINTENANCE		PURCHASED MAINTENANCE COSTS		TOOL ROOM	
	HOURS	$ ALLOC	HOURS	$ ALLOC	% OF DEPT CHARGE	$	HOURS	$ ALLOC
General & Administrative	8,728	240,733	200	4,876	10.0%	488	X X X	X X X
General Factory Overhead	X X X	X X X	X X X	X X X	10.0%	X X X	X X X	X X X
Engineering	X X X	X X X	200	4,876	10.0%	488	X X X	X X X
Maintenance	X X X	X X X	X X X	X X X	10.0%	X X X	X X X	X X X
Tool Room	X X X	X X X	399	9,751	10.0%	975	X X X	X X X
Production Control	0	0	399	9,751	10.0%	975	X X X	X X X
Quality Assurance	0	0	399	9,751	10.0%	975	X X X	X X X
Shipping & Receiving	0	0	393	9,751	10.0%	975	X X X	X X X
TOTAL STAFF & INDIRECT	8,728	240,733	1,995	48,755		4,875	0	0
Welding	3,741	103,171	998	24,377	20.0%	4,875	831	17,106
Assembly	1,247	34,390	998	24,377	20.0%	4,875	831	17,106
Direct Press Labor	0	0	X X X	X X X	X X X	X X X	X X X	X X X
Press Operations	2,494	68,781	2,494	60,943	100.0%	60,943	3,563	73,313
CNC Machining	2,494	68,781	1,496	36,566	50.0%	18,283	1,425	29,326
TOTAL PRODUCTION	9,975	275,123	5,988	146,264		88,977	6,650	136,851
TOTAL	18,703	515,856	7,980	195,019		93,853	6,650	136,851
Other direct costs	1,247	34,390	998	24,377			831	17,106
Tooling projects	2,494	68,781	X X X	X X X			9,144	188,171
Capital projects	2,494	68,781	998	24,377			X X X	X X X
TOTALS	24,937	687,808	9,975	243,773		93,853	16,625	342,128

173

100 hours of maintenance might take place in both Production Control and Press Operations. In Production Control, purchased maintenance would most likely be nominal because that cost center has no major equipment that would require expensive repair parts or special outside expertise. On the other hand, repairs in Press Operations would more likely require expensive parts, rental of rigging equipment, services of outside experts, and so on. The same amount of effort (as measured in hours) by the Maintenance function in these two areas would result in vastly different purchased maintenance costs.

As a result, separate purchased maintenance cost percentages are developed for each cost center. These percentages reflect the average amount of outside maintenance costs that accompany the internal maintenance costs for each cost center. For example, the Production Control cost center mentioned in the previous paragraph might have purchased maintenance that amounts to 10% of Maintenance charges. Press Operations, on the other hand, might have a factor closer to 100% of Maintenance charges. Using this feature, the model not only can vary the distribution of the Maintenance service center as demand for its services change, but it can also change the overall amount, as well as distribution, of purchased maintenance costs.

Once developed, *the purchased maintenance cost percentages are entered into the model.* The model then calculates and forwards directly to Schedule DC–1 the amount and distribution of this cost element.

The results of this schedule's calculations add the purchased maintenance costs to each cost center and distribute all service center costs to other cost centers and cost objectives. The distribution has no impact on total costs and should result in no cost remaining in any service center.

Schedule AL–3: Production Support Distribution

Schedule AL–3 (Exhibits 13.5 and 13.6) is used to distribute the costs of the production support activities to cost centers. Conversion costs, including outside processing costs, were selected as drivers for these costs. The cost centers included are Production Control, Quality Assurance, and Shipping and Receiving.

The schedule brings forward the conversion costs through the distribution of service centers (Level V) from Schedule DC–1 for each of the Level VIII production cost centers except Direct Press Labor. Press support costs are distributed on the basis of Press Operations' conversion cost. Schedule AL–3 also brings forward total outside manufacturing services from Schedule AL–5. Because the data from Schedule AL–5 is entered independent of any calculations made in Schedule AL–3, no problem results from using the data from a schedule coming later in the model.

Percentages are calculated for each cost center's portion of the group's total conversion costs. Total costs of each production support cost center are brought forward from Schedule DC–1 and distributed to the various cost centers based on the calculated percentages.

The results of these distributions then go to Schedule DC–2: Indirect Cost Rate Calculations, where the appropriate amounts are added to each cost center and the totals subtracted from Production Control, Quality Assurance, and Shipping and Receiving. This updating is done on Schedule DC–2 which, in addition to performing the calculation of indirect costing rates, is a continuation of Schedule DC–1. This distribution has no impact on total costs and should result in no cost remaining in any production support cost center.

Schedule AL–4: Administrative Support Distribution

Schedule AL–4 (Exhibits 13.7 and 13.8) is used to distribute the costs of the administrative support activities to cost centers. Conversion costs (this time excluding outside processing costs) were selected as drivers for these costs. The only cost center included is General/Administration.

The schedule brings forward the revised conversion costs through the distribution of production support activities (Level VI) from the updated data on Schedule AL–3 for each of the Level VIII production cost centers, including Direct Press Labor. Percentages are calculated for each cost center's portion of the group's total conversion costs. The total cost of General/Administration is brought forward from Schedule DC–1 and distributed to the various cost centers based on the calculated percentages.

Exhibit 13.5   Schedule AL—3 Information

PURPOSE: To distribute the cost of production support activities to cost centers

MANUAL INPUT: None

INPUT FROM:
Schedule AL—4   Schedule DC—2

OUTPUT TO:
Schedule AL—4   Schedule DC—2

LEVEL: VI—Production
Support Activities

A81 PR-1 Personnel & Gross Pay	T81 AL-1 General Factory Overhead	
A161 PR-2 Overtime Information	T161 AL-2 Service Center Billings	
A241 PR-3 Shift Premium	T241 AL-3 Production Support Activity Distribution	
A321 PR-4 Direct Working Indirect	T321 AL-4 Administrative Support Activity Distribution	
A401 FB-1 Vacation, Holiday and Sick Pay	T401 AL-5 Direct Material and Outside Processing	
A481 FB-2 Fringe Rate Calculations	T481 AL-6 Machine Time Information	
A561 SA-1 Square Footage Information	T561 Departmental Cost Accumulation	DC-1
A641 SA-2 Depreciation Expense	T641 Indirect Cost Rate Calculations	DC-2
A721 SA-3 Leases and Rentals	T721 DC-3 Rate/Cost Reconciliation	
A801 SA-4 Other Fixed Allocations		
A881 SA-5 Utilities		
A961 SA-6 Supplies		
A1041 SA-7 Budgeted Expenses		

Exhibit 13.6 Schedule AL—3

	CONVERSION COSTS	%	PRODUCTION CONTROL	QUALITY ASSURANCE	SHIPPING & RECEIVING	PS COST DISTRIB	REVISED CONV COSTS
Costs to Distribute			192,860	339,522	81,563	613,945	
Welding	942,089	31.5%	60,798	107,033	25,712	193,543	1,135,632
Assembly	616,929	20.6%	39,814	70,090	16,838	126,742	743,671
Direct Press Labor	N/A	0.0%	0	0	0	0	0
Press Operations	549,326	18.4%	35,451	62,410	14,993	112,854	662,179
CNC Machining	480,092	16.1%	30,983	54,544	13,103	98,630	578,723
Outside Manufacturing Services	400,000	13.4%	25,814	45,445	10,917	82,176	482,176
TOTAL	2,988,436	100.0%	192,860	339,522	81,563	613,945	3,602,381

Exhibit 13.7　Schedule AL—4 Information

PURPOSE:　To distribute the cost of administrative support activities to cost centers

MANUAL INPUT:　None

INPUT FROM:
Schedule DC—1　　　　　　　Schedule AL—3

OUTPUT TO:　Schedule DC—2

LEVEL:　VII—Administrative
Support Activities

A81　　　　　　PR-1 　Personnel & Gross Pay	T81　　　　　　AL-1 　General Factory Overhead	
A161　　　　　PR-2 　Overtime Information	T161　　　　　AL-2 　Service Center Billings	
A241　　　　　PR-3 　Shift Premium	T241　　　　　AL-3 　Production Support Activity 　Distribution	
A321　　　　　PR-4 　Direct Working Indirect	T321　　　　　AL-4 　Administrative Support 　Activity Distribution	
A401　　　　　FB-1 　Vacation, Holiday and 　Sick Pay	T401　　　　　AL-5 　Direct Material and 　Outside Processing	
A481　　　　　FB-2 　Fringe Rate Calculations	T481　　　　　AL-6 　Machine Time Information	
A561　　　　　SA-1 　Square Footage Information	T561　　　　　　　　　DC-1 　Departmental Cost Accumulation	
A641　　　　　SA-2 　Depreciation Expense	T641　　　　　　　　　DC-2 　Indirect Cost Rate 　Calculations	
A721　　　　　SA-3 　Leases and Rentals	T721　　　　　DC-3 　Rate/Cost Reconciliation	
A801　　　　　SA-4 　Other Fixed Allocations		
A881　　　　　SA-5 　Utilities		
A961　　　　　SA-6 　Supplies		
A1041　　　　SA-7 　Budgeted Expenses		

Exhibit 13.8 Schedule AL—4

	REVISED CONV COSTS	%	GEN & ADMIN COSTS	TOTAL COST POOL
Costs to Distribute			1,181,059	
Welding	1,135,632	29.2%	344,611	1,480,243
Assembly	743,671	19.1%	225,669	969,340
Direct Press Labor	771,866	19.8%	234,225	1,006,091
Press Operations	662,179	17.0%	200,940	863,119
CNC Machining	578,723	14.9%	175,615	754,338
Outside Manufacturing Services	N/A	0.0%	0	0
	3,892,071	100.0%	1,181,059	5,073,130

179

Exhibit 13.9   Schedule AL—5 Information

PURPOSE: To input data not subject to the cost accumulation process but needed as part of base for rate distribution

MANUAL INPUT: Annual direct material purchases
Annual direct outside services purchases
Annual tooling purchases

INPUT FROM: No other schedule

OUTPUT TO: Schedule AL—3   Schedule DC—2

LEVEL: None—data input only

A81 PR-1 Personnel & Gross Pay	T81 AL-1 General Factory Overhead	
A161 PR-2 Overtime Information	T161 AL-2 Service Center Billings	
A241 PR-3 Shift Premium	T241 AL-3 Production Support Activity Distribution	
A321 PR-4 Direct Working Indirect	T321 AL-4 Administrative Support Activity Distribution	
A401 FB-1 Vacation, Holiday and Sick Pay	T401 AL-5 Direct Material and Outside Processing	
A481 FB-2 Fringe Rate Calculations	T481 AL-6 Machine Time Information	
A561 SA-1 Square Footage Information	T561 Departmental Cost Accumulation	DC-1
A641 SA-2 Depreciation Expense	T641 Indirect Cost Rate Calculations	DC-2
A721 SA-3 Leases and Rentals	T721 DC-3 Rate/Cost Reconciliation	
A801 SA-4 Other Fixed Allocations		
A881 SA-5 Utilities		
A961 SA-6 Supplies		
A1041 SA-7 Budgeted Expenses		

Exhibit 13.10   Schedule AL—5

DIRECT MATERIAL PURCHASES   3,000,000

DIRECT OUTSIDE SERVICES   400,000

TOOLING PURCHASES   150,000

The results of this distribution then go to Schedule DC–2: Indirect Cost Rate Calculations, where the appropriate amounts are added to each cost center and the total subtracted from General/Administration. This distribution has no impact on total costs and should result in no cost remaining in the General/Administration cost center.

Schedule AL–5: Direct Material and Outside Processing

Schedule AL–5 (Exhibits 13.9 and 13.10) is used to enter certain direct cost information into the model. *Annual direct material, direct outside processing, and purchased tooling cost are entered.* These costs go directly to Schedule DC–2: Indirect Cost Rate Calculations.

Schedule AL–6: Machine Time Information

Schedule AL–6 (Exhibits 13.11 and 13.12) is used to calculate the total chargeable machine hours that are the base for calculating hourly rates for the machine hour–driven production cost centers. These amounts are also used as drivers for the calculation of automatically variable utility and supply expenses. The two production cost centers to which machine time information applies are Press Operations and CNC Machining.

The number of pieces of equipment in each cost center whose operation is used to charge the cost center's indirect costs is entered. Annual hours available for each piece of equipment on each shift are calculated using data brought forward from Schedule FB–1. This is done by subtracting holiday (but not vacation) hours from Schedule FB–1 from the standard 2,080-hour work year. *The number of shifts*

Exhibit 13.11   Schedule AL—6 Information

PURPOSE: To establish the chargeable machine hours for use in calculating machine hour rates and driving other automatically variable costs

MANUAL INPUT: Number of pieces of equipment in each applicable cost center

Average shifts in operation for each cost center

Percentage downtime by cause for each cost center

INPUT FROM: Schedule FB—1

OUTPUT TO:

Schedule SA—5   Schedule SA—6   Schedule DC—2

LEVEL: None—data input only

A81	PR-1	T81	AL-1
Personnel & Gross Pay		General Factory Overhead	
A161	PR-2	T161	AL-2
Overtime Information		Service Center Billings	
A241	PR-3	T241	AL-3
Shift Premium		Production Support Activity Distribution	
A321	PR-4	T321	AL-4
Direct Working Indirect		Administrative Support Activity Distribution	
A401	FB-1	T401	AL-5
Vacation, Holiday and Sick Pay		Direct Material and Outside Processing	
A481	FB-2	T481	AL-6
Fringe Rate Calculations		Machine Time Information	
A561	SA-1	T561	DC-1
Square Footage Information		Departmental Cost Accumulation	
A641	SA-2	T641	DC-2
Depreciation Expense		Indirect Cost Rate Calculations	
A721	SA-3	T721	DC-3
Leases and Rentals		Rate/Cost Reconciliation	
A801	SA-4		
Other Fixed Allocations			
A881	SA-5		
Utilities			
A961	SA-6		
Supplies			
A1041	SA-7		
Budgeted Expenses			

Exhibit 13.12   Schedule AL—6

	PRESS OPERATIONS	CNC MACHINING
TOTAL PIECES OF EQUIPMENT	10	4
ANNUAL HOURS PER PIECE/SHIFT	1,984	1,984
SHIFTS IN OPERATION	2.0	2.0
TOTAL ANNUAL HOURS AVAILABLE	39,680	15,872
NON-PRODUCTION HOURS (%):		
Set-up time	10%	10%
Maintenance	5%	5%
Normal excess capacity	20%	20%
Other	0%	0%
NON-PRODUCTION HOURS (%):		
Set-up time	3,968	1,587
Maintenance	1,984	794
Normal excess capacity	7,936	3,174
Other	0	0
TOTAL ANNUAL CHARGEABLE HOURS:		
Percentage	65%	65%
Hours	25,792	10,317

the department will be in operation is entered, and the total annual hours available for the cost center are calculated by the model.

The percentage of total hours that the equipment in each cost center does not operate is entered by downtime category. These categories are setup, maintenance, normal excess capacity, and other. The model translates these percentages into downtime hours, then subtracts the downtime hours from the available hours to determine the total annual chargeable hours.

These hours go directly to Schedule DC–2: Indirect Cost Rate Calculations.

14

Building the Cost Accumulation Model: Production Activities and Rate Calculations

At this point in the model, all operating costs of Costa Manufacturing have been entered, manipulated, and distributed. What remains are the schedules on which all this earlier work is summarized and Costa's indirect costing rates calculated.

Schedule DC–1: Departmental Cost Accumulation

Schedule DC–1 (Exhibits 14.1, 14.2, and 14.3) is the heart of the model. All roads lead to this schedule or its partner, Schedule DC–2. On this schedule, all specific assignment costs are accumulated and cost distributions through Level V are made. Cost distributions for Levels VI and VII are made on Schedule DC–2, which is a continuation of Schedule DC–1 as well as a schedule for calculating indirect costing rates.

Hourly and salary fringe benefit costs are brought forward from Schedule FB–2. Departmental salaries are brought forward from Schedule PR–1. Because a portion of the indirect hourly payroll cost becomes vacation and holiday pay, it cannot

185

Exhibit 14.1   Schedule DC—1 Information

PURPOSE: To accumulate labor, fringe and specific assignment costs by cost center and document the distribution of costs through Level V

MANUAL INPUT: None

INPUT FROM:

Schedule PR—1	Schedule PR—2	Schedule PR—3
Schedule PR—4	Schedule FB—1	Schedule FB—2
Schedule SA—2	Schedule SA—3	Schedule SA—4
Schedule SA—5	Schedule SA—6	Schedule SA—7
Schedule AL—1	Schedule AL—2	

OUTPUT TO:

Schedule AL—1	Schedule AL—2	Schedule AL—3
Schedule AL—4	Schedule DC—2	

LEVEL: VIII—Production Activities

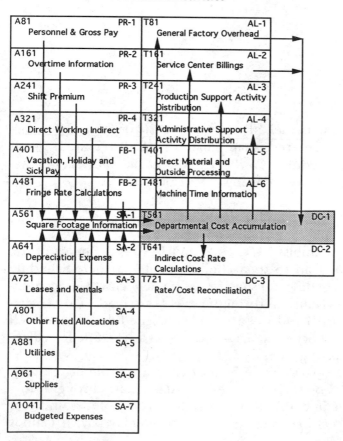

Exhibit 14.2   Schedule DC—1 (Part 1)

	FRINGE BENEFITS / HOURLY	FRINGE BENEFITS / SALARY	GEN & ADMIN	GENERAL FACTORY OVERHEAD	ENGINEERING	MAINTENANCE	TOOL ROOM	PRODUCTION CONTROL	QUALITY ASSURANCE	SHIPPING & RECEIVING	WELDING
FRINGE BENEFIT COSTS:											
Group health insurance	273,500	88,300									
Workers' compensation	88,700	1,900									
State unemployment	33,800	10,600									
Federal unemployment		1,700									
Employer portion FICA	158,200	87,200									
401(k) contribution	6,200										
Group life insurance		2,700									
Long-term disability											
Pension/profit sharing	23,800	171,000									
Other benefit(s)	68,691										
Vacation pay	84,392										
Holiday pay											
Sick pay											
INDIRECT LABOR COSTS:											
Departmental salaries 92.20%			500,000	120,000	280,000	72,000	189,748	72,000	96,000	30,979	0
Indirect labor – net @					154,896	85,193	189,748	34,852	96,810	30,979	35,700
Indirect charges by direct labor											35,700
Total Indirect Labor 31.88%		(363,401)	500,000	120,000	134,896	157,193	189,748	106,852	192,810	30,979	35,700
Hourly fringes @ 41.04%	(742,584)		159,386	38,253	89,256	22,952	77,868	22,952	30,952	12,713	146,504
					63,566	34,561		14,102	39,729		
TOTAL INDIRECT LABOR W/FRINGES			659,386	158,253	587,718	215,106	267,616	144,106	263,141	43,692	182,204
SPECIFIC ASSIGNMENT COSTS:											
Overtime premium			0	0	4,000	2,200	4,900	300	2,500	800	17,600
Shift premium			4,000	2,000	8,000	2,700	8,000	2,000	3,900	4,000	6,600
Building depreciation			5,000	5,000	3,438	6,000	10,000	10,300	10,000	10,000	10,000
Equipment depreciation			488		3,030	5,000	975	375	975	975	50,000
Purchased maintenance costs			3,800								4,875
Leases and rentals			1,443	443	443	443	885	885	885	885	5,050
Real property taxes			1,400	700	2,834	2,100	2,808				3,500
Personal property taxes			354	354	334	334	-708	-708	1,708	1,708	4,040
Utilities:											
Electricity			180	90	330	270	330	90	180	180	28,597
Other			400	200	840	600	800	200	400	400	1,000
Supplies:											
Argon compounds			0	0	0	0	0	0	0	0	96,389
Drills and cutters			0	4,000	16,000	6,000	10,000	4,000	5,000	2,000	32,100
Other			10,000	2,000	54,000	3,000		10,000	26,000	2,000	
Budgeted expenses			250,000								
TOTAL SPECIFIC ASSIGNMENT COSTS			276,065	14,787	35,215	28,667	43,398	30,458	55,948	23,848	259,752
DEPARTMENTAL COSTS THROUGH SPECIFIC ASSIGNMENT			935,451	173,040	632,933	243,773	311,014	174,564	319,089	67,540	441,956
GENERAL FACTORY OVERHEAD ALLOCATION			240,713	(173,040)	(515,856)	(195,019)	21,364	8,545	10,682	4,272	34,181
			4,876		4,876						
SERVICE CENTERS:											
Engineering support – time							9,751	9,751	9,751	9,751	103,171
Repairs and maintenance support					(68,781)	(24,377)	(156,85)				24,377
Tooling support					(68,781)	(24,377)	(188,17)				17,106
Tooling projects					(24,383)		(17,106)				
Capital projects											
Other direct costs											
NET OVERHEAD COST PER BOOKS	(1) 1,181,059	(1) 1,181,059	(1) 1,181,059	0	0	(0)	1	192,840	339,322	81,563	620,791

187

Exhibit 14.3 Schedule DC—1 (Part 2)

	ASSEMBLY	DIRECT PRESS LABOR	PRESS OPERATIONS	CNC MACHINING	O/S PROC OVERHEAD	TOTAL INDIRECT COSTS	DIRECT LABOR	DIRECT MATERIAL	OTHER DIRECT COSTS	TOTAL COST
FRINGE BENEFIT COSTS:										
Group health insurance										
Workers compensation										
State unemployment										
Federal unemployment										
Employer portion FICA										
401(k) corporation										
Group life insurance										
Long/short term disability										
Pension/profit sharing										
Other benefit(s)										
Vacation pay										
Holiday pay										
Sick pay										
INDIRECT LABOR COSTS:										
Indirect salaries @ 92.20%						1,140,000				1,140,000
Indirect labor-net						673,614				673,614
Indirect charges by direct labor	29,209	48,682	0	0		113,590				113,590
Total Indirect Labor	29,209	48,682	0	81,136		1,927,204				1,927,204
Salary fringes @ 31.88%						363,401				363,401
Hourly fringes @ 41.04%	119,867	199,778	0	33,296		742,584				742,584
TOTAL INDIRECT LABOR W/FRINGES	149,076	248,460	0	114,432		3,033,189				3,033,189
SPECIFIC ASSIGNMENT COSTS:										
Overtime premium	14,400	24,000	0	4,000		75,300				75,300
Shift premium	15,000	10,000	0	2,000		30,600				30,600
Building depreciation	20,000		20,000	75,288		100,000				100,000
Equipment depreciation	4,875		60,943	18,280		280,000				280,000
Purchased maintenance costs						93,853				93,853
Leases and rentals						25,008				25,008
Insurance	2,020		6,313	6,313		35,000				35,000
Real property taxes	5,600		7,000	5,600		20,004				20,004
Personal property taxes	11,616		5,050	5,050						
Utilities:										
Electricity	23,406		91,806	36,711		182,170				182,170
Other	1,600		2,000	1,600		10,000				10,000
Supplies:										
Drawing compounds	0	0	0	0		96,389				96,389
Drills and cutters	0	0	77,376	51,585		77,376				77,376
Other	0	0	25,800	10,300		51,585				51,585
Budgeted expenses	0	0	(25,000)	(10,000)		175,200				175,200
						318,000				318,000
TOTAL SPECIFIC ASSIGNMENT COSTS	94,918	34,000	346,288	222,442		1,525,786				1,525,786
DEPARTMENTAL COSTS THROUGH SPECIFIC ASSIGNMENT	243,994	282,460	346,288	336,874		4,558,975				4,558,975
GENERAL FACTORY OVERHEAD ALLOCATION	34,181	51,272	0	8,545		2				2
SERVICE CENTERS:										
Engineering support	34,390	0	68,781	68,781		0				0
Repairs and maintenance - time	24,377		60,943	38,566		0				0
Tooling support	17,106		73,313	29,326		0				0
Tooling projects						(256,952)			256,952	0
Capital projects						(110,264)			110,264	0
Other direct costs						(58,767)			58,767	0
NET OVERHEAD COST PER BOOKS	354,048	333,732	549,326	480,092		4,132,993			425,984	4,558,977

simply be brought forward from Schedules PR–1 and PR–2. The amounts from these schedules can, however, be multiplied by the percentage of wages for distribution from Schedule FB–1 to arrive at indirect labor for each cost center. Indirect labor worked by direct personnel can be brought forward directly from Schedule PR–4.

Salary fringe benefits are charged to cost centers by applying the salary fringe benefit rate from Schedule FB–2 to the salary costs already brought forward to Schedule DC–1. The sum of these cost center charges is then subtracted from the salary fringe benefit cost center. This should "zero out" this salary fringe benefit cost center.

Hourly fringe benefits use the hourly fringe benefit rate brought forward from Schedule FB–2, but instead of applying the rate only to the indirect labor costs calculated on Schedule DC–1, it is also applied to the cost center's direct labor as recorded on Schedule DC–2. This calculation is consistent with the treatment of fringe benefits for direct hourly employees established in the cost flow-down analysis. The sum of these cost center charges is then subtracted from the hourly fringe benefit cost center. This should zero out this hourly fringe benefit cost center.

Specific assignment costs are brought forward from various schedules as follows:

Cost	From
Overtime premium	Schedule PR–2
Shift premium	Schedule PR–3
Building depreciation	Schedule SA–2
Equipment depreciation	Schedule SA–2
Purchased maintenance costs	Schedule AL–2
Leases and rentals	Schedule SA–3
Insurance	Schedule SA–4
Real property taxes	Schedule SA–4
Personal property taxes	Schedule SA–4
Utilities	Schedule SA–5
Supplies	Schedule SA–6
Budgeted expenses	Schedule SA–7

Exhibit 14.4   Schedule DC—2 Information

PURPOSE: To complete cost distributions for Levels VI and VII and to calculate Level VIII indirect cost application rates

MANUAL INPUT: None

INPUT FROM:

Schedule PR—4	Schedule AL—3	Schedule AL—4
Schedule AL—5	Schedule AL—6	Schedule DC—1

OUTPUT TO: Schedule DC—3

LEVEL: VIII—Production Activities

A81   PR-1
   Personnel & Gross Pay
	T81 AL-1
	   General Factory Overhead

A161   PR-2
   Overtime Information
	T161 AL-2
	   Service Center Billings

A241   PR-3
   Shift Premium
	T241 AL-3
	   Production Support Activity
	   Distribution

A321   PR-4
   Direct Working Indirect
	T321 AL-4
	   Administrative Support
	   Activity Distribution

A401   FB-1
   Vacation, Holiday and
   Sick Pay
	T401 AL-5
	   Direct Material and
	   Outside Processing

A481   FB-2
   Fringe Rate Calculations
	T481 AL-6
	   Machine Time Information

A561   SA-1
   Square Footage Information
	T561 DC-1
	   Departmental Cost Accumulation

A641   SA-2
   Depreciation Expense
	T641 DC-2
	   Indirect Cost Rate
	   Calculations

A721   SA-3
   Leases and Rentals
	T721 DC-3
	   Rate/Cost Reconciliation

A801 SA-4 Other Fixed Allocations	
A881 SA-5 Utilities	
A961 SA-6 Supplies	
A1041 SA-7 Budgeted Expenses	

Exhibit 14.5 Schedule DC—2 (Part 1)

	GEN & ADMIN	GENERAL FACTORY OVERHEAD	ENGINEERING	MAINTENANCE	TOOL ROOM	PRODUCTION CONTROL	QUALITY ASSURANCE	SHIPPING & RECEIVING	WELDING
NET OVERHEAD COST PER BOOKS	1,181,059	0	0	(0)	1	192,860	339,522	81,563	620,791
Production Support Activity Distribution:									
Production Control						(192,860)			60,798
Quality Assurance							(339,522)		107,033
Shipping & Receiving								(81,563)	25,712
General & Administrative Distribution	(1,181,059)								344,611
OVERHEAD COST AFTER CONVERSION ALLOCATIONS	0	0	0	0	(0)	1	0	0	1,158,944
DIRECT LABOR DOLLARS									321,298
Overhead as a % of Direct Labor									361%
MACHINE HOURS									
Overhead cost per Machine Hour									
OUTSIDE PROCESSOR OVERHEAD:									
Outside processing costs									
Overhead as a % of o/s costs									
DIRECT MATERIAL PURCHASES									
TOOLING PURCHASES									
OUTSIDE MANUFACTURING SERVICES									
TOTAL MANUFACTURING COSTS	(1)	(1)	0	0	(0)	1	0	0	1,158,944

191

Exhibit 14.6   Schedule DC—2 (Part 2)

	ASSEMBLY	DIRECT PRESS LABOR	PRESS OPERATIONS	CNC MACHINING	O/S PROC OVERHEAD	TOTAL INDIRECT COSTS	DIRECT LABOR	DIRECT MATERIAL	OTHER DIRECT COSTS	TOTAL COST
NET OVERHEAD COST PER BOOKS	354,048	333,732	549,326	480,092		4,132,993			425,984	4,558,977
Production Support Activity Distri									0	0
Production Control	39,814	0	35,451	30,983	25,814				(0)	(0)
Quality Assurance	70,090	0	62,410	54,544	45,445					
Shipping & Receiving	16,838	0	14,993	13,103	10,917					
General & Administrative Distribut	225,669	234,225	200,940	175,615		(0)			0	0
OVERHEAD COST AFTER CONVERSION ALLOC	706,459	567,956	863,119	754,338	82,176	4,132,993			425,984	4,558,977
DIRECT LABOR DOLLARS	262,881	438,134					1,022,314			1,022,314
Overhead as a % of Direct Labor	269%	130%								
MACHINE HOURS			25,792	10,317						
Overhead cost per Machine Hour			33.46	73.12						
OUTSIDE PROCESSOR OVERHEAD:										
Outside processing costs					400,000					
Overhead as a % of o/s costs					20.5%					
DIRECT MATERIAL PURCHASES								3,000,000		3,000,000
TOOLING PURCHASES									150,000	150,000
OUTSIDE MANUFACTURING SERVICES									400,000	400,000
TOTAL MANUFACTURING COSTS	706,459	567,956	863,119	754,338	82,176	4,132,993	1,022,314	3,000,000	975,984	9,131,291

192

The distribution of General Factory Overhead is brought forward from Schedule AL–1. The distributed service center costs are brought forward from Schedule AL–2. At this point, General Factory Overhead, Engineering, Tool Room, and Maintenance cost centers should be zeroed out.

Schedule DC–2: Indirect Cost Rate Calculations

Schedule DC–2 (Exhibits 14.4, 14.5, and 14.6) begins by completing the distribution begun on Schedule DC–1. Balances remaining in each cost center are brought forward. The distribution of production support activities is brought forward from Schedule AL–3. The administrative support activity distribution is brought forward from Schedule AL–4. Upon completion of these distributions, costs should remain only in the production activities.

Using chargeable direct labor dollars brought forward from Schedule PR–4, the direct labor–based cost centers' indirect cost application rates are calculated. Using machine hour information brought forward from Schedule AL–6, the machine hour–based cost centers' indirect cost application rates are calculated. Using the outside processing costs brought forward from Schedule AL–5, the outside processing indirect cost application rate is calculated.

The direct material and purchased tooling costs are brought forward from Schedule AL–5 to complete the summarization of total operating cost for Costa Manufacturing.

Schedule DC–3: Rate/Cost Reconciliation

Schedule DC–3 (Exhibits 14.7 and 14.8) is used to check the completeness of the rate structure developed by the model. All direct costs and indirect cost application bases are brought forward from Schedule DC–2. The indirect cost application rates are also brought forward from Schedule DC–2 and applied against their bases to calculate the indirect costs. The total cost accumulated in this fashion is compared with the total cost shown on Schedule DC–2. If the difference is close to zero, the calculations have accounted for all of Costa's operating costs. If the difference is more than could be caused by rounding, a problem exists in the model's mechanics and needs to be located and corrected.

Exhibit 14.7   Schedule DC—3 Information

PURPOSE: To check the completeness of the rate structure developed by the model

MANUAL INPUT: None

INPUT FROM: Schedule DC—2

OUTPUT TO: No other schedules

LEVEL: None—analysis only

A81 PR-1 Personnel & Gross Pay	**T81** AL-1 General Factory Overhead	
A161 PR-2 Overtime Information	**T161** AL-2 Service Center Billings	
A241 PR-3 Shift Premium	**T241** AL-3 Production Support Activity Distribution	
A321 PR-4 Direct Working Indirect	**T321** AL-4 Administrative Support Activity Distribution	
A401 FB-1 Vacation, Holiday and Sick Pay	**T401** AL-5 Direct Material and Outside Processing	
A481 FB-2 Fringe Rate Calculations	**T481** AL-6 Machine Time Information	
A561 SA-1 Square Footage Information	**T561** DC-1 Departmental Cost Accumulation	
A641 SA-2 Depreciation Expense	**T641** DC-2 Indirect Cost Rate Calculations	
A721 SA-3 Leases and Rentals	**T721** DC-3 Rate/Cost Reconciliation	
A801 SA-4 Other Fixed Allocations		
A881 SA-5 Utilities		
A961 SA-6 Supplies		
A1041 SA-7 Budgeted Expenses		

Exhibit 14.8   Schedule DC—3

```
NON-PRODUCTION DIRECT COSTS:
  Direct material and purchased parts                              3,000,000
  Tooling purchases                                                  150,000
  Capitalized costs                                                  425,984
                                                                  ----------
TOTAL NON-PRODUCTION DIRECT COSTS                                  3,575,984


OUTSIDE MANUFACTURING COSTS                    400,000    120.5%     482,176

DIRECT MANUFACTURING LABOR/OVERHEAD:

                               Overhead
                               % DLabor   D. Labor   Overhead
                               --------  ----------  ---------
  Welding                        361%      321,298  1,158,944   1,480,242
  Assembly                       269%      262,881    706,459     969,340
  Direct Press Labor             130%      438,134    567,956   1,006,090

CYCLE TIME OVERHEAD:

                       Hours               $/Hour
                     ----------          ----------
  Press Operations      25,792             33.46               863,119
  CNC Machining          10,317             73.12               754,338
                                                             ----------
                                                              9,131,289
TOTAL COSTS                                                  ==========


         TOTAL COSTS PER DC - 2                          9,131,291
                                                         ==========
```

15

Completion of the Model: Does the Company Have Activity-Based Costing Yet?

With the completion of Schedule DC–3, Costa's cost accumulation model is complete. Thus far, however, Costa has done nothing to change its day-to-day accounting operations. What else must the company do to complete the implementation of activity-based costing? The answer in one word is *nothing!*

Although many other things can be done to improve Costa's new activity-based costing system, the company now has an abc system that generates cost information vastly superior to that provided by its previous system. This improvement has been accomplished without any changes in day-to-day accounting operations. New input data can be developed for the model as time passes (at least annually) using basically the same procedures used to gather the information for the original model.

The original goal of activity-based costing at Costa was to develop a more effective means of determining the cost of individual products. Using the model to develop new costing rates and applying them to the correct drivers for each product accomplishes this objective. A massive system conversion is unnecessary. The same financial accounting–oriented system can be used for valuing the organization's inventory and determining its overall cost of goods sold. For individual measurement periods, the results might not agree with those that would have been obtained with a fully integrated activity-based costing system, but over time, the generalized system will accurately report overall results. The results should, however, be much more favorable than they would have been otherwise because individual decisions are not being made with the financial-oriented system. Individual decisions are being made with the other, "off-line" system: the activity-based costing system.

What each additional step toward integration can do is to further improve the accuracy of activity-based costing information over time and provide the capability of incorporating more relevant and effective performance measurement techniques in the future.

The first important step for Costa would be to begin collecting machine time information. The system already collects the direct labor information relevant for Welding, Assembly, and Direct Press Labor, but Costa needs some history on Press Operations and CNC Machining to ensure the quality of data for this important new cost driver.

Another change, which would improve the accuracy of Costa's cost data, is the restructuring of cost centers to agree with those in the model. This change would provide for the collection of actual costs that can confirm or correct the estimates made in establishing the initial model.

One more change that would materially enhance cost data accuracy would be the collection of time information for the service centers Maintenance, Engineering, and the Tool Room. This would provide for the collection of actual demand data that can confirm or correct the demand estimates made in establishing the initial model.

With only these three changes, the activity-based costing data generated by the cost accumulation model can improve in accuracy and provide management with even more confidence in its relevance.

I am not saying that a full integration of activity-based costing principles and practices into the day-to-day accounting system should be discouraged. Each organization must make its own cost–benefit analysis to determine whether integration will improve decision making enough to make the investment worthwhile.

In Section III of this book, I discuss ways in which activity-based costing, whether off-line, fully integrated, or somewhere in between, can be used to improve a company's decision-making process. But before I do that, I take a brief look at how the abc approach to implementing activity-based costing can be used in service organizations.

16

Activity-Based
Costing in Service
Organizations

Unfortunately, most literature on activity-based costing empha-
sizes its use in a manufacturing setting. Even I am guilty of writ-
ing from a manufacturing perspective, as evidenced by the case
study of Costa Manufacturing used in this book to demonstrate
the principles and techniques of abc. It is important to note, however, that activity-based costing, including the abc approach described in this book, applies to all types of business (and even
nonbusiness) organizations, not only manufacturers. The same
principles and practices can be used to develop relevant cost systems for insurance companies, banks, sports teams, restaurants,
car dealerships, consulting firms, leasing companies, printers,
public utilities, warehousers/distributors, or medical clinics.

   To demonstrate this point, I use the abc techniques to show
how activity-based systems can be developed for the last two types
of service business mentioned above: a warehouser/distributor
and a medical clinic. The examples are intended not to be in-
depth case studies, but to be demonstrations of how the abc
methodology can be used in a service industry setting. As a result,
detailed discussions of the reasoning behind each system design
decision are not included.

Exhaust Systems

Exhaust Systems is an $11 million aftermarket distributor of exhaust pipes, catalytic converters/mufflers, tail pipes, and the hardware necessary to install them. It sells to a large number of "jobbers" throughout the country. One important product characteristic to keep in mind is that the irregular sizes and shapes of exhaust pipes make them much more cumbersome to handle and more inefficient to store than the other three products.

Financial results for Exhaust Systems's most recent fiscal year are summarized below.

Sales	$11,000,000
Cost of products sold	7,500,000
Gross margin	3,500,000
Warehousing costs	2,000,000
Operating profit	1,500,000
General/administration expenses	1,000,000
Profit before interest and income taxes	$ 500,000

In developing its abc system, Exhaust Systems followed the ten steps outlined in Chapter 6.

Step 1. Identify and Define Relevant Activities   The following were identified as the major activities necessary in operating the organization:

Accounts payable	Human resources
Billing	Internal sales
Cash disbursements	Inventory control
Collections	Lift-truck maintenance
Credit	Material handling
Data processing	Order picking
Exterior maintenance	Order processing
Facilities maintenance	Packing/marking/staging
Forecasting	Payroll
General accounting	Purchasing
General management	Put-away

Receiving
Sales and marketing
Security
Shipping
Storage–Exhaust pipes

Storage–Hardware
Storage–Mufflers/converters
Storage–Tail pipes
Treasury duties
Warehouse supervision

Step 2. Organize Activities by Cost Center   Once the activities were established, Exhaust Systems grouped them into logical cost centers.

General / Administration
   Cash disbursements
   Collections
   General accounting
   General management
   Forecasting
   Inventory control
   Payroll
   Treasury duties
   Human resources
   Sales and marketing
   Warehouse supervision
Facilities
   Exterior maintenance
   Facilities maintenance
   Security
Data Processing
   Data processing
Material Handling
   Lift-truck maintenance
   Material handling
Procurement
   Accounts payable
   Purchasing
Incoming Handling
   Put-away
   Receiving

Outgoing Handling
   Order picking
   Packing/marking/staging
   Shipping
Order Processing
   Billing
   Credit
   Internal sales
   Order processing
Product Line–Exhaust Pipes
   Storage–Exhaust pipes
Product Line–Tail Pipes
   Storage–Tail pipes
Product Line–Mufflers / Converters
   Storage–Mufflers/converters
Product Line–Hardware
   Storage–Hardware

Step 3. Identify Major Elements of Cost   Major elements of cost
at Exhaust Systems were identified as follows:

   Salaries and wages
   Fringe benefits
   Depreciation
   Purchased maintenance
   Leases and rentals
   Insurance
   Property taxes
   Utilities (including fuel for lift-truck fleet)
   Supplies
   Various budgeted expenses

Step 4. Determine Relationships between Activities and Costs
The relationships between activities and costs at Exhaust Systems
were fairly straightforward. Salaries, wages, and fringe benefits belonged in the cost centers where the employees were working. Depreciation of the building was charged to Facilities (later
to be redistributed on the basis of square footage). Equipment

depreciation was distributed on the basis of each asset's location. Purchased maintenance was distributed on the basis of where the maintained assets were located, and lease and rental costs were charged to the activities requiring the leased or rented items. Building insurance was charged to Facilities, and other general insurance costs were charged to General/Administration.

Real property taxes were distributed in the same manner as building depreciation, whereas personal property taxes were distributed on the basis of asset values. In this setting, electric, gas, and water utilities were primarily for general use, not for the operation of major equipment. As a result, these utilities were charged to Facilities. Fuel for operating the lift-truck fleet was charged to Material Handling. Supplies and budgeted expenses were distributed to the consuming or benefiting activities.

Step 5. Identify Cost Drivers to Assign Costs to Activities and Activities to Products   The usual drivers were used to assign costs to activities. Headcounts, labor dollars, and labor hours were used to assign and sometimes determine costs related to wages and fringe benefits. Headcounts were used in determining and assigning supplies. Utilities were determined by the number of shifts in operation. Lift-truck fuel was determined by the number of lift-truck drivers employed.

The more difficult decisions were in establishing drivers for assigning activities to other activities and to products. Data Processing served General/Administration, Procurement, and Order Processing cost centers (by this time activities had been grouped into cost centers). Material Handling served Incoming and Outgoing Handling cost centers as well as General/Administration (for reorganizing or inventorying stock). Procurement benefited the entire organization in its purchase of general items, but spent the bulk of its time in negotiating and administering the purchase of products for resale. As a result of these characteristics, the system designer decided that these three cost centers were driven by demand and, as a result, should be treated as service centers and their costs assigned to other cost centers on the basis of their estimated demand.

General/Administration's costs were incurred in support of the entire organization. The system designer decided to distribute these costs to the operations centers on the basis of each center's "activity cost," a warehouser/distributor's equivalent of a manufacturer's conversion cost.

Orders processed was determined to be the driver of Order Processing. Although a large order would require somewhat more processing than a small one, it was believed that the majority of order processing activity was fixed for each order and that using a more complex driver (e.g., both orders and line items) would add precision without adding much accuracy.

Units of product handled was selected as the most appropriate driver for assigning the cost of the remaining operations cost centers to the product. A problem arose, however, in the fact that the handling of one exhaust pipe requires more effort than the handling of muffler or tail pipe and much more effort than the handling of one unit of hardware. By simply using units to assign Income Handling and Outgoing Handling costs to the product, not enough cost would be assigned to the difficult-to-handle exhaust pipes and too much would be charged to the other product types, especially hardware.

The solution to this problem was the use of driver multipliers. These multipliers were used to convert units of product to activity units, a concept similar to the consumption units discussed earlier in this book. Thus, Exhaust Systems could devise a method for more equitably assigning Incoming and Outgoing Handling costs. For example, an exhaust pipe requires about twice as much effort as a muffler/converter. If the level of effort necessary to handle one muffler/converter is used as a base, the driver multiplier for mufflers/converters is 100% and that for exhaust pipes 200%.

Actual units handled, without any multiplier, was determined to be an effective driver for assigning the Product Line Costs cost centers to products.

Step 6. Establish the Cost Flow Pattern   The costs and cost centers of Exhaust Systems were organized into the cost flow pattern shown in Exhibit 16.1.

Steps 7 through 9. Select the Appropriate Tools/Plan the Cost Accumulation Model/Gather the Necessary Data   The appropriate tools for effecting the cost flow pattern were selected, the cost accumulation model was planned, and the data necessary to drive

Exhibit 16.1   Cost flow-down diagram/Exhaust Systems

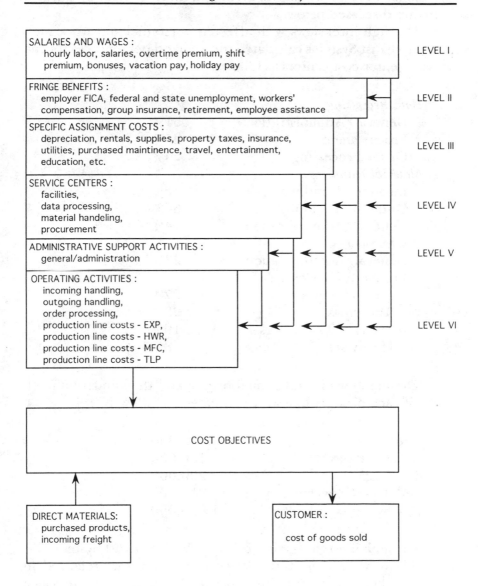

the model were collected. Some of the more critical or unusual items are discussed below.

Through interviews with affected personnel and work sampling, Exhaust Systems calculated the demand percentages for the service center cost centers as follows:

Data Processing
General/Administration	51%
Procurement	25%
Order Processing	24%

Material Handling
Incoming Handling	36%
Outgoing Handling	60%
General/Administration	4%

Procurement
General/Administration	23%
Product Line Costs	
Exhaust Pipes	27%
Tail Pipes	23%
Muffler/Converters	19%
Hardware	8%

The number of total annual orders and the annual unit volumes of each product line were estimated as follows:

Orders	42,000
Exhaust Pipes	180,000
Tail Pipes	200,000
Mufflers/Converters	210,000
Hardware	1,800,000

Through interviews and work sampling, Exhaust Systems was also able to determine the relative levels of effort required in handling the four product lines, using Mufflers/Converters as a base (100%), as follows:

Exhaust Pipes	200%
Tail Pipes	100%

Mufflers/Converters	100%
Hardware	5%

Step 10. Establish the Cost Accumulation Model   With the necessary data collected, Exhaust Systems was then able to build a cost accumulation model. A condensed version of Schedules DC–1 and DC–2 from the model are provided in Exhibits 16.2 and 16.3.

Results of Exhaust Systems's abc Analysis   The results of Exhaust Systems's abc analysis showed that the cost of processing each order was approximately $14.50, and the overhead incurred in purchasing, handling, and storing one unit of each product line was approximately as follows:

Exhaust Pipes	$5.52
Tail Pipes	$2.83
Mufflers/Converters	$2.71
Hardware	$ .15

Using this abc approach to develop the cost of a customer order results in a cost "buildup" as shown in Exhibit 16.4.

The distribution of indirect costs developed through this abc analysis results in an infinitely more accurate measure of costs than does any generalized method. Fortunately, the ability to perform such an analysis using abc methodology is well within the capabilities and resources of a small or mid-sized warehousing and distributing organization.

Main Street Health Clinic

Main Street Health Clinic is a $4 million provider of a variety of the most commonly needed health care services. These include general practice, pediatrics, gynecology/obstetrics, and physical therapy. The clinic has radiology and laboratory facilities and a full administrative staff. Nursing services are provided by a pool of staff nurses, each of whom can work in two or more of the service areas.

Financial results for the clinic's most recent fiscal year are summarized on page 212.

Exhibit 16.2 Schedule DC—1/Exhaust Systems, Inc.

	FRINGE BENEFITS/ HOURLY	FRINGE BENEFITS/ SALARY	GEN & ADMIN	FACILITY COST	DATA PROCESSING	MATERIAL HANDLING	PROCURE-MENT	INCOMING HANDLING	OUTGOING HANDLING	ORDER PROCESSING	PROD LINE COSTS/ EXST PIPE	PROD LINE COSTS/ TAIL PIPE	PROD LINE COSTS/ MUF/CONV	PROD LINE COSTS/ HARDWARE	TOTAL
FRINGE BENEFIT COSTS:															
Various	180,000	240,000													
LABOR COSTS:															
Departmental salaries			540,000		90,000		120,000			180,000					930,000
Hourly labor					45,000	240,000		120,000	120,000						525,000
TOTAL LABOR COSTS			540,000		135,000	240,000	120,000	120,000	120,000	180,000					1,455,000
Salary fringes		(240,000)	140,000		23,000		31,000			46,000					240,000
Hourly fringes	(180,000)				15,000	83,000		41,000	41,000						180,000
TOTAL LABOR W/FRINGES	0	0	680,000	0	173,000	323,000	151,000	161,000	161,000	226,000	0	0	0	0	1,875,000
SPECIFIC ASSIGNMENT COSTS:															
Overtime premium			0	0	2,000	12,000	0	6,000	6,000	0	0	0	0	0	26,000
Shift premium			0	0	0	6,000	0	3,000	3,000	0	0	0	0	0	12,000
Depreciation			2,000	120,000	16,000	30,000	6,000	6,000	12,000	6,000	30,000	18,000	18,000	6,000	270,000
Purchased maintenance			0	20,000	5,000	30,000	0	0	0	0	0	0	0	0	55,000
Leases and rentals			6,000	10,000	20,000	5,000	0	0	0	0	10,000	0	0	5,000	56,000
Insurance			60,000	30,000	0	0	0	0	0	0	0	0	0	0	90,000
Property taxes			0	12,000	2,000	3,000	1,000	1,000	1,000	1,000	3,000	2,000	2,000	1,000	29,000
Utilities			0	60,000	0	10,000	0	0	0	25,000	0	0	0	0	95,000
Supplies			20,000	20,000	35,000	30,000	10,000	5,000	10,000	0	0	0	0	0	130,000
Budgeted expenses			222,000	22,000	33,000	30,000	8,000	4,000	3,000	18,000	4,000	7,000	7,000	4,000	362,000
COSTS THROUGH SPECIFIC ASSIGNMENT COSTS			990,000	294,000	286,000	479,000	176,000	186,000	196,000	276,000	47,000	27,000	27,000	16,000	3,000,000
OPERATION SUPPORT ACTIVITIES:															
Facilities			30,000	(294,000)	10,000	15,000	10,000	15,000	15,000	10,000	90,000	37,000	38,000	24,000	0
Data Processing			151,000		(296,000)		75,000			70,000					0
Material Handling			14,000			(494,000)		180,000	300,000						0
Procurement			61,000				(261,000)				70,000	60,000	50,000	20,000	0
COSTS THROUGH OPERATION SUPPORT DISTRIBUTIONS			1,246,000	0	0	0	0	381,000	511,000	356,000	207,000	124,000	115,000	60,000	3,000,000
GENERAL AND ADMINISTRATION			(1,246,000)					271,000	363,000	253,000	147,000	88,000	82,000	42,000	0
COSTS THROUGH GENERAL AND ADMINISTRATION DISTRIBUTION			0	0	0	0	0	652,000	874,000	609,000	354,000	212,000	197,000	102,000	3,000,000

210

Exhibit 16.3 Schedule DC—2/Exhaust Systems, Inc.

	FRINGE BENEFITS/ HOURLY	FRINGE BENEFITS/ SALARY	GEN & ADMIN	FACILITY COST	DATA PROCESSING	MATERIAL HANDLING	PROCURE- MENT	INCOMING HANDLING	OUTGOING HANDLING	ORDER PROCESSING	PROD LINE COSTS / EXST PIPE	PROD LINE COSTS / TAIL PIPE	PROD LINE COSTS / MUF/CONV	PROD LINE COSTS / HARDWARE	TOTAL
COSTS THROUGH GENERAL AND ADMINISTRATION DISTRIBUTION								652,000	874,000	609,000	354,000	212,000	197,000	102,000	3,000,000
Orders										42,000					
Units											180,000	200,000	210,000	1,800,000	
Activity Units								860,000	860,000						
Unit Cost								0.76	1.32	14.50	1.97	1.06	0.94	0.06	

	ANNUAL VOLUME	ACTIVITY UNIT MULTIPLIER	ACTIVITY UNIT VOLUME	INCOMING HANDLING	OUTGOING HANDLING	ORDER PROCESSING	PROD LINE COSTS / EXST PIPE	PROD LINE COSTS / TAIL PIPE	PROD LINE COSTS / MUF/CONV	PROD LINE COSTS / HARDWARE	TOTAL/ UNIT	EXTENSION
ORDERS	42,000					14.50					14.50	609,000
EXHAUST PIPES	180,000	2.00	360,000	1.52	2.03		1.97				5.52	992,791
TAIL PIPES	200,000	1.00	200,000	0.76	1.02			1.06			2.83	566,884
MUFFLERS/CONVERTERS	210,000	1.00	210,000	0.76	1.02				0.94		2.71	569,628
HARDWARE	1,800,000	0.05	90,000	0.04	0.05					0.06	0.15	261,698
TOTAL			860,000									3,000,000

211

Exhibit 16.4

Item	Mdse Unit Qty	Mdse Unit Cost	Prod Line Cost	Extended Item Cost
Exhaust Pipe A	3	$24.00	$5.52	$88.56
Exhaust Pipe B	4	18.00	5.52	94.08
Tail Pipe A	2	9.00	2.83	23.66
Tail Pipe B	4	11.50	2.83	57.32
Muffler/Converter A	2	45.00	2.71	95.42
Muffler/Converter B	1	37.50	2.71	40.21
Muffler/Converter C	3	28.90	2.71	94.83
Hardware–misc	80	1.05	.15	96.00
Order processing				14.50
Total cost				$604.58

Revenues	$4,000,000
Costs and expenses	
Physician salaries	1,200,000
Nursing salaries	360,000
Administrative salaries	656,000
Fringe benefits	172,000
Operating expenses	1,326,000
Profit before interest and income taxes	$ 286,000

Charges for services were governed by the local market and the charges allowed by the patients' insurance carriers. The clinic's management, however, had not been able to determine its profitability by type of service. To correct this deficiency in knowledge of their own operations, the clinic's management decided to develop service line costs using the abc methodology. Like Exhaust Systems, the clinic followed the ten steps outlined in Chapter 6.

Step 1. Identify and Define Relevant Activities   The following were identified as the major activities necessary in operating the clinic:

Facility maintenance
General accounting
General administration
Housekeeping
Insurance administration
Nursing services
Patient accounting
Patient waiting
Professional services–General practice
Professional services–Physical therapy
Professional services–Pediatrics
Professional services–Gynecology
Professional services–Obstetrics
Professional services–Radiology
Professional services–Laboratory
Records
Scheduling

Step 2. Organize Activities by Cost Center   Main Street Health
Clinic then grouped the activities into logical cost centers.

General / Administration
    General accounting
    General administration
    Patient waiting
    Scheduling
Facility
    Facility maintenance
    Housekeeping
Medical Records
    Records
Patient Financial Services
    Insurance administration
    Patient accounting
Nursing Support
    Nursing services
General Practice
    Professional services–General practice

Pediatrics
  Professional services–Pediatrics
Physical Therapy
  Professional services–Physical therapy
Gynecology
  Professional services–Gynecology
Obstetrics Surcharge
  Professional services–Obstetrics
Radiology
  Professional services–Radiology
Laboratory
  Professional services–Laboratory

The Obstetrics Surcharge cost center requires further discussion. Obstetric and gynecological services are provided by the same physicians in the same examining rooms with the same nursing assistance and the same basic equipment. Thus, it would seem logical that the cost of the two types of services would be the same. However, two elements of cost are materially different for obstetric and gynecological services: malpractice insurance and attorneys' fees. Although obstetric and gynecological services carry approximately the same cost, the obstetrics portion of the practice should carry a disproportionate amount of attorneys' fees and malpractice insurance cost.

In establishing cost centers, the clinic decided that the activities of the obstetrics/gynecology group would all be included in Gynecology, but that the malpractice insurance and legal costs specifically attributable to the practice of obstetrics would be accumulated in a separate cost center, Obstetrics Surcharge. These costs would be added to the basic Gynecology cost for patients requiring obstetric services.

Step 3. Identify Major Elements of Cost   Major elements of cost at the clinic were identified as follows:

Salaries and wages   Purchased maintenance
Fringe benefits   Purchased housekeeping
Depreciation   Leases and rental

Property taxes   Supplies
Insurance–Malpractice   Attorneys' fees
Insurance–Other   Various budgeted expenses
Utilities

Step 4. Determine Relationships between Activities and Costs
The relationships between activities and costs at Main Street
Health Clinic were fairly straightforward. Salaries, wages, and
fringe benefits belonged in the cost centers where the employees
were working. Building depreciation and purchased housekeeping
were charged to Facilities. Equipment depreciation was distributed on the basis of each asset's location. Purchased maintenance was distributed on the basis of where the maintained assets
were located, and lease and rental costs were charged to the cost
centers requiring the leased or rented items.

Like building depreciation, real property taxes were distributed to Facilities, whereas personal property taxes were
distributed on the basis of asset values. Utilities were charged to
Facilities. Supplies and budgeted expenses were distributed
to the consuming or benefiting cost centers.

As mentioned above, special situations arose in connection
with attorneys' fees and malpractice insurance. Although a portion of the clinic's attorneys' fees are for general business purposes, most are related to professional liability matters. As a result,
only those fees related to general business matters are charged to
General/Administration. The balance of the fees are distributed
to the cost centers established for the professional services that
require them.

Each type of health service provided by the clinic has a different level of malpractice risk. As a result, the cost of malpractice
insurance (a cost approaching 10% of the clinic's total expenditures) must be carefully distributed to the professional service
cost centers according to that level of risk. Most prominent among
the cost centers in this respect is Obstetrics Surcharge, which was
established for the sole purpose of accumulating malpractice insurance costs and attorneys' fees relating to the clinic's practice of
obstetrics.

Step 5. Identify Cost Drivers to Assign Costs to Activities and Activities to Products   Many of the usual drivers were used to assign costs to the cost centers. Headcounts and labor dollars were used to assign and sometimes determine costs related to wages and fringe benefits. The number of operation hours was used to determine general utility costs, whereas the number of patient visits was used to establish additional utility costs required in Radiology. Patient visits was also used in determining and assigning supplies.

Square footage was the basis for assigning the accumulated cost of Facilities (waiting area square footage was assigned to General/Administration). Medical Records and Patient Financial Services were assigned to professional service cost centers on the basis of patient visits. Nursing supported all of the professional service cost centers and was assigned on the basis of each center's estimated demand for its services.

The final internal distribution of costs was General/Administration, which was also assigned to professional service cost centers on the basis of patient visits.

In general, patient visits was determined to be the most appropriate driver for assigning professional service cost center costs to the final cost objective. A problem arose, however, in the performance of services in Laboratory and Radiology. In both of these cost centers, a variety of services are performed for the patient. Some services require only a small amount of effort and support cost, whereas others require much more effort and support cost.

The concept of driver multipliers was used to overcome this problem. Each procedure performed in Laboratory and Radiology was given a "degree of effort" rating of 1, 2, or 3. A rating of 1 indicated a fairly simple procedure, a 2 indicated average complexity, and a 3 indicated the most complex procedures. Once assigned, these ratings were used to convert patient visits to these cost centers into "service units."

For example, Radiology had 3,000 patient visits, 1,000 of each rating. The clinic determined that procedures rated 2 required twice the effort of procedures rated 1 and procedures rated 3 required four times the effort of those rated 1. Service units were then calculated as follows:

Rating	Multiplier	Visits	Service Units
1	100%	1,000	1,000
2	200%	1,000	2,000
3	400%	1,000	4,000
Total service units			7,000

A cost per service unit was established, and one service unit was charged for each procedure rated 1, two service units for each procedure rated 2, and four service units for each procedure rated 3.

The number of patient visits (without any multiplier) was determined to be an effective driver for assigning the other professional service cost centers to final cost objectives.

Step 6. Establish the Cost Flow Pattern   The costs and cost centers of the Main Street Health Clinic were organized into the cost flow pattern shown in Exhibit 16.5.

Steps 7 through 9. Select the Appropriate Tools/Plan the Cost Accumulation Model/Gather the Necessary Data   The appropriate tools for effecting the cost flow pattern were selected, the cost accumulation model was planned, and the data necessary to drive the model were collected. Some of the more critical or unusual items are discussed below.

Through interviews with Nursing personnel and work sampling, Main Street Health Clinic calculated the demand percentages for the Nursing Support cost center as follows:

General Practice	30%
Pediatrics	20%
Physical Therapy	5%
Gynecology	30%
Radiology	5%
Laboratory	10%

Exhibit 16.5   Cost flow-down diagram/Main Street Health Clinic

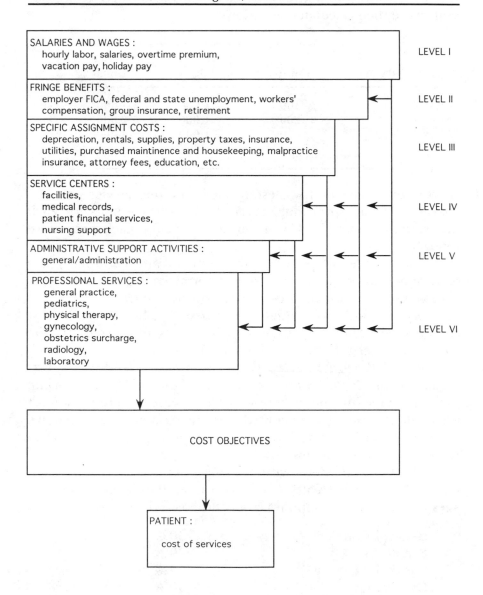

The number of patient visits in each of the professional service cost centers were estimated as follows:

General Practice	22,000
Pediatrics	16,000
Physical Therapy	9,600
Gynecology	20,000
Obstetrics	6,000
Radiology	7,600
Laboratory	19,200

It should be noted that the Obstetrics visits are also included in the count for Gynecology.

Square footage occupied by the various cost centers was measured as follows:

General/Administration	1,800
Medical Records	900
Patient Financial Services	750
General Practice	1,350
Pediatrics	900
Physical Therapy	1,350
Gynecology	900
Radiology	600
Laboratory	450
Total	9,000

Interviews with Radiology and Laboratory personnel resulted in grouping their procedures into the three effort-level ratings with effort multipliers as follows:

Rating	Radiology	Laboratory
1	100%	100%
2	180%	200%
3	320%	350%

Exhibit 16.6 Schedule DC—1/Main Street Health Clinic

	FRINGE BENEFITS	GEN & ADMIN	FACILITY COST	MEDICAL RECORDS	PATIENT FINANCIAL SERVICES	NURSING SUPPORT	GENERAL PRACTICE	PEDIATRICS	PHYSICAL THERAPY	GYNECOLOGY	OBSTETRICS SURCHARGE	RADIOLOGY	LABORATORY	TOTAL
FRINGE BENEFITS:														
Various	172,000													0
LABOR COSTS:														
Departmental salaries and wages		120,000		72,000	96,000	360,000	360,000	360,000	160,000	360,000		200,000	128,000	2,216,000
Fringe benefits	(172,000)	12,000		12,000	16,000	48,000	13,000	13,000	15,000	13,000		14,000	16,000	172,000
TOTAL LABOR W/FRINGES	0	132,000	0	84,000	112,000	408,000	373,000	373,000	175,000	373,000	0	214,000	144,000	2,388,000
SPECIFIC ASSIGNMENT COSTS:														
Overtime premium		3,000		4,000	4,000	14,000			2,000			6,000	2,000	35,000
Depreciation		5,000	110,000	5,000	5,000		5,000	5,000	10,000	5,000		20,000	10,000	180,000
Purchased maintenance		1,000	12,000		3,000							18,000	6,000	40,000
Purchased housekeeping			24,000											24,000
Leases and rentals		6,000	12,000	3,000	9,000				2,000			24,000	4,000	60,000
Property taxes		1,000	20,000	1,000	1,000		1,000	1,000	3,000	1,000		6,000	3,000	38,000
Insurance - malpractice							50,000	50,000	10,000	75,000	125,000	35,000	5,000	350,000
Insurance - other		15,000	10,000											25,000
Utilities			24,000									12,000		36,000
Supplies		24,000	4,000	8,000	12,000		24,000	18,000	14,000	46,000		120,000	30,000	300,000
Attorneys' fees		12,000					6,000	4,000		9,000	24,000	9,000	6,000	70,000
Budgeted expenses		60,000	12,000	6,000	6,000	12,000	12,000	8,000	6,000	24,000		16,000	6,000	168,000
COSTS THROUGH SPECIFIC ASSIGNMENT COSTS	0	259,000	228,000	111,000	152,000	434,000	471,000	459,000	222,000	533,000	149,000	480,000	216,000	3,714,000
OPERATION SUPPORT ACTIVITIES:														
Facilities		46,000	(228,000)	23,000	19,000		34,000	23,000	34,000	23,000		15,000	11,000	0
Medical records				(134,000)			29,000	21,000	13,000	35,000		10,000	26,000	0
Patient financial services					(171,000)		37,000	27,000	16,000	45,000		13,000	33,000	0
Nursing support						(434,000)	130,000	87,000	22,000	130,000		22,000	43,000	0
COSTS THROUGH OPERATION SUPPORT DISTRIBUTIONS	0	305,000	0	0	0	0	701,000	617,000	307,000	766,000	149,000	540,000	329,000	3,714,000
GENERAL AND ADMINISTRATION		(305,000)					67,000	49,000	29,000	79,000		23,000	58,000	0
COSTS THROUGH GENERAL AND ADMINISTRATION DISTRIBUTIONS	0	0	0	0	0	0	768,000	666,000	336,000	845,000	149,000	563,000	387,000	3,714,000

Exhibit 16.7 Schedule DC—2/Main Street Health Clinic

	FRINGE BENEFITS	GEN & ADMIN	FACILITY COST	MEDICAL RECORDS	FINANCIAL SERVICES	NURSING SUPPORT	GENERAL PRACTICE	PEDIATRICS	PHYSICAL THERAPY	GYNECOLOGY	OBSTETRICS SURCHARGE	RADIOLOGY	LABORATORY	TOTAL
COSTS THROUGH GENERAL AND ADMINISTRATION DISTRIBUTIONS							768,000	666,000	336,000	845,000	149,000	563,000	387,000	3,714,000
Paitent Visits							22,000	16,000	9,600	20,000	6,000	7,600	19,200	
Service Units							22,000	16,000	9,600	20,000	6,000	11,840	37,800	
Service Unit Costs							34.91	41.63	35.00	42.25	24.83	47.55	10.24	

RATE SUMMARY

General Practice	34.91	per visit
Pediatrics	41.63	per visit
Physical Therapy	35.00	per visit
Gynecology	42.25	per visit
Obstetrics Surcharge	24.83	per visit
Obstetrics	67.08	per visit
Radiology:		
Level 1 Procedure	47.55	per procedure
Level 2 Procedure	85.59	per procedure
Level 3 Procedure	152.16	per procedure
Laboratory:		
Level 1 Procedure	10.24	per procedure
Level 2 Procedure	20.48	per procedure
Level 3 Procedure	35.83	per procedure

221

Historical data regarding the frequency of each procedure and estimated patient visits resulted in the following estimate of visits to Radiology and Laboratory cost centers by procedure rating:

Rating	Radiology	Laboratory
1	4,400	6,000
2	2,000	9,600
3	1,200	3,600

Step 10. Establish the Cost Accumulation Model   With the necessary data collected, Main Street Health Clinic was then able to build a cost accumulation model. A condensed version of Schedules DC–1 and DC–2 from the model are provided in Exhibits 16.6 and 16.7.

Results of Main Street Health Clinic's abc Analysis   As a result of the abc analysis, Main Street Health Clinic was able to determine the costs involved in the various health services it provides and compare them with the pricing allowed by market conditions and its patients' insurance carriers. As was the case with Exhaust Systems, the ability to perform such an analysis using abc methodology is well within the capabilities and resources of this mid-sized health organization.

Activity-based costing, whether it takes the form of ABC or abc, is equally as valuable a management tool in service organizations as it is in manufacturing firms. The same methodology can be followed in developing an activity-based costing approach for either type of organization. The same cost flow concepts can be followed, and the same tools can be used. All that differs are the particulars: patient visits instead of machine hours, units shipped instead of direct labor, activity costs instead of conversion costs, service units instead of consumption units. These represent different incarnations of the same basic concepts, which can be put to good use by any organization that needs to understand and control its costs.

Part III

USING THE COST
ACCUMULATION MODEL

17

Product Costing and Product Line Profitability

Product costing and product line profitability are so closely related that I cover both subjects simultaneously. I do this by treating Costa Manufacturing's four product lines as if each was a single product. The concepts and practices involved are the same whether each product line comprises many products or only one product.

In recent years, Costa's profit margins have been eroding to the point that, in the year just completed, its profit before interest and income taxes amounted to less than 2.8% of sales. As a first step in attempting to understand this problem, Costa's management analyzed profitability by product line using the company's traditional cost accounting methods. As discussed in Chapter 9, Costa had been using direct labor as a base for charging products with indirect manufacturing costs, and conversion cost as a base for distributing both Engineering and General/Administration costs. These rates were as follows:

Manufacturing overhead: 236.1% of direct labor dollars

Engineering overhead: 13.8% of manufacturing conversion cost input

General/Administration: 22.2% of total conversion cost input

The results of this product line profitability analysis are summarized in Exhibit 17.1.

This analysis clearly showed that two of Costa's product lines, Product Lines B and D, were barely breaking even. Undoubtedly, after distributing a share of the company's interest expense, both lines would prove to be losers. On the other hand, Product Line A seems to be carrying the entire company. Although it is only 28% of the company's total sales, it contributes over 64% of the profit. Product Line C, Costa's smallest product line, contributes 15% of the profit with less than 10% of the sales.

As a result of this analysis, Costa's management decided to concentrate its efforts on improving the profitability of Product Lines B and D through price increases and reductions in each product line's direct labor content.

Exhibit 17.1   Product Line Profitability under Traditional Cost System/ Costa Manufacturing Company

	Product Line A	Product Line B	Product Line C	Product Line D	Total
Sales	2,470,000	2,880,000	830,000	2,620,000	8,800,000
Cost of goods sold					
Direct material	750,000	1,000,000	350,000	900,000	3,000,000
Outside services		200,000	50,000	150,000	400,000
Direct labor					
Welding	197,840	30,030		93,428	321,298
Assembly	82,590	144,002		36,289	262,881
Press		162,450	71,630	204,054	438,134
Machine	54,125	14,512	12,500		81,137
Total direct labor	334,555	350,994	84,130	333,771	1,103,450
Overhead @ 236.1%	789,884	828,697	198,631	788,033	2,605,245
Total cost of goods sold	1,874,439	2,379,691	682,761	2,171,804	7,108,695
Gross margin	595,561	500,309	147,239	448,196	1,691,305
Engineering @ 13.8%	155,173	162,797	39,021	154,809	511,800
General/Admin @ 22.2%	284,074	298,032	71,436	283,408	936,950
Profit before interest and income taxes	156,314	39,480	36,782	9,979	242,555
Profit % to sales	6.33%	1.37%	4.43%	0.38%	2.76%

Product Line Profitability under abc

After completing its design of an activity-based approach to costing and developing its cost accumulation model, Costa's management began to have some doubts as to the validity of the original product line profitability analysis. They decided to take another look at profitability by product line, this time with product cost buildups developed using the abc analysis' bases and rates. The results of this reevaluation are summarized in Exhibits 17.2 through 17.7.

Exhibit 17.2   Product A Profitability/Costa Manufacturing Company

Product Line A		Old System		abc System
Sales		2,470,000		2,470,000
Direct material		750,000		750,000
Outside services		0		0
Overhead @			20.5%	0
Direct Labor				
Welding		197,840		197,840
Assembly		82,590		82,590
Press		0		0
Machine		54,125		
Direct labor overhead				
Welding @	236.1%	467,100	361.0%	714,202
Assembly @	236.1%	194,995	269.0%	222,167
Press @	236.1%	0	130.0%	0
Machine @	236.1%	127,789		
Machine time overhead				
Press	0 hours @		33.46	0
CNC Machine	6,882 hours @		73.12	503,212
Engineering	13.8%	155,173		
General/admin	22.2%	284,074		
Total product cost		2,313,685		2,470,011
Profit before interest and income taxes		156,315		(11)
Profit % to sales		6.33%		0.00%

Exhibit 17.3   Profit B Profitability/Costa Manufacturing Company

Product Line B		Old System		abc System
Sales		2,880,000		2,880,000
Direct material		1,000,000		1,000,000
Outside services		200,000		200,000
Overhead @			20.5%	41,000
Direct labor				
Welding		30,030		30,030
Assembly		144,002		144,002
Press		162,450		162,450
Machine		14,512		
Direct labor overhead				
Welding @	236.1%	70,901	361.0%	108,408
Assembly @	236.1%	339,989	269.0%	387,365
Press @	236.1%	383,544	130.0%	211,185
Machine @	236.1%	34,263		
Machine time overhead				
Press	9,563 hours @		33.46	319,978
CNC Machine	1,845 hours @		73.12	134,906
Engineering	13.8%	162,797		
General/admin	22.2%	298,032		
Total product cost		2,840,521		2,739,324
Profit before interest and income taxes		39,479		140,676
Profit % to sales		1.37%		4.88%

Exhibit 17.4   Product C Profitability/Costa Manufacturing Company

Product Line C		Old System		abc System
Sales		830,000		830,000
Direct material		350,000		350,000
Outside services		50,000		50,000
Overhead @			20.5%	10,250
Direct labor				
Welding		0		0
Assembly		0		0
Press		71,630		71,630
Machine		12,500		
Direct labor overhead				
Welding @	236.1%	0	361.0%	0
Assembly @	236.1%	0	269.0%	0
Press @	236.1%	169,118	130.0%	93,119
Machine @	236.1%	29,513		
Machine time overhead				
Press	4,217 hours @		33.46	141,101
CNC Machine	1,590 hours @		73.12	116,261
Engineering	13.8%	39,021		
General/admin	22.2%	71,436		
Total product cost		793,218		832,361
Profit before interest and income taxes		36,782		(2,361)
Profit % to sales		4.43%		−0.28%

Exhibit 17.5   Product D Profitability/Costa Manufacturing Company

Product Line D		Old System		abc System
Sales		2,620,000		2,620,000
Direct material		900,000		900,000
Outside services		150,000		150,000
Overhead @			20.5%	30,750
Direct labor				
Welding		93,428		93,428
Assembly		36,289		36,289
Press		204,054		204,054
Machine		0		
Direct labor overhead				
Welding @	236.1%	220,584	361.0%	337,275
Assembly @	236.1%	85,678	269.0%	97,617
Press @	236.1%	481,771	130.0%	265,270
Machine @	236.1%	0		
Machine time overhead				
Press	12,012 hours @		33.46	401,922
CNC Machine	0 hours @		73.12	0
Engineering	13.8%	154,809		
General/admin	22.2%	283,408		
Total product cost		2,610,021		2,516,605
Profit before interest and income taxes		9,979		103,395
Profit % to sales		0.38%		3.95%

Exhibit 17.6   Product Line Profitability under "abc" System/Costa Manufacturing Company

	Product Line A	Product Line B	Product Line C	Product Line D	Total
Sales	2,470,000	2,880,000	830,000	2,620,000	8,800,000
Direct material	750,000	1,000,000	350,000	900,000	3,000,000
Outside services	0	200,000	50,000	150,000	400,000
Overhead	0	41,000	10,250	30,750	82,000
Direct labor					
Welding	197,840	30,030	0	93,428	321,298
Assembly	82,590	144,002	0	36,289	262,881
Press	0	162,450	71,630	204,054	438,134
Machine	0	0	0	0	0
Direct labor overhead					
Welding	714,202	108,408	0	337,275	1,159,885
Assembly	222,167	387,365	0	97,617	707,149
Press	0	211,185	93,119	265,270	569,574
Machine	0	0	0	0	0
Machine time overhead					
Press	0	319,978	141,101	401,922	863,001
CNC Machine	503,212	134,906	116,261	0	754,379
Total product cost	2,470,011	2,739,324	832,361	2,516,605	8,558,301
Profit before interest and income taxes	(11)	140,676	(2,361)	103,395	241,699
Profit % to sales	0.00%	4.88%	−0.28%	3.95%	2.75%
Machine time					
Press	0	9,563	4,217	12,012	25,792
CNC Machine	6,882	1,845	1,590	0	10,317
Total machine time	6,882	11,408	5,807	12,012	36,109

Exhibit 17.7   Comparative Product Line Profitability—"abc" System v.
Traditional Cost System/Costa Manufacturing Company

	Sales	Profit		Profit % to Sales	
		Old System	New System	Old System	New System
Product Line A	2,470,000	156,314	(11)	6.33%	0.00%
Product Line B	2,880,000	39,480	140,676	1.37%	4.88%
Product Line C	830,000	36,782	(2,361)	4.43%	−0.28%
Product Line D	2,620,000	9,979	103,395	0.38%	3.95%
Totals	8,800,000	242,555	241,699	2.76%	2.75%

The results using the abc bases and rates tell an entirely different story from those using traditional methods. Instead of carrying the organization, Product Lines A and C are losing money while the traditional system's apparent losers, Product Lines B and D, are generating 58% and 43% of the profits, respectively. The following sections look at each product line individually to see how this turnabout could have occurred.

Product Line A   After combining line items for the same processes and applying the old system's Engineering and General/Administration costs to each cost center individually, the two systems' results can be compared as follows:

	Old System	New System	Variance
Direct material	$750,000	$750,000	$ 0
Welding	925,000	912,000	13,000
Assembly	386,000	305,000	81,000
Machine	253,000	503,000	(250,000)
Total	$2,314,000	$2,470,000	$(156,000)

Costa's old system accumulated all manufacturing overhead in a single pool and applied it to products on the basis of their direct labor content. Indirect costs were charged only as direct labor operations were performed, and the same percentage of direct labor dollars was charged regardless of where the direct labor took place. The overhead percentage attributed to direct assembly work was the same as that used for work done by a welder, a pressman, or a machine operator. These practices occurred despite the facts that (1) the cost of operating each cost center is vastly different and (2) direct labor is not necessarily the most appropriate base for distributing the cost center's indirect costs.

Product Line A requires a great deal of machining. In fact, the 6,882 hours of machine time needed to manufacture the product line represents 67% of Costa's total machine time. Because Costa's machining takes place on CNC Machine centers, very few direct labor dollars would be charged under the old system. As a result, an inadequate amount of machining overhead was charged to the product line. Compounding this shortfall, the rate used to charge the costs for each direct labor dollar was significantly diluted by the other, lower cost operations. The net result is that the old system applied only $253,000, less than 34% of the cost center's total cost, to a product line that required 67% of the cost center's time and resources.

Under the abc system, the cost of CNC machining not only is calculated as a separate cost center, but is applied to the product line on the more relevant machine hour basis. Using the abc system, a more realistic charge for CNC machining is applied to Product Line A. The $503,000 charge is approximately 67% of the cost center's total cost, representative of the 67% of total machine hours required by Product Line A.

Assembly, on the other hand, is a low-overhead operation. Although both costing systems agree that direct labor is the proper distribution basis, the rates under each system are significantly different. Under abc, an indirect cost application rate of 269% was determined using cause–effect relationships. When burdened with Engineering and General/Administration charges, assembly operations under the old system carried a rate of 365% ($303 overhead/$83 direct labor), resulting in a substantial overcharge.

Although these two distortions were in opposite directions, the understatement of machining costs was much higher than the overstatement of assembly costs, resulting in a seriously undercosted product line.

The bottom-line impact is that Product Line A, thought to be Costa's most profitable when measured by traditional cost accounting methods, is, in reality, losing money.

Product Line B Following the same methods used with Product Line A, the results of the two costing methods for Product Line B can be summarized as follows:

	Old System	New System	Variance
Direct material	$1,000,000	$1,000,000	$ 0
Outside services	200,000	241,000	(41,000)
Welding	140,000	138,000	2,000
Assembly	673,000	531,000	142,000
Press	760,000	694,000	66,000
Machine	68,000	135,000	(67,000)
Total	$2,841,000	$2,739,000	$ 102,000

Product Line B requires almost 55% of Costa's total assembly time. As mentioned when discussing Product Line A, Costa's old system significantly overcharged products for assembly operations (365% vs. 269% of direct labor), which has clearly distorted the cost of Product Line B. The product line was overcharged 27% for assembly work.

A more modest 9.5% overcharge was made for press operations. The use of a single, plantwide rate, combined with the fact that almost half of the press operation's cost is driven by the operation of the presses, not activities of employees, results in this overcharge.

In the other direction, the old system failed to provide for the costs of planning, procuring, scheduling, and handling products sent for outside processing. The combination of this factor and abc's higher cost distribution for machining operations (as discussed under Product Line A) partially offset the old system's overcosting for press and assembly operations.

The net impact of these differences is that Product Line B, shown by the old system as barely breaking even, is Costa's most profitable product line, in terms of both dollars and percentage to sales.

Product Line C   The results of the two costing methods for Product Line C can be summarized as follows:

	Old System	New System	Variance
Direct material	$350,000	$350,000	$ 0
Outside services	50,000	60,000	(10,000)
Press	335,000	306,000	29,000
Machine	58,000	116,000	(58,000)
Total	$793,000	$832,000	$(39,000)

As was the case with Product Line A, the failure of the old system to adequately charge machining costs to products is the major factor in distorting the profitability of Product Line C. Although the abc system resulted in somewhat lower press costs, the serious undercosting of machining operations (also present in Product Lines A and B) and the addition of the outside services overhead cost changed this product line from showing marginal profit to being a loser.

Product Line D   The comparative results for Product Line D are as follows:

	Old System	New System	Variance
Direct material	$ 900,000	$ 900,000	$ 0
Outside services	150,000	181,000	(31,000)
Welding	437,000	430,000	7,000
Assembly	170,000	134,000	36,000
Press	953,000	872,000	81,000
Total	$2,610,000	$2,517,000	$(93,000)

The overcosting of press operations under the old system, which was a minor factor with the other product lines, becomes a major factor with Product Line D which consumes 46% of Costa's press operation time. As mentioned in discussing Product Line B, the use of a single, plantwide rate and the fact that almost half the cost of press operations is driven by machine time, not direct labor, combine to cause this distortion.

The old system's problem of overcosting assembly operations, a problem that also impacted Product Lines A and B, further overstated Product Line D's costs. In this case, the distortion is about the same amount as the undercosting resulting from the old system's failure to take into account overhead relating to outside services.

Thus, Product Line D, which the old system showed as breaking even, is shown by the abc approach to be one of Costa's two profitable product lines.

Summary

It is interesting that the indirect cost rates for Welding were almost identical under both systems. After adding the impact of the Engineering and General/Administration rates, the effective plantwide rate under the old system is approximately 367%. This compares with the 361% rate calculated for Welding under the abc system. As a result, welding operations were not a major factor in any product line cost distortions uncovered in Costa's product line profitability analyses. This occurrence, however, is purely coincidental and should not be considered as indicating that the old system's treatment of Welding was appropriate.

Comparison of these two sets of product line cost buildups shows the impact of a dysfunctional cost system on determining individual product costs. Not only do the distortions of the old system lead to improper product pricing decisions, but they lead management in the wrong directions when the system is used to direct cost control efforts. In Costa's case, concentration would have been diverted from those products in most trouble through management's use of the misleading information generated by its traditional cost accounting system.

Product costing is not the only area in which an abc approach and the development of a cost accumulation model can be of help in cost management efforts. As mentioned earlier, activity-based costing is based on the premise that products cause activities and activities cause costs. Although a product line profitability analysis can help management identify ways of reducing the consumption of activities by products, another method must be developed to assist in looking for ways of reducing the costs of the activities themselves. An approach available under abc is the subject of Chapter 18.

As mentioned repeatedly throughout this book, the goal of activity-based costing is accuracy, not precision. As a result, percentages used to represent indirect cost application rates are not carried to a large number of decimal places. Unfortunately, this sometimes makes it difficult for the reader who wishes to confirm his or her understanding by independently performing calculations made in the text or accompanying figures and exhibits.

The impact of these rounded rates is not always limited to a few dollars. For example, when the direct press labor overhead rate in Costa's cost accumulation model is carried to thousandths of a percent, it is 129.631%. Because such a level of precision does not enhance accuracy in activity-based costing, no decimals are used, and this rate is rounded to 130%. When the .369% rate differential is applied to the $438,134 direct labor base, it generates a difference of $1,617. As a result, the reader will not always be able to tie in amounts exactly.

One reconciliation worth including is that between the total abc costs in the product profitability analysis and the total costs according to the cost accumulation model. The differences in this case involved more than simply rounding, and are set forth below.

Product costs per product line analysis		$8,558,301
Model costs not in product cost		
Tooling material	$150,000	
Tooling projects	256,952	
Capital projects	110,264	
Other direct costs	58,767	575,983
Rate rounding variance		(2,996)
Other rounding		3
Total cost per model		$9,131,291

18

Rate Decomposition and Process Value Analysis

For decades, direct labor was the first area of attention when managers were challenged with reducing the cost of a problem product. By reducing direct labor, management thought that a proportionate amount of indirect cost relating to the product would also disappear. Although this may have been true in the accounting records, it was not true in reality.

Using direct labor as a base for assigning indirect costs gives the illusion that a reduction in direct labor results in a reduction in those indirect costs. If a company's overhead rate is 300% of direct labor dollars and the company reduces direct labor by $1.00, there will be a $3.00 reduction in the amount of overhead *charged to the product* by the accounting system. Unfortunately, it is very unlikely that there will be a $3.00 reduction in the amount of overhead *incurred by the organization*. Reducing direct labor by $1.00 will more likely reduce total indirect costs by an amount closer to only $.50 or $1.00, depending on the employees' fringe benefit package.

During the earlier discussion of cost drivers, I indicated that their purpose was twofold: to determine where the cost should be distributed and to help determine how much the cost will be. When direct labor is selected as the basis for assigning a cost center's costs to products, it is usually because of its appropriateness

239

as a where-to driver. Direct labor is seldom the best how-much driver for a majority of costs in a cost center. As a result, a reduction in direct labor headcount does little other than reduce the amount of direct labor cost and its related fringe benefits.

Thus, the preoccupation with reducing direct labor content as a means of reducing product cost has distracted management from a more fertile area for cost reduction, that is, reducing the cost of the activities needed to produce the organization's products or provide its services. Remember, *products require activities and activities require costs.* By moving backward from the product to the activities needed to produce it and from there to the costs needed to support each activity, management can direct itself to areas where cost reduction efforts will have the most impact on the organization.

The concept of process value analysis (PVA) has been evolved to assist management in moving the emphasis of its cost reduction efforts in this direction. Briefly defined, process value analysis is a management technique for analyzing and improving processes in an organization by (1) identifying those activities that add value to process output and those that merely add cost and no value, (2) eliminating or minimizing cost drivers related to non–value added activities, and (3) optimizing cost drivers related to value added activities.

PVA is a valuable technique for effecting continuous improvements in an organization. However, like ABC, PVA is a detailed, time-intensive process that many small and mid-sized organizations will find beyond their means. Fortunately, there are ways in which these small to mid-sized organizations can use the cost accumulation model developed for activity-based costing purposes to assist them in implementing a PVA approach to identifying cost reduction opportunities.

Cost Reduction Opportunities: Operating Activities

Each operating center's indirect cost application rate is the result of a flow-down process in which the costs of higher level cost centers were accumulated and distributed to lower level cost centers using cause–effect relationships. In the cost accumulation model, the sources of the costs of each operating activity are readily identified. For example, Costa Manufacturing has a CNC Machining cost center with a total cost of $754,337. Schedules DC–1 and DC–2 of Costa's cost accumulation model indicate that the source of these costs is as follows:

Indirect labor	$ 81,136
Fringe benefits	33,296
Specific assignment costs	222,442
General factory overhead	8,545
Engineering support	68,781
Repairs and maintenance	36,566
Tooling support	29,326
Production control support	30,983
Quality assurance support	54,544
Shipping and receiving support	13,103
General/administration support	175,615
Total costs	$754,337

This simple summary goes a long way toward compartmentalizing Costa's three-quarters of a million dollars of CNC Machining costs in a way that lends itself to meaningful analysis.

Of the $745,337 total CNC machining costs, only $336,874 (or 45%) are costs incurred directly in the cost center. These include indirect labor with associated fringe benefits and specific assignment costs. These costs can be summarized by major element as follows:

Indirect labor w/fringes	$114,432	34%
Electricity	36,711	11%
Drills and cutters	51,585	15%
Other variable costs	36,183	11%
Scrap income	(10,000)	(3%)
Total controllable costs	$228,911	68%
Depreciation expense	$ 91,000	27%
Other fixed costs	16,963	5%
Total fixed costs	$107,963	32%
Cost incurred directly by CNC Machining	$336,874	100%

This summary highlights three elements of cost that make up over 60% of the costs incurred directly by the cost center: indirect labor, electricity, and drills and cutters. These three elements can be selected as targets for cost reduction using a PVA approach. A simple way of applying this approach is by posing some basic questions about each element.

Indirect Labor. Why is indirect labor needed in this cost center? Is it for material handling? for parts loading and unloading? for setup? for monitoring readouts? Is there a way to eliminate or reduce the need for any of these activities? Can it be done by relocating equipment? by mechanizing a process? by negotiating a change to the labor agreement? by centralizing the readouts in a control center?

Electricity. What causes electrical consumption to be at this level? Is it equipment processing time? "up-but-idle" time? the size and type of motor? maximum demand? Are there ways to reduce this consumption with the same product throughput? Can the company reduce up-but-idle time? install more efficient motors? improve scheduling? streamline CNC programs for more efficient processing?

Drills and Cutters. What causes wear on drills and cutters? Is it the hardness of the metal? the quality of the tools? the processing time? the handling of the tools? Is maximum life squeezed out of every tool? Is the proper tool used in all circumstances? Are alternative tools necessary? Are they possible or desirable? Can more expensive tools prove to be cost-effective? Can better physical control of drills and cutters increase their life?

Questions such as these can help to identify the true drivers of each cost, drivers that are often more detailed than those used in the cost accumulation model. These are the root-cause drivers that ABC might use in cost accumulation, but that abc uses only in cost reduction. By selectively identifying these drivers after being directed toward them through the cost accumulation model, a company gains the knowledge necessary to control costs without incurring the cost of identifying and maintaining them as part of its day-to-day activity-based system.

Further analysis of CNC Machining indicates that $134,673 (18% of its total cost) are charged to it by service centers on a demand basis as follows:

Engineering	$ 68,781	51%
Maintenance	36,566	27%
Tool Room	29,326	22%
Total service center charges	$134,673	100%

Again, some basic questions can be posed regarding the demand for these services to solicit ideas for methods of reducing or eliminating the cost center's demand.

Engineering. What kind of engineering support is provided? Why must this support be provided? Is it necessary support, or is it merely something that has always been done? Are there changes that can be made in CNC Machining that will reduce the cost center's demand for these services? Are there specific processes that need this support? Can those processes be changed to reduce that need?

Maintenance. What kind of maintenance support is provided? Why must it be provided? Is it preventative in nature or a reaction to breakdowns? Is it concentrated on particular equipment? Would it be best to replace that equipment? Can that equipment be handled differently to reduce its need for maintenance?

Tool Room. What type of tool room support is provided? Why must it be provided? Do particular tools cause the demand? Does the demand come from particular types of tools? Can they be changed to demand less support? Are there quality problems with the tools? What can be done to improve their quality?

As was the case with the costs considered earlier, questions such as these can help identify cost drivers. In this case, however, the drivers are for the demand portion of the cost equation. CNC Machining does not have direct control over the hourly cost of service center time, but it does have considerable control over the demand for those hours. By controlling the demand, the cost center can exercise control over much of the cost.

The same type of analysis can be performed for each operating cost center. The categorization of cost by element and cost center that results from developing the cost accumulation model makes it possible to efficiently select candidates for cost reduction analyses. This ability to "zero in" on these areas at Costa would have been nonexistent had all manufacturing costs remained in the single manufacturing cost center of its old system. Exhibit 18.1 is a

Exhibit 18.1 Cost Reduction Opportunity Analysis—Operating Activities/Costa Manufacturing Company

	Welding	Assembly	Direct Press Labor	Press Operations	CNC Machining	Outside Processing
Variable costs through specific assignment costs						
Indirect labor	35,700	29,209	48,682		81,136	
Overtime premium	17,600	14,400	24,000		4,000	
Shift premium	6,600	5,400	10,000		2,000	
Fringe benefits	146,504	119,867	199,778		33,296	
Specific assignment costs						
Electricity	28,597	23,406		91,806	36,711	
Argon	96,389			77,376		
Drawing compounds						
Drills and cutters					51,585	
Other supplies	32,100			25,800	10,300	
Maintenance materials	4,875	4,875		60,943	18,283	
Other variable costs	1,000	1,600		(23,000)	(8,400)	
Total variable costs through specific assignment costs	369,365	198,757	282,460	232,925	228,911	0
Demand-driven costs						
Maintenance	24,377	24,377		60,943	36,566	
Engineering	103,171	34,390		68,781	68,781	
Tool Room	17,106	17,106		73,313	29,326	
Total demand-driven costs	144,654	75,873	0	203,037	134,673	0
Total "controllable" costs	514,019	274,630	282,460	435,962	363,584	0

	Col 1	Col 2	Col 3	Col 4	Col 5	Col 6
Fixed costs						
Depreciation	60,000	36,000		95,000	91,000	
Other fixed costs	12,590	9,236		18,363	16,963	
Total fixed costs	72,590	45,236	0	113,363	107,963	0
Distributions						
General Factory Overhead	34,181	34,181	51,272	35,451	8,545	25,814
Production Control	60,798	39,814		62,410	30,983	45,445
Quality Assurance	107,033	70,090		14,993	54,544	10,917
Shipping & Receiving	25,712	16,838	234,225		13,103	
General/Administration	344,611	225,669		200,940	175,615	
Total distributions	572,335	386,592	285,497	313,794	282,790	82,176
Total cost center cost	1,158,944	706,458	567,957	863,119	754,337	82,176
Controllable costs						
Indirect labor w/ fringes and premiums	17.8%	23.9%	49.7%	0.0%	16.0%	0.0%
Variable specific assign. costs	14.1%	4.2%	0.0%	27.0%	14.4%	0.0%
Demand-driven costs	12.5%	10.7%	0.0%	23.5%	17.9%	0.0%
Controllable costs	44.4%	38.8%	49.7%	50.5%	48.3%	0.0%
Noncontrollable costs						
Fixed Costs	6.3%	6.4%	0.0%	13.1%	14.3%	0.0%
Distributions	49.3%	54.8%	50.3%	36.4%	37.4%	100.0%
Total costs	100.0%	100.0%	100.0%	100.0%	100.0%	100.0%

summary of operating activity costs that could be used as a guide for locating these potential cost reduction opportunities.

Cost Reduction Opportunities: Service Centers and Support Activities

Fixed costs and the distribution of operating support and administrative support activities are not generally controllable at the operating cost center level. Demand for service center activities is within control of the operating activities, but the hourly cost of those services is not. As a result, steps must also be taken to locate the cost reduction opportunities in these support and service activities.

The steps necessary in this process are the same as with the operating activities: summarize the costs in an appropriate manner, select the most likely candidates for cost reduction, and then ask many questions. Exhibits 18.2 and 18.3 are summaries that can serve as guides for finding cost reduction candidates in Costa's service centers and support activities, respectively.

Questions that should be answered for each material element of cost in each of these operating and administrative support and service center activities include:

- o What material or service is being "bought" with this cost?
- o Why is this material or service necessary? What is its driver?
- o Could other materials or services serve the same need? If so, would they be more cost-effective?
- o Is there a way to reduce the need for this material or service (reduce or eliminate its driver)?

Without the indirect cost matrix that results from the cost accumulation model, cost information is too generalized to be a guide for cost reduction efforts. Even if these cost details are not kept in the day-to-day accounting records, the reasoning and logic that go into the model's development and the cause–effect relationships that result in the categorization of costs by element and cost center provide a valuable navigational aid in directing the organization's efforts toward continuous cost improvement.

Exhibit 18.2   Cost Reduction Opportunity Analysis—Service Centers/Costa Manufacturing Company

	Maintenance	Engineering	Tool Room
Varible costs through specific assignment costs			
Salaries	72,000	280,000	
Indirect labor	85,193	154,896	189,748
Overtime premium	2,200	4,000	4,900
Shift premium	2,700		
Fringe benefits	57,913	152,822	77,868
Specific assignment costs			
Other supplies	6,000	16,000	10,000
Budgeted Expenses	3,000	54,000	4,000
Other variable costs	870	1,618	2,105
Total variable costs through specific assignment costs	229,876	663,336	288,621
Demand-driven costs			
Maintenance		4,876	9,751
Total demand-driven costs	0	4,876	9,751
Total "controllable" costs	229,876	668,212	298,372
Fixed costs			
Depreciation	11,000	13,000	18,000
Other fixed costs	2,897	6,597	4,393
Total fixed costs	13,897	19,597	22,393
Distributions			
General Factory Overhead			21,364
Total distributions	0	0	21,364
Total cost center cost	243,773	687,809	342,129
Controllable costs			
Salary and hourly labor w/fringes and premiums	90.3%	86.0%	79.7%
Variable specific assign. costs	4.0%	10.4%	4.7%
Demand-driven costs	0.0%	0.7%	2.9%
Controllable costs	94.3%	97.1%	87.3%
Noncontrollable costs			
Fixed costs	5.7%	2.9%	6.5%
Distributions			6.2%
Total costs	100.0%	100.0%	100.0%

Exhibit 18.3 Cost Reduction Opportunity Analysis—Administrative and Operations Support Activities/Costa Manufacturing Company

	General/ Administrative	General Factory Overhead	Prod Control	Quality Assurance	Shipping/ Receiving
Variable costs through specific assignment costs					
Salaries	500,000	120,000	72,000	96,000	
Indirect labor			34,852	96,810	30,979
Overtime premium			900	2,500	800
Shift premium				3,900	
Fringe benefits	159,386	38,253	37,254	70,331	12,713
Specific assignment costs					
Other supplies	10,000	4,000	4,000	5,000	2,000
Budgeted expenses	250,000	2,000	10,000	26,000	2,000
Other variable costs	1,068	290	1,265	1,555	1,555
Total variable costs through specific assignment costs	920,454	164,543	160,271	302,096	50,047
Demand-driven costs					
Maintenance	4,876		9,751	9,751	9,751
Engineering	240,733				
Total demand-driven costs	245,609	0	9,751	9,751	9,751
Total "controllable" costs	1,166,063	164,543	170,022	311,847	59,798

Fixed costs					
Depreciation	9,000	7,000	12,000	14,000	14,000
Other fixed costs	5,996	1,497	2,293	2,993	3,493
Total fixed costs	14,996	8,497	14,293	16,993	17,493
Distributions					
General Factory Overhead			8,545	10,682	4,272
Total distributions	0	0	8,545	10,682	4,272
Total cost center cost	1,181,059	173,040	192,860	339,522	81,563
Controllable costs					
Salary and hourly labor w/fringes and premiums	55.8%	91.5%	75.2%	79.4%	54.5%
Variable specific assign. costs	22.1%	3.6%	7.9%	9.6%	6.8%
Demand-driven costs	20.8%	0.0%	5.1%	2.9%	12.0%
Controllable costs	98.7%	95.1%	88.2%	91.9%	73.3%
Noncontrollable costs					
Fixed costs	1.3%	4.9%	7.4%	5.0%	21.4%
Distributions			4.4%	3.1%	5.3%
Total costs	100.0%	100.0%	100.0%	100.0%	100.0%

19

Decision Support Analyses

Thus far, the cost accumulation model has been used to determine product cost and product line profitability and to guide continuous cost improvement activities. If properly designed, the cost accumulation model also can serve as a valuable tool for use in supporting an even wider variety of management decisions.

In the discussion of consumption units in Chapter 8, I suggested that, in developing an abc system, it is useful to divide the category of costs normally termed variable costs into two separate categories: those that vary only when management actions are taken as a result of the volume change, and those that vary automatically with a change in volume or after a management action is taken.

If volume changes, personnel levels and composition will not change unless management takes action to increase or reduce the number of employees. Likewise, unless directed by management, overtime will not be increased or decreased, shifts will not be added or deleted, and equipment will not be added or sold.

On the other hand, if headcount, labor hours, or equipment operating times change, a variety of other cost elements will change automatically. For example, a change in headcount, labor hours, or labor dollars will result in a change in fringe benefit costs. Because these costs are driven by the number and type of employees as well as the organization's payroll dollars, they will change as a result of the change in their driver. A change in direct labor or operating time will result in a change in certain volume-related specific assignment costs, such as utilities and supplies.

When these automatically variable costs are properly built into the cost accumulation model, the model can be used to simulate the results of management decisions. This chapter discusses how this can be done in two instances, specifically, in evaluating the benefits of a proposed capital expenditure and in deciding whether to add employees or to increase overtime in response to an increase in volume.

Capital Expenditure Evaluation

Costa Manufacturing's management has learned of new electronic controls that will enable the company to operate presses with less direct labor personnel. Management estimates that by adding the new controls to two of their ten presses, the company can use two

Exhibit 19.1

	Fixed	Variable	Total
Salaries	$360,000		$ 360,000
Indirect labor		$ 551,172	551,172
Fringe benefits		793,777	793,777
Overtime and shift premium		101,900	101,900
Depreciation	358,000		358,000
Maintenance materials		92,877	92,877
Leases and rentals	500		500
Insurance	24,122		24,122
Property taxes	50,096		50,096
Utilities		190,460	190,460
Supplies		324,550	324,550
Recaptured costs		(254,031)	(254,031)
Other		12,000	12,000
Totals	$792,718	$1,812,705	2,605,423
Direct labor base		$1,103,450	
Variable overhead rate		164%	

fewer direct personnel on each of the two shifts the presses operate. The cost to purchase and install each new control is $125,000, for a total of $250,000. The controls will have an estimated useful life of ten years.

Before the development of the abc system, Costa's analysis might have begun with a traditional division of manufacturing overhead costs into fixed and variable elements. The segregation of the costs into these two categories would then have been used to develop a variable overhead rate, in a manner similar to Exhibit 19.1.

With this rate, Costa would have calculated the savings from the addition of these controls as follows:

Annual wages per press operator	$ 20,000
Reduction in headcount	4
Direct labor savings	$ 80,000
Variable overhead @ 164%	131,200
Less: depreciation on new controls	(25,000)
Net Savings	$ 186,200
Investment	$ 250,000
Return on investment	74%

With the cost accumulation model at its disposal, however, Costa's management can take a different look at the benefits that would result from this expenditure. After making a few minor changes to the model's input, Costa can compare the total cost of operating the organization before and after the proposed expenditure to determine the actual dollars that would be saved. The changes required would be:

o Schedule PR–1: Reduce direct hourly headcount in direct press labor from 24.0 to 20.0 and reduce direct hourly wages from $480,000 to $400,000.

o Schedule PR–3: Reduce second-shift headcount in direct press labor from 10.0 to 8.0.

o Schedule SA–2: Increase press operations depreciation expense from 75,000 to 100,000 and original asset cost from 500,000 to 750,000.

After processing the changes total costs as reflected on Schedules DC–1 and DC–2 before and after the investment can be summarized as shown in Exhibit 19.2.

When looked at through the cost accumulation model, the savings are a little more than half those calculated using Costa's traditional accounting system. The reasons are fairly simple. In the old system's variable overhead rate of 164%, many elements of cost have not changed as press direct labor has been reduced. Looking at these elements individually helps explain where phantom savings would arise.

Indirect labor reductions would be limited to the reduced amount of direct-working-indirect expense that would result from having fewer direct individuals. The old system assumed that for each $1.00 of direct labor saved, $.50 in indirect labor would also be saved. In reality, unless management found that less indirect support is required and then acted on that finding, no other indirect labor savings would occur. This savings is correctly calculated by using the cost accumulation model.

Fringe benefit reductions would be limited to the fringe benefits that pertain to the four employees whose services would no longer be needed. Using the variable manufacturing overhead rate, Costa inadvertently included indirect and salary fringe benefits, resulting in a fringe benefit reduction of $.72 for each $1.00

Exhibit 19.2

	Before	After	Savings
Direct labor	$1,022,314	$ 948,262	$ 74,052
Direct working indirect	113,590	105,362	8,228
Hourly fringes	742,584	710,993	31,591
Overtime premium	75,300	71,300	4,000
Shift premium	30,600	28,600	2,000
Depreciation expense	280,000	305,000	(25,000)
Other costs	6,866,903	6,866,016	887
Total	$9,131,291	$9,035,533	$ 95,758
Investment			$250,000
Return on investment			38%

of direct labor, instead of the $.41 reflected in the hourly fringe benefit rate.

In the press operation, *maintenance materials, utilities,* and most *supplies* are not driven by direct labor. These elements are driven primarily by the presses' operating time, a factor that would not change after the proposed investment is made. As a result, these cost elements were erroneously included in the savings calculation using the old system. Use of the cost accumulation model correctly excluded these cost elements from the calculated cost savings.

It is easy to see how the cause–effect reasoning that went into the design of the abc system and its representation in the cost accumulation model results in a much more accurate estimate of savings to be gained from this proposed capital investment. Using the model, the time required to "crunch the numbers" to arrive at these much more accurate savings estimates is a matter of minutes. Following this general approach (measuring total costs with and without the proposed investment), the cost accumulation model can be used to provide realistic estimates of the savings that will be realized from almost any capital expenditure opportunity that is justified by cost reductions in a consistent and timely manner.

Overtime versus Additional Manpower

One of Costa's competitors announced that it was going out of business. As a result, the competitor's customers needed to re-source their work. One such customer requested that Costa take over the production of a product that required a significant amount of welding for the final year of the contract. This was to be a one-year windfall with no guarantee of a permanent increase in Costa's base business. Because this company was also one of Costa's regular customers, Costa agreed to the request.

Costa estimated that approximately $80,000 of additional straight-time direct labor would be required in Welding to complete the final year of this production program. Under normal circumstances, the company would add four direct employees (at $22,000 each annually) to perform this work. Because this was not a permanent increase in business, however, the company was hesitant to add four employees only to lay them off in a year's time. An informal survey indicated that current Welding personnel were willing to increase their workday to 10 or 11 hours if requested.

Before deciding on a course of action, Costa decided that this would be another decision in which the cost accumulation model would help. Management "leaned" toward the overtime option, but would decide in its favor only if there were not substantial savings involved in adding the four temporary employees.

To determine the additional cost involved in adding four more welders, the company changed the base model's Schedule PR–1, increasing direct hourly headcount in Welding from 16.0 to 20.0 and Welding's direct hourly wages from 352,000 to 440,000. The model calculated that the addition of four welders would increase direct labor cost by $80,325, enough to meet the requirements of the additional work.

The resulting change in total costs is displayed on Costa's revised Schedules DC–1 and DC–2. These revised schedules indicate that the addition of the four welders would increase costs from $9,131,291 to $9,298,292, an increase of $167,001.

Returning to the base model, Costa then determined the percentage of overtime that would be required to add an additional $80,000 to available straight-time direct labor in Welding. On Schedule PR–2, the company increased direct and indirect overtime percentages for Welding until the increase in direct labor dollars on Schedule DC–2 approximated $80,000. By increasing the overtime percentage from 10% to 36.3%, direct labor dollars would total $80,416, approximately the additional straight-time direct labor required by the program.

The resulting change in total costs is displayed on the revised Schedules DC–1 and DC–2. These revised schedules show that by increasing overtime in Welding to 36.3% to provide the estimated $80,000 of straight-time labor required by the program, costs would increase from $9,131,291 to $9,324,120, an increase of $192,829.

A summary of the results from the three model runs is provided in Exhibit 19.3, which compares changes in the major elements of cost. The analysis indicates that adding four more indirect personnel in Welding would cost Costa about $26,000

Exhibit 19.3

	Before	Add Four Welders	Increase Overtime	Add Four Welders	Increase Overtime
Direct labor	1,022,314	1,102,639	1,102,730	80,325	80,416
Indirect labor	787,204	796,129	798,331	8,925	11,127
Hourly fringe benefits	742,584	777,733	760,339	35,149	17,755
Overtime premium	75,300	79,700	121,600	4,400	46,300
Electricity	182,170	188,195	188,155	6,025	5,985
Argon	96,389	120,487	119,830	24,098	23,441
Other supplies	125,200	133,300	133,000	8,100	7,800
Other costs	6,100,130	6,100,109	6,100,135	(21)	5
Total facility cost	9,131,291	9,298,292	9,324,120	167,001	192,829

less than providing the additional direct labor through extra overtime.

This overtime-versus-additional-manpower comparison and the earlier analysis of the model's estimate of Costa's capital expenditure's benefit show the effectiveness of the cost accumulation model in projecting the results of alternative courses of action. These two examples should also add confidence in the model's capability of simulating the impact on the organization's costs of a myriad of other potential management decisions and in its value as a management decision-support tool.

20

Long-Term Costing and Pricing: Determining Activity and Resource Requirements

One problem facing many organizations today is the long-term pricing commitments increasingly required by their customers. This is especially true of the small and mid-sized organization that serves as a supplier to one or more major corporations. These major corporations often require multi-year fixed prices or even guaranteed annual price reductions from their suppliers as a means of controlling their own costs.

Although these customer demands create opportunities for small and mid-sized organizations, the long-term commitments involved can also make these opportunities dangerous. Decisions based on bad information today could lead to tremendous problems, if not total disaster, tomorrow. This is especially true when the organization is considering a single, long-term project that cannot be modified to any significant extent during its period of performance.

Activity-based costing and the cost accumulation model can be valuable tools for evaluating the risk of making long-term pricing commitments. When coupled with a forward-costing model,

259

they can be used to anticipate future resource requirements and to quantify the costs of providing those resources during the periods that they are required. Costa Manufacturing is again used as an example of how this can be accomplished.

One of Costa Manufacturing's largest customers has asked it to quote on a five-year program that the customer expects will result in $7–11 million in sales over the five years for the supplier to whom the contract is awarded. If Costa is awarded this business, it would be in addition to its core business, which is expected to remain at current levels throughout the forseeable future. The customer provided Costa with the product specifications and a forecast of shipments by quarter. It also indicated that the bid must provide for a 2% annual decrease in the product's unit price during each of the five years of the program.

In considering the bid request, Costa's management noted that, if awarded, this program would put Costa at an operating level 20% above its current and planned levels. Their initial reaction was that, if they priced the product using their current abc rates, they would be able to reduce the price by 2% per year because of the economies of scale that would develop at the higher operating levels.

After engineering personnel determined the necessary processes and their times, as well as required direct material, purchased parts, and outside processing, an initial unit price for this product was developed as follows:

Direct material		$ 7.3000
Purchased parts		.3875
Outside services		1.8500
Outside service overhead @ 20.5%		.3793
Direct labor		
Welding	.100 hr @ $10.58	1.0580
Assembly	.080 hr @ $ 8.65	.6920
Direct press labor	.020 hr @ $ 9.62	.1924
Direct labor overhead		
Welding	@ 361%	3.8194
Assembly	@ 269%	1.8615
Direct press labor	@ 130%	.2501

Machine time overhead		
Press operations	.010 hr @ $33.46	.3346
CNC Machining	.100 hr @ $73.12	7.3120
Total unit cost		$25.4368
Required margin	@ 12.5%	3.6338
Initial unit price		$29.0706

Costa assumed that any required tooling costs would be covered by the overhead overabsorption that would result from this program.

Based on this calculation, the unit price schedule for the five years of the program would be:

1992	$ 29.0706
1993	28.4892
1994	27.9194
1995	27.3610
1996	26.8138

Before acting on this information, however, Costa's management realized that factors other than economies of scale would be involved. Changing economic situations would impact the various elements of cost. Shipments would not be made evenly throughout the period. Volume would slowly pick up, level off for a few years, and then slowly decline as the program winds down. As a result, management decided to seek a way to use the cost accumulation model to estimate the economies of scale generated by the increased volume, provide for anticipated economic changes by cost element, and take into account the varying level of shipments for each year during the program's life cycle.

Costa needed to project the cost structure of its manufacturing facility during each year the contract would run. Because management expected no significant change in its core business during the next five years, Costa believed that, after the impact of economics was factored into the major cost elements, the current cost accumulation model could be used to represent the cost structure for each of the next five years without the new program. The only thing that needed to be added to establish a costing structure for each of the five years was the additional volume.

This last requirement was not as easy to determine as Costa first thought. Now that Costa had multiple cost centers with a variety of rates and bases for applying indirect costs to individual products, management could not simply raise overall volume by a percentage to determine future rate structures. The new program would generate different incremental volumes for each cost center, resulting in a different impact on each cost center's rate. In addition, new capital equipment, more direct employees, and additional support staff might be required. These additions could cause further, significant changes in specific cost center rates.

To perform the necessary analysis, Costa could again take advantage of personal computer spreadsheet software. Keeping in mind the technique of developing a series of interactive worksheets on a single spreadsheet file that worked so well for the cost accumulation model, Costa could develop a computerized set of easily followed green sheets to assist in this endeavor. This set of computerized green sheets is called the forward-costing model.

Outline for Long-Term Cost Estimating

The first step in estimating Costa's future rate structure was to determine the additional activities and resources required by the new program. These required activities and resources were calculated in the first portion of the forward-costing model. In this series of worksheets, unit activity and resource requirements (hours of production activity time, raw materials, purchased parts, or outside services) were extended by the units to be produced each year to determine the total additional activities and resources that would be demanded by the new program. Once these requirements were determined, two steps were necessary before the forward-costing model could be continued.

The second step in the long-term cost estimating process was to determine how the additional activities established in the first step would be provided. This required a separate spreadsheet analysis (the resource requirement analysis) that took the resources that provide the activities in each base-year model and allowed Costa to adjust those resources to provide the activities demanded by the new program. For example, additional welding hours (the activity) could be provided by more personnel, extra overtime, or a combination of both (the resources). The resource requirement analysis allowed Costa to measure the impact of various combinations of resources for all of the production activity centers to determine what resources would need to be added to each year's base model to make production of the new program possible.

The third step involved updating each year's base cost accumulation model to forecast the indirect cost rate structure that would exist during each year. Once the new rate structures for the years of the program were determined, it was possible to return to the forward-costing model and complete the process.

In the fourth step, each year's forecasted cost structure and rates were entered into the forward-costing model and then used, along with the data previously entered into the model during the first step, to project the program's cost during the five years of its life cycle.

The fifth and final step was to use the forward-costing data to determine the prices to be quoted under the alternative pricing strategies being considered by Costa's management.

The first step in this long-term costing process is discussed in the remainder of this chapter. Each of the remaining four steps is discussed, respectively, in one of the next four chapters.

Determining Activity and Resource Requirements

As noted in the outline, Costa's first step was to determine the additional resources (costs) that would be needed in each year of the program. This was necessary before Costa could begin forecasting rates for those years. To determine the resources, Costa needed to determine the increase in activity that would be demanded by the addition of the new program. Activity-based costing's basic premise holds true here: The new program would require activities, and the activities would require costs.

Information was available to work backward from the product, to the driver, to the needed resource or cost. The customer had given Costa product specifications and unit requirements by quarter. In preparing the preliminary cost buildup, Costa's personnel determined the needed processes and their times, as well as the direct material, purchased parts, and outside processing requirements. All that may have been overlooked were the needed Tool Room resources. With this information, Costa could begin mapping out its green sheet analysis.

Mapping Out the Forward-Costing Model

In mapping out a green sheet analysis to determine the activity requirements, Costa developed the following series of worksheets:

- *Schedule 1: Unit Production Requirements*—This schedule provided a summary of the unit production information by quarter that was provided by the customer.

- *Schedule 2: Direct Labor and Machine Time Requirements*— The time required by each unit of product in each operating cost center was entered. This time was provided in terms of direct labor hours or machine hours as appropriate for the particular cost center.

- *Schedule 3: Direct Material Requirements*—This schedule included the current cost of each type of raw material required for one unit of product. Inflation factors were added for each year to forecast the cost of direct material during each year the program would be in production.

- *Schedule 4: Purchased Part Requirements*—This schedule included the current cost of each purchased part required for a single unit of product. Inflation factors were added for each year to forecast the cost of purchased parts during each year the program would be in production.

- *Schedule 5: Outside Service Requirements*—This schedule included the current cost of each type of outside service required for one unit of product. Inflation factors were added for each year to forecast the cost of outside services during each year the program would be in production.

Exhibit 20.1   Forward costing model—Schedule 7: Additional Activity Requirements/Costa Manufacturing Company

| | Years Ending thru | | | | | |
	Dec-92	Dec-93	Dec-94	Dec-95	Dec-96	Total Program
DIRECT LABOR HOURS REQUIRED:						
Welding	4,250	7,250	7,250	6,500	3,750	29,000
Assembly	3,400	5,800	5,800	5,200	3,000	23,200
Direct Press Labor	850	1,450	1,450	1,300	750	5,800
TOTAL DIRECT LABOR HOURS	8,500	14,500	14,500	13,000	7,500	58,000
MACHINE HOURS REQUIRED:						
Press Operations	425	725	725	650	375	2,900
CNC Machining	4,250	7,250	7,250	6,500	3,750	29,000
TOTAL MACHINE HOURS	4,675	7,975	7,975	7,150	4,125	31,900
TOOL ROOM HOURS REQUIRED	3,750	0	0	0	0	3,750
DIRECT MATERIALS/PURCHASED PARTS ($)	327,000	585,000	626,000	598,000	367,000	2,503,000
DIRECT OUTSIDE SERVICES ($)	79,000	141,000	151,000	144,000	88,000	603,000
PURCHASES OF TOOLING AND TOOL MATERIAL ($)	50,000	0	0	0	0	50,000

o *Schedule 6: Tool Room Requirements* — The additional Tool Room hours necessary to develop and produce the tooling for this program and required tooling material and purchased tooling were entered for each year of the program.

o *Schedule 7: Additional Activity Requirements* — The production requirements as set forth in Schedule 1 were extended by the appropriate unit processing time or unit cost from Schedules 2 through 5 to calculate the additional direct labor or machine time in each operating activity and the additional direct material, purchased parts, and outside service costs needed during each year of the program. The additional Tool Room hour requirements for each year were brought forward from Schedule 6. Exhibit 20.1 shows the layout and data accumulated in Schedule 7.

After this portion of the analysis was complete, the activity data necessary to determine the additional resources required during the course of the program were available. Because Costa's system used outside service cost as a basis for applying certain indirect costs to products, it was included as an activity. The reason for including direct material and purchased parts is less obvious. They were included to serve as a gauge for determining the possible need for additional indirect personnel in production support activities.

Exhibit 20.2   Forward costing model—Layout and flow through Schedule 7

A61 — Schedule 1	Unit Production Requirements
A121 — Schedule 2	Direct Labor and Machine Time Requirements
A181 — Schedule 3	Direct Material Requirements
A241 — Schedule 4	Purchased Part Requirements
A301 — Schedule 5	Outside Service Requirements
A361 — Schedule 6	Tool Room Requirements
A421 — Schedule 7	Additional Activity Requirements

The general layout and flow of data between these schedules is shown in Exhibit 20.2. Because the flow of information is more straightforward in the forward-costing model than in the cost accumulation model, the method of documentation is less elaborate or detailed. The narrative provided above for each schedule together with Exhibit 20.2's flow diagram should provide the needed information for both understanding and creating this first portion of the forward-costing model.

21

Long-Term Costing and Pricing: Providing the Required Activities

Additional Activity Requirements, Schedule 7 of the forward-costing model, sets out the additional direct labor, machine, and tool room hours that would be required during each year if the five-year program was awarded to Costa. The schedule also shows the cost of direct materials/purchased parts, direct outside services, and tooling/tool material purchases that would be required during each of the five years of the program in then-year (adjusted-for-inflation) dollars. This information represents either additional activities or indicators of additional activities that would be required as a result of the program. The next step was to determine how Costa would provide these additional activities.

Ideally, an organization would have a cost accumulation model established to support each year of its long-range plan. These models would include all of the recurring core business, as well as projected new products and programs. They would not, however, include unexpected opportunities such as the one presenting itself to Costa. The absence of such a large, unanticipated program dictates the need to adjust each year's cost structures and rates to include this additional business.

Because Costa had only recently begun its use of abc, it had not yet developed cost accumulation models to support each year of its long-range plan. Fortunately (at least for this purpose), Costa expected no significant increase or decrease in its business during the next few years. As a result, it was confident that the assumptions regarding manpower and equipment resources in its current cost accumulation model would hold true in future years if no unexpected, large programs were awarded. This meant that it could replicate the current model for use as a base for each of the five years that the program would run.

Once Costa determined how these additional activities would be provided during each year of the program, the company added the necessary resources to each year's base cost accumulation model to determine that year's cost and rate structure. The result was annual rates established under the assumption that Costa had been awarded the program. These rates were then used in the forward-costing model to develop the product costs during the program's period of performance.

A personal computer worksheet was again a valuable tool in determining the actions that would need to be taken if the contract was awarded. I call this worksheet the resource requirement analysis. The first activities to be addressed on the worksheet were the additional direct labor and tool room labor requirements.

Additional Direct Manpower Resources

Costa could increase direct labor to meet the annual requirements of the new program by (1) adding more direct labor personnel, (2) having employees work more overtime, or (3) doing both. A decision was needed for each of the four direct labor cost centers (including Tool Room) for each of the five years of the program. Thus, 20 separate manpower decisions were needed. The first section of the resource requirement analysis was designed to simplify this decision-making process.

The number of additional annual direct labor hours that would be provided by adding one direct labor employee depended on other information included in the applicable year's cost accumulation model. For example, Costa's straight-time work year is 2,080 hours. However, adding a direct labor employee would not increase available direct labor hours by 2,080. Costa must also consider overtime, time paid for not working, and direct-working-indirect time. The first section of the analysis took these factors into account so that the impact of changes in headcount and over-time percentages could be readily determined.

Costa brought forward the necessary information from each year's cost accumulation model. Information brought forward for each direct labor cost center and its source schedules are as follows:

Average annual straight-time hours	Given at 2,080
Current overtime percentage	Schedule PR–2
Current gross overtime hours	Schedule PR–2
Direct working indirect percentage	Schedule PR–4
Chargeable direct percentage	Schedule FB–1

Using the cost accumulation model's 1992 data for Welding as an example, the calculations were as follows:

(1) Chargeable direct percentage	92.2%
(2) Direct working indirect percentage	10.0%
(3) Gross/net reduction percentage: $(1) \times [100\% - (2)]$	83.0%
(4) Average annual straight-time hours	2,080
(5) Straight-time hours per head: $(3) \times (4)$	1,726
(6) Addition to headcount	2
(7) Additional straight-time hours: $(5) \times (6)$	3,452
(8) Current overtime percentage	10.0%
(9) Additional overtime hours: $(7) \times (8)$	345
(10) Additional direct hours: $(7) + (9)$	3,797

The results at this point reflected the additional hours generated by adding two direct employees in Welding who would work the same level of overtime as the employees already included in the model.

As calculated on Schedule 7 of the forward-costing model, 4,250 additional hours would be needed in Welding during the first year of the program. The addition of the two welders would still leave Costa 453 hours short during the first year. By adding a third welder to the calculation shown above, 1,898 hours were added, over 1,400 hours more than needed. The best answer most likely would be a slightly higher level of overtime for all welders, including the two newly added welders. The impact of an overtime change was added to the earlier analysis:

(11) Additional overtime percentage points	1.0%
(12) Percentage overtime change: (11)/(8)	10.0%
(13) Current gross overtime hours	3,328
(14) Net overtime hours per model: (13) × (3)	2,762
(15) Total overtime hours after headcount additions: (9) + (14)	3,107
(16) Additional overtime hours: (12) × (15)	311
(17) Total additional hours: (10) + (16)	4,108

As can be seen, increasing Welding's overtime to 11% would still leave it 142 hours short of the additional 4,250 needed. Increasing the overtime by 2 percentage points, however, would result in a total of 4,418 hours, more than enough for the additional volume.

By mechanizing the required calculations in the resource requirement analysis worksheet, Costa created a tool for efficiently testing headcount/overtime adjustment combinations for each direct labor cost center in each year until the desired combinations were determined.

Once the data from each year's base cost accumulation model were entered, the only decision variables were the additional headcount and overtime percentage change. The decisions resulting from this analysis are shown in Exhibit 21.1. All the figures shown represent percentage point changes from the base year, not from the previous year.

Additional Machine Time Resources

As with direct labor hours, Costa could increase machine hours to meet the annual requirements of the new program in one of three

Exhibit 21.1

	1992	1993	1994	1995	1996
Welding					
Headcount change	+2.0	+3.5	+3.5	+3.5	+2.0
Overtime change	+2.0%	+2.0%	+2.0%	0.0%	0.0%
Assembly					
Headcount change	+2.0	+3.0	+3.0	+3.0	0.0
Overtime change	−1.0%	+1.0%	+1.0%	−1.0%	+1.0%
Direct Press Labor					
Headcount change	0.0	0.0	0.0	0.0	0.0
Overtime change	+2.0%	+4.0%	+4.0%	+3.0%	+2.0%
Tool Room					
Headcount change	+2.0	0.0	0.0	0.0	0.0
Overtime change	−1.0%	0.0%	0.0%	0.0%	0.0%

ways: (1) by adding more machines, (2) by running each machine more hours, or (3) by doing both. Decisions were needed for both machine time–driven cost centers for all five years of the program. This meant ten separate decisions.

One factor that must be considered in decisions regarding machine time resources is the relative permanence of equipment additions. When making direct manpower decisions, increases or decreases in headcount can be made over a relatively short period of time. An organization can increase its labor force for a number of months or years and then return to its former manpower levels by attrition or layoffs. Once equipment is added, however, it usually stays for a long time, even if the reason for its acquisition disappears. As a result, the decision between additional equipment and more uptime will have more long-term ramifications than the decision between direct manpower's additional headcount and more overtime.

The second section of the resource requirement analysis worksheet was prepared to support decisions for providing the additional machine time required by the new program. The information needed for the analysis was found on Schedule AL–6 of the cost accumulation model. Using, for example, the data for Costa's

CNC Machining cost center and the program's second-year requirements for additional machine time, the calculations began as follows:

(1)	Pieces of equipment	4
(2)	Annual hours/piece/shift	1,984
(3)	Shifts in operation	2.0
(4)	Annual hours available: $(1) \times (2) \times (3)$	15,872
(5)	Percentage of nonproduction hours	35%
(6)	Original chargeable hours available: $(4) \times [100\% - (5)]$	10,317

The results at this point represented the situation as it existed in the base model. Using this information, Costa could test additional equipment–adjusted uptime combinations to determine the one most suited for providing the needed additional machine hours.

(7)	Additional piece(s) of equipment	2
(8)	Additional hours provided by new equipment: $(2) \times (3) \times [1 - (5)] \times (7)$	5,158

This additional 5,158 hours of machine time would not be enough to meet the 7,250 hours required by the new program in its second year. The addition of a third new piece of equipment would bring the total additional hours to 7,737, 487 hours more than needed.

   As mentioned earlier, there is a permanence to the addition of a new piece of equipment. Once the need is gone, the equipment is still there. Costa considered this program to be a one-time opportunity, not a permanent increase in its level of operations. Thus, Costa wanted to add the minimum of new equipment.

   One way to get the most out of the CNC equipment would be to increase the cost center's overall uptime. Schedule AL–6 of the cost accumulation model indicates that there is 20% normal excess capacity in the cost center. As a result, it should be possible for

Costa to increase its available CNC machining hours by using some of this excess capacity.

(9) Additional uptime percentage points   9%

(10) Total machine hours available:
   $[(1) + (7)] \times (2) \times (3)$ 23,808

(11) Additional hours from increased uptime:
   $(9) \times (10)$ 2,143

(12) Total additional hours: $(8) + (11)$ 7,301

The addition of two more pieces of CNC equipment and a 9 percentage point increase in overall utilization of CNC equipment would enable Costa to meet the CNC machining requirements of the new program. By mechanizing the required calculations in the resource requirement analysis worksheet, Costa could create a tool for efficiently testing equipment–uptime adjustment combinations for each machine time cost center in each year until the desired combinations were determined.

Once the data from each year's base cost accumulation model were entered, the only decision variables were the additional pieces of equipment and changes in uptime. The decisions resulting from this analysis are shown in Exhibit 21.2. These changes are from the base year, not the previous year.

Before leaving the subject of machine time, two other items must be considered. If Costa were to add two more CNC machining

Exhibit 21.2

	1992	1993	1994	1995	1996
Press Operations					
Additional equipment	0	0	0	0	0
Change in uptime	+1.0%	+2.0%	+2.0%	+2.0%	+1.0%
CNC Machine					
Additional equipment	2	2	2	2	2
Change in uptime	−4.0%	+9.0%	+9.0%	0.0%	−6.0%

centers, it would need to invest some money in capital equipment. Once the required capital investment was determined, Costa must then decide how its cost would be recaptured as part of product cost.

Each CNC machine center would cost $100,000, so the capital equipment cost of $200,000 was easily determined. The depreciation of this equipment, however, has a different impact on costing and pricing decisions than on simple compliance with GAAP and tax regulations.

Proper treatment for financial and tax reporting is dictated by rules and regulations. This equipment would undoubtedly be capitalized in the CNC Machining cost center and depreciated using the most advantageous method for the optimum depreciable life. Costa's management, on the other hand, viewed the acquisition of these two new CNC machine centers somewhat differently. As mentioned several times, management viewed this program as a one-time opportunity, not a permanent increase in business volume. As a result, management believed that this additional equipment would be surplus after the program was completed. Therefore, they wanted to recover the entire cost of the new equipment in the pricing of this one program.

There are two methods for satisfying this requirement. The new equipment could be amortized over the parts produced on a piece-rate basis, or it could be depreciated into the cost center's rate structure over a five-year period. Neither method would be theoretically correct. The amortization method would charge to the new program the entire cost of the two new machines, as well as a pro-rata charge of all the other equipment whose costs are included in the cost center. This would result in a disproportionate charge of depreciation to the new program. On the other hand, depreciating the equipment over five years would spread the increased depreciation cost to all products manufactured in CNC Machining during the period, not only to the new program.

Management decided that the second method would be preferable, especially in that both current and new products could be produced on either the old or the new equipment and the increased volume would result in reduced rates for all products manufactured during the five years of the program. As a result, the CNC Machining cost center's annual depreciation would be increased by $40,000 ($200,000/5 years) for each year of the program.

Other Additional Costs and Indirect Resources

Schedule 7 of the forward-costing model also indicates the additional direct material/purchased parts, direct outside services, and purchased tooling/tool material required by the new program. The increased activity indicated by these additional direct labor hours, machine hours, and other direct costs would require some increase in indirect labor support. As discussed earlier, the cost accumulation model does not automatically change these indirect headcounts because they are not automatically variable. Action would be needed by management to increase or decrease the number of indirect personnel. As a result, Costa's management needed to review the activity increases that would result from the program and decide what indirect labor changes would be necessary to support these increases. The headcount changes decided upon by Costa's management are summarized in Exhibit 21.3. Again, these are changes from the base year, not the previous year.

  One final analysis was necessary before Costa could proceed to update each year's cost accumulation model. As mentioned, Costa did not have a cost accumulation model for each of the next five years. Instead, the belief that the company's core of business would remain relatively stable during the next five years made the current cost accumulation model representative of each year's base. Although this may be correct for measuring the level of

Exhibit 21.3

	1992	1993	1994	1995	1996
Engineering	+1.0	+1.0	+1.0	+1.0	0.0
Production control	+1.0	+1.0	+1.0	+1.0	+0.5
Quality assurance	+1.0	+1.0	+1.0	+1.0	0.0
Shipping and receiving	0.0	+1.0	+1.0	+1.0	+0.5
CNC Machine	+1.0	+1.0	+1.0	+1.0	+1.0

resources and activities, changes in economic conditions on certain costs must also be factored in before the models would be truly representative of future operations.

Five cost elements warranted consideration for changing cost levels—salaries, hourly wages, health insurance, utilities, and supplies. Each of these elements of cost is material and would likely undergo significant unit cost increases during the next five years. After remaining at current levels for the first year, the annual increases anticipated by management for each cost element were as follows:

Salaries	5%
Hourly wages	4%
Health insurance	10%
Utilities	3%
Supplies	2%

To incorporate these inflationary increases into each year's base cost accumulation model, Costa needed to develop a series of factors for each cost element that would adjust each year's unit cost to reflect the compounded rates of increase. The resulting factors are shown in Exhibit 21.4.

With the information included in the resource requirement analysis, Costa was ready to move forward and update the information in each year's base cost accumulation model to simulate the cost structure and forecast the indirect cost application rates under the assumption that the new, five-year program had been awarded.

Exhibit 21.4

	1992	1993	1994	1995	1996
Salaries	1.000	1.050	1.103	1.158	1.216
Hourly wages	1.000	1.040	1.082	1.125	1.170
Health insurance	1.000	1.100	1.121	1.331	1.464
Utilities	1.000	1.030	1.061	1.093	1.126
Supplies	1.000	1.020	1.040	1.061	1.082

22

Long-Term Costing and Pricing: Updating the Base-Year Models

Thus far, Costa had determined the additional activities that would be required if it were awarded this five-year program and the management actions that would be taken in each year to provide those additional activities. What needed to be determined next was the impact those management actions would have on the cost structure and rates for those years during which this program would be performed.

As noted earlier, the existing cost accumulation model would be used by Costa as the base for each of the program's five years. As a result, Costa first made five copies of the model, one for each year 1992 through 1996. Once these copies were made, Costa could begin changing model input to incorporate the decisions documented in the resource requirement analysis developed in Chapter 21.

A summary of the additional resource requirements resulting from this program is included in Exhibit 22.1. Using 1994 as an example, Costa made the following changes to incorporate the projected management actions.

- o Schedule PR–1: Increased the direct hourly headcount in Welding by 3.5 and in Assembly by 3.0. Also increased

Exhibit 22.1

	1992	1993	1994	1995	1996
Additional direct headcount					
Welding	2.0	3.5	3.5	3.5	2.0
Assembly	2.0	3.0	3.0	3.0	0.0
Direct Press Labor	0.0	0.0	0.0	0.0	0.0
Tool Room	2.0	0.0	0.0	0.0	0.0
Change in overtime percentage					
Welding	2%	2%	2%	0%	0%
Assembly	−1%	1%	1%	−4%	1%
Direct Press Labor	2%	4%	4%	3%	2%
Tool Room	−1%	0%	0%	0%	0%
Additional pieces of equipment					
Press Operations	0	0	0	0	0
CNC Machine	2	2	2	2	2
Change in uptime					
Press Operations	1%	2%	2%	2%	1%
CNC Machine	−4%	9%	9%	0%	−6%
Additional depreciation expense					
Press Operations	0	0	0	0	0
CNC Machine	40,000	40,000	40,000	40,000	40,000
Additional material/ purchased parts	327,000	585,000	626,000	598,000	367,000
Additional outside services	79,000	141,000	151,000	144,000	88,000
Additional tooling/ tooling material	50,000	0	0	0	0
Other additional personnel					
Engineering	1.0	1.0	1.0	1.0	0.0
Production Control	1.0	1.0	1.0	1.0	0.5
Quality Assurance	1.0	1.0	1.0	1.0	0.0
Shippng and Receiving	0.0	1.0	1.0	1.0	0.5
CNC Machine	1.0	1.0	1.0	1.0	1.0
Variable cost inflation factors					
Salaries	1.000	1.050	1.103	1.158	1.216
Hourly wages	1.000	1.040	1.082	1.125	1.170
Health insurance	1.000	1.100	1.210	1.331	1.464
Utilities	1.000	1.030	1.061	1.093	1.126
Supplies	1.000	1.020	1.040	1.061	1.082

direct hourly payroll in Welding by $77,000 and in Assembly by $54,000 (increased headcount multiplied by average annual wage for the respective cost center). Increased the salary headcount in Engineering by 1.0 and increased Engineering's salary payroll by $35,000 (1.0 × average annual Engineering salary). Increased the indirect hourly headcounts in Production Control, Quality Assurance, Shipping and Receiving, and CNC Machining by 1.0 each. Also increased indirect hourly payroll in Production Control by $18,000, Quality Assurance by $33,333, Shipping and Receiving by $16,000, and CNC Machining by $20,000 (each amount representing the cost of one indirect employee in the respective cost center according to the base model).

- Schedule PR–2: Changed the overtime percentage in Welding from 10% to 12%, in Assembly from 10% to 11%, and in Direct Press Labor from 10% to 14%.
- Schedule SA–2: Increased depreciation expense in CNC Machining from $75,000 to $115,000 and that cost center's original equipment cost from $500,000 to $700,000.
- Schedule AL–2: Updated the distribution of hours for each service center to account for the activities of the additional individual in Engineering and changes caused by the additional CNC equipment and other activity increases.
- Schedule AL–5: Increased direct material purchases from $3,000,000 to $3,626,000 and direct outside services from $400,000 to $551,000.
- Schedule AL–6: Increased the pieces of equipment in CNC Machining from four to six. Also reduced the excess capacity percentage in Press Operations from 20% to 18% and in CNC Machining from 20% to 11%.

Once these changes were entered, Costa could adjust the model for the impact of economic changes on the key cost elements. This was done by using the variable cost inflation factors calculated on the resource requirement analysis. Costa made the following price-level changes for 1994:

- o Schedule PR–1: Multiplied the total of each cost center's salary payroll cost by 1.103 and the total of each cost center's direct and indirect hourly payroll cost by 1.082.
- o Schedule FB–2: Multiplied the $3,073 hourly and $3,154 salary health insurance costs per employee by 1.210.
- o Schedule SA–5: Multiplied the $30,000 fixed electric cost, the $150-per-unit variable electric cost, and the $10,000 other utilities cost by 1.061.
- o Schedule SA–6: Multiplied the $6.00-per-unit argon cost, the $3.00-per-unit drawing compound cost, the $5.556-per-unit drills and cutters cost, and the $1.00-per-unit other supplies cost by 1.040.

After completing these changes, the cost accumulation model was recalculated to determine the cost structure and rates for 1994 under the assumption that Costa would receive the contract.

Exhibit 22.2

	1992	1993	1994	1995	1996
Direct Labor Rates					
Welding	10.58	11.00	11.44	11.90	12.38
Assembly	8.65	9.00	9.36	9.74	10.13
Direct Press Labor	9.62	10.00	10.40	10.82	11.25
Direct Labor Overhead					
Welding	341%	331%	334%	336%	345%
Assembly	253%	242%	244%	245%	258%
Direct Press Labor	125%	124%	125%	124%	126%
Machine Time Rates					
Press Operations	32.31	33.04	34.06	35.12	35.81
CNC Machine	64.31	56.70	58.41	65.60	71.70
Outside Manufacturing					
Overhead %	21.0%	20.1%	20.2%	20.7%	20.0%
Service Center Rates					
Engineering	27.62	28.39	29.67	31.09	32.07
Tool Room	18.99	20.89	21.76	22.69	23.49
Maintenance	24.42	25.09	26.22	27.45	28.39

By following this procedure for each of the five years of the program, Costa developed a forecast of the product costing rates that would be in effect during each year of the program's life cycle. The results of incorporating the resource requirement analysis and economic changes into Costa's models are summarized in Exhibit 22.2. These rates were taken from Schedules PR–2, AL–2, and DC–3 of the cost accumulation models.

Once these rates were established, Costa was ready to return to the forward-costing model to project the cost of this multi-year program.

23

Long-Term Costing and Pricing: Projecting Multi-Year Program Costs

During the first three stages of Costa's long-term costing and pricing analysis, the company (1) identified and quantified the additional activities that would be necessary should they receive the contract, (2) determined in detail how they would provide those activities, and (3) calculated the impact on each year's costing rates of the higher volume, additional resources, and inflationary cost increases. Their next step was to apply those projected costing rates to the additional activity that this contract would generate during its life cycle.

This was accomplished by continuing to develop the forward-costing model begun in Chapter 20. Thus far, this model had been developed through Schedule 7, Additional Activity Requirements. For this stage, Costa picked up the model at Schedule 8 and proceeded as follows:

- ○ *Schedule 8: Indirect Cost Application Rate Forecast*—On this schedule, the direct labor rate, direct labor overhead rate, machine time overhead rate, outside manufacturing overhead rate, and service center rate for each cost center and each year in the forward-costing model (as calculated by the five cost accumulation models) were entered. With the entry of this information, Costa had sufficient information to project the cost of this program, by quarter, for its duration. No further data needed to be entered. The balance of the costing portion of the model uses information provided in Schedules 1 through 8.

o *Schedule 9: Tooling Investments* — Tool Room hours required for each quarter were brought forward from Schedule 6. These were then extended by the appropriate year's Tool Room rate from Schedule 8. Tooling material/purchased tooling requirements were also brought forward from Schedule 6.

o *Schedule 10: Direct Labor and Manufacturing Overhead Cost* — On this series of schedules (one for each year), unit direct labor and machine time requirements were brought forward from Schedule 2 and extended by each quarter's unit production from Schedule 1. The resulting quarterly time requirements were then extended by the appropriate year's direct labor and/or overhead rate from Schedule 8 to determine the direct labor and manufacturing overhead cost amounts for each quarter.

o *Schedule 11: Direct Material Costs* — The appropriate year's direct material cost per unit was brought forward from Schedule 3 and extended by each quarter's unit production requirements from Schedule 1 to determine direct material cost by quarter.

o *Schedule 12: Purchased Parts Costs* — The appropriate year's purchased parts cost per unit was brought forward from Schedule 4 and extended by quarterly unit production requirements from Schedule 1 to determine purchased parts cost by quarter.

o *Schedule 13: Outside Service Costs* — The appropriate year's direct outside service cost per unit was brought forward from Schedule 5 and extended by each quarter's unit production requirements from Schedule 1 to determine the direct outside service cost by quarter.

○ *Schedule 14: Outside Service Overhead Cost*—Outside service costs from Schedule 13 were brought forward and extended by the appropriate year's outside services overhead rate from Schedule 8 to calculate outside service overhead cost by quarter.

○ *Schedule 15: Forward Costing Summary*—On this series of schedules (one for each year), the quarterly data for each element of cost were brought forward from Schedules 10 through 14 to form annual summaries, by quarter, of product cost. Direct material cost was brought forward from Schedule 11, purchased parts cost from Schedule 12, outside services cost from Schedule 13, direct labor and overhead costs from Schedule 10, and outside processing overhead from Schedule 14. These amounts were totaled and divided by production units brought forward from Schedule 1 to develop an annual cost per unit. Schedule 15e (the fifth year's summary) is included as Exhibit 23.1.

○ *Schedule 16: Cumulative Program Cost Summary*—This schedule picked up the quarterly manufacturing cost totals from Schedule 15 and added them to the quarterly tooling investments from Schedule 9 to determine the cumulative total program costs at the end of each quarter during the program's life cycle. This summary schedule is included as Exhibit 23.2.

The general layout and flow of data between these schedules and those schedules developed earlier (Schedules 1 through 7) are shown in Exhibits 23.3 through 23.6. As with Schedules 1 through 7 in Chapter 20, the information flow is more straightforward in the forward-costing model than in the cost accumulation model. As a result, the method of documentation continues to be less elaborate or detailed than it was in that model. The narrative provided above for each schedule, together with the flow diagrams in Exhibits 23.3 through 23.6, should provide the information needed for both understanding and creating this portion of the forward-costing model.

Exhibit 23.1 Forward costing model—Schedule 15e: Forward Costing Summary (Year 5)/Costa Manufacturing Company

	Rates	Year Ending: Dec-96					TOTAL PROGRAM
		Quarter 1	Quarter 2	Quarter 3	Quarter 4	Total Year	
DIRECT COSTS:							
Direct material		116,280	116,280	63,768	46,512	348,840	2,377,168
Purchased parts		6,171	6,171	3,703	2,469	18,514	126,176
Outside services		29,469	29,469	17,681	11,788	88,406	602,438
DIRECT LABOR:							
Welding	12.36	15,475	15,475	9,285	6,190	46,425	331,430
Assembly	10.13	10,130	10,130	6,078	4,052	30,390	216,936
Direct Press Labor	11.25	2,813	2,813	1,688	1,125	8,438	60,261
TOTAL DIRECT LABOR		28,418	28,418	17,051	11,367	85,253	608,627
DIRECT LABOR OVERHEAD:							
Welding	42.71	53,389	53,389	32,033	21,356	160,166	1,114,385
Assembly	26.14	26,135	26,135	15,681	10,454	78,406	535,688
Direct Press Labor	14.18	3,544	3,544	2,126	1,418	10,631	75,124
TOTAL DIRECT LABOR OVERHEAD		83,068	83,068	49,841	33,227	249,204	1,725,197
MACHINE TIME OVERHEAD:							
Press Operations	35.81	4,476	4,476	2,686	1,791	13,429	98,636
CNC Machining	71.70	89,625	89,625	53,775	35,850	268,875	1,803,140
TOTAL MACHINE TIME OVERHEAD		94,101	94,101	56,461	37,641	282,304	1,901,776
OUTSIDE PROCESSING OVERHEAD		5,894	5,894	3,536	2,358	17,682	122,724
TOTAL ANNUAL COSTS		363,401	363,401	218,040	145,361	1,090,202	7,464,105
UNITS PRODUCED		12,500	12,500	7,500	5,000	37,500	290,000
COST/UNIT		29.0721	29.0721	29.0720	29.0721	29.0721	25.7383

Exhibit 23.2   Forward costing model—Schedule 16: Cumulative Program
Cost Summary/Costa Manufacturing Company

		Years Ending			
	Dec-92	thru	Dec-96		
	Dec-92	Dec-93	Dec-94	Dec-95	Dec-96
	-----------	-----------	-----------	-----------	-----------
FIRST QUARTER:					
Manufacturing Costs Incurred	121,108	481,133	506,514	542,852	363,401
Tooling Costs Incurred	59,990	0	0	0	0
FIRST QUARTER COSTS	181,098	481,133	506,514	542,852	363,401
ACCUMULATED PROGRAM COSTS					
THROUGH END OF QUARTER	181,098	1,635,512	3,405,000	5,277,450	6,862,266
SECOND QUARTER:					
Manufacturing Costs Incurred	181,662	481,133	506,514	542,852	363,401
Tooling Costs Incurred	49,980	0	0	0	0
SECOND QUARTER COSTS	231,642	481,133	506,514	542,852	363,401
ACCUMULATED PROGRAM COSTS					
THROUGH END OF QUARTER	412,740	2,116,645	3,911,513	5,820,301	7,225,667
THIRD QUARTER:					
Manufacturing Costs Incurred	242,215	360,850	379,885	407,139	218,040
Tooling Costs Incurred	9,995	0	0	0	0
THIRD QUARTER COSTS	252,210	360,850	379,885	407,139	218,040
ACCUMULATED PROGRAM COSTS					
THROUGH END OF QUARTER	664,950	2,477,495	4,291,399	6,227,440	7,443,707
FOURTH QUARTER:					
Manufacturing Costs Incurred	484,431	420,992	443,199	271,426	145,361
Tooling Costs Incurred	4,998	0	0	0	0
FOURTH QUARTER COSTS	489,428	420,992	443,199	271,426	145,361
ACCUMULATED PROGRAM COSTS					
THROUGH END OF THE YEAR	1,154,379	2,898,486	4,734,598	6,498,865	7,589,067
CUMULATIVE MANUFACTURING COST	1,029,416	2,773,524	4,609,636	6,373,903	7,464,105
PROGRAM-TO-DATE AVERAGE UNIT COST	24.2216	24.1176	24.5847	25.2432	25.7383

Exhibit 23.3   Forward costing model—Layout and flow through Schedule 10e/Costa Manufacturing Company

A61	Schedule 1	Unit Production Requirements
A121	Schedule 2	Direct Labor and Machine Time Requirements
A181	Schedule 3	Direct Material Requirements
A241	Schedule 4	Purchased Part Requirements
A301	Schedule 5	Outside Service Requirements
A361	Schedule 6	Tool Room Requirements
A421	Schedule 7	Additional Activity Requirements
A481	Schedule 8	Indirect Cost Application Rate Forecast
A541	Schedule 9	Tooling Investments
A601	Schedule 10a	Direct Labor and Manufacturing Overhead Cost - (Year 1)
A661	Schedule 10b	Direct Labor and Manufacturing Overhead Cost - (Year 2)
A721	Schedule 10c	Direct Labor and Manufacturing Overhead Cost - (Year 3)
A781	Schedule 10d	Direct Labor and Manufacturing Overhead Cost - (Year 4)
A841	Schedule 10e	Direct Labor and Manufacturing Overhead Cost - (Year 5)

Exhibit 23.4   Forward costing model—Layout and flow through Schedule
14/Costa Manufacturing Company

A61	Schedule 1	Unit Production Requirements
A121	Schedule 2	Direct Labor and Machine Time Requirements
A181	Schedule 3	Direct Material Requirements
A241	Schedule 4	Purchased Part Requirements
A301	Schedule 5	Outside Service Requirements
A361	Schedule 6	Tool Room Requirements
A421	Schedule 7	Additional Activity Requirements
A481	Schedule 8	Indirect Cost Application Rate Forecast
A541	Schedule 9	Tooling Investments
A601	Schedule 10a	Direct Labor and Manufacturing Overhead Cost - (Year 1)
A661	Schedule 10b	Direct Labor and Manufacturing Overhead Cost - (Year 2)
A721	Schedule 10c	Direct Labor and Manufacturing Overhead Cost - (Year 3)
A781	Schedule 10d	Direct Labor and Manufacturing Overhead Cost - (Year 4)
A841	Schedule 10e	Direct Labor and Manufacturing Overhead Cost - (Year 5)
A901	Schedule 11	Direct Material Costs
A961	Schedule 12	Purchased Parts Costs
A1021	Schedule 13	Outside Service Costs
A1081	Schedule 14	Outside Service Overhead Cost

Exhibit 23.5   Forward costing model—Layout and flow through Schedule
15e/Costa Manufacturing Company

Box	Schedule	Description
A61	Schedule 1	Unit Production Requirements
A121	Schedule 2	Direct Labor and Machine Time Requirements
A181	Schedule 3	Direct Material Requirements
A241	Schedule 4	Purchased Part Requirements
A301	Schedule 5	Outside Service Requirements
A361	Schedule 6	Tool Room Requirements
A421	Schedule 7	Additional Activity Requirements
A481	Schedule 8	Indirect Cost Application Rate Forecast
A541	Schedule 9	Tooling Investments
A601	Schedule 10a	Direct Labor and Manufacturing Overhead Cost - (Year 1)
A661	Schedule 10b	Direct Labor and Manufacturing Overhead Cost - (Year 2)
A721	Schedule 10c	Direct Labor and Manufacturing Overhead Cost - (Year 3)
A781	Schedule 10d	Direct Labor and Manufacturing Overhead Cost - (Year 4)
A841	Schedule 10e	Direct Labor and Manufacturing Overhead Cost - (Year 5)
A901	Schedule 11	Direct Material Costs
A961	Schedule 12	Purchased Parts Costs
A1021	Schedule 13	Outside Service Costs
A1081	Schedule 14	Outside Service Overhead Cost
A1141	Schedule 15a	Forward Costing Summary (Year 1)
A1201	Schedule 15b	Forward Costing Summary (Year 2)
A1261	Schedule 15c	Forward Costing Summary (Year 3)
A1321	Schedule 15d	Forward Costing Summary (Year 4)
A1381	Schedule 15e	Forward Costing Summary (Year 5)

Exhibit 23.6   Forward costing model—Layout and flow through Schedule 16/Costa Manufacturing Company

A61	Schedule 1	Unit Production Requirements
A121	Schedule 2	Direct Labor and Time Machine Requirements
A181	Schedule 3	Direct Material Requirements
A241	Schedule 4	Purchased Part Requirements
A301	Schedule 5	Outside Service Requirements
A361	Schedule 6	Tool Room Requirements
A421	Schedule 7	Additional Activity Requirements
A481	Schedule 8	Indirect Cost Application Rate Forecast
A541	Schedule 9	Tooling Investments
A601	Schedule 10a	Direct Labor and Manufacturing Overhead Cost - (Year 1)
A661	Schedule 10b	Direct Labor and Manufacturing Overhead Cost - (Year 2)
A721	Schedule 10c	Direct Labor and Manufacturing Overhead Cost - (Year 3)
A781	Schedule 10d	Direct Labor and Manufacturing Overhead Cost - (Year 4)
A841	Schedule 10e	Direct Labor and Manufacturing Overhead Cost - (Year 5)
A901	Schedule 11	Direct Material Costs
A961	Schedule 12	Purchased Parts Costs
A1021	Schedule 13	Outside Service Costs
A1081	Schedule 14	Outside Service Overhead Cost
A1141	Schedule 15a	Forward Costing Summary (Year 1)
A1201	Schedule 15b	Forward Costing Summary (Year 2)
A1261	Schedule 15c	Forward Costing Summary (Year 3)
A1321	Schedule 15d	Forward Costing Summary (Year 4)
A1381	Schedule 15e	Forward Costing Summary (Year 5)
A1441	Schedule 16	Cumulative Program Cost Summary

24

Long-Term Costing and Pricing: Life-Cycle Pricing

After carrying the forward-costing model through Schedule 16, Costa had a well-constructed forecast of the program's cost for each of the five years. The next issue was what unit price Costa should quote for the program.

In Chapter 20, Costa developed an initial cost estimate of $25.4368 per unit. Using a target margin of 12.5%, Costa arrived at an initial unit price of $29.0706. If Costa were awarded the program with an initial unit price of $29.0706 and with the required annual 2% price reductions, the total program revenue under this scenario would be calculated as follows:

Year	Unit Shipments	Unit Price	Sales
1992	42,500	29.0706	1,235,501
1993	72,500	28.4892	2,065,466
1994	72,500	27.9194	2,024,157
1995	65,000	27.3610	1,778,466
1996	37,500	26.8138	1,005,517
Total program sales			8,109,107

Based on Schedule 16 of the forward-costing model, the total cost of the program during the entire five years was projected at

295

$7,589,067. This would result in only a $520,040 (6.4%) margin during the program's run, far below the desired margin of 12.5%.

A year by year review of the forward-costing model shows the following changes in average cost per unit (excluding tooling) during the program's life cycle:

Year	Avg Unit Cost	% Change
1992	24.2216	
1993	24.0567	−0.68%
1994	25.3257	+5.28%
1995	27.1426	+7.17%
1996	29.0721	+7.11%

It is apparent that during the five years of the program, costs would not decrease enough to keep pace with the required 2% annual price reductions. In fact, unit costs would increase significantly after the first two years of the program, causing a fast and deep decline in margins. How, then, should Costa go about pricing this program?

Although Costa wanted to realize a 12.5% margin on the program, the facts are that the company could not show a 12.5% margin during each year of the program. Decreasing prices and increasing costs made this impossible. Instead, Costa needed to set its prices to provide for a 12.5% margin *during the life cycle of the program.* In that Costa had already projected total program costs, including tooling, at $7,589,067, their pricing needed to generate total revenues of $8,673,220 over the program's life cycle to realize the desired margin.

The forward-costing model was used to develop the mechanics for determining the five-year pricing schedule that would result in the desired margin. This was done by adding a final schedule to the model: Schedule 17, the Life Cycle Pricing Analysis. This schedule brought forward the basic cost information needed to test various first-year prices under a variety of margin and future price behavior assumptions.

The position and data flow into Schedule 17 is shown in Exhibit 24.1. Exhibit 24.2 shows the format for Schedule 17 developed by Costa. Variables that can be entered to test different answers are boxed on Costa's schedule.

Schedule 17 brought forward annual unit requirements from Schedule 1 and annual tooling requirements and annual manufacturing costs from Schedule 16. Management then entered the total program's desired margin percentage. After totaling the tooling and manufacturing costs for the program, the schedule then calculated the gross revenues necessary to attain the desired margin percentage.

Costa then entered the desired price behavior, expressed as an annual percentage change, and a *provisional* first-year price. The annual unit price percentage changes were then used to calculate each subsequent year's unit price. By multiplying these prices by the annual units, annual and total project revenues were determined.

The schedule then compared the annual revenues required with the annual revenues that would be generated by the provisional first-year price and displayed the resulting shortfall or excess of revenue. After several trial-and-error cycles, the first-year price that would generate revenues close to those needed for the desired margin were determined. In Costa's case, that first-year price came to $31.10.

To determine the impact of this pricing decision on reported margins, the model first had to establish a tooling cost per unit by dividing total tooling cost by total program units. This cost was then multiplied by each year's unit shipments to establish the tooling cost applicable to each year's sales. Annual manufacturing costs were then brought forward and added to these annual tooling costs to determine the total annual project costs. These annual project costs were then subtracted from the annual revenues to establish annual margins and margin percentages.

In Costa's case, the first-year price of $31.10 would generate a margin of 20.73%. However, by the final year of the program, margins would have fallen to −2.85%. Over the life cycle of the program, they would net to the desired 12.5%. Had Costa proceeded with the original $29.0706 unit price, first-year margins would have been a healthy 15.2%, but by the fifth year, they would have dropped to −10%. The overall profit would have fallen over $560,000 short of its target.

Exhibit 24.1   Forward costing model—Layout and flow through Schedule 17/Costa Manufacturing Company

Code	Schedule	Description
A61	Schedule 1	Unit Production Requirements
A121	Schedule 2	Direct Labor and Time Machine Requirements
A181	Schedule 3	Direct Material Requirements
A241	Schedule 4	Purchased Part Requirements
A301	Schedule 5	Outside Service Requirements
A361	Schedule 6	Tool Room Requirements
A421	Schedule 7	Additional Activity Requirements
A481	Schedule 8	Indirect Cost Application Rate Forecast
A541	Schedule 9	Tooling Investments
A601	Schedule 10a	Direct Labor and Manufacturing Overhead Cost - (Year 1)
A661	Schedule 10b	Direct Labor and Manufacturing Overhead Cost - (Year 2)
A721	Schedule 10c	Direct Labor and Manufacturing Overhead Cost - (Year 3)
A781	Schedule 10d	Direct Labor and Manufacturing Overhead Cost - (Year 4)
A841	Schedule 10e	Direct Labor and Manufacturing Overhead Cost - (Year 5)
A901	Schedule 11	Direct Material Costs
A961	Schedule 12	Purchased Parts Costs
A1021	Schedule 13	Outside Service Costs
A1081	Schedule 14	Outside Service Overhead Cost
A1141	Schedule 15a	Forward Costing Summary (Year 1)
A1201	Schedule 15b	Forward Costing Summary (Year 2)
A1261	Schedule 15c	Forward Costing Summary (Year 3)
A1321	Schedule 15d	Forward Costing Summary (Year 4)
A1381	Schedule 15e	Forward Costing Summary (Year 5)
A1441	Schedule 16	Cumulative Program Cost Summary
A1501	Schedule 17	Life Cycle Pricing Analysis

Exhibit 24.2 Life cycle pricing analysis/Costa Manufacturing Company

	Dec-92	Years Ending thru	Dec-96			
	Dec-92	Dec-93	Dec-94	Dec-95	Dec-96	Total Program
Units shipped	42,500	72,500	72,500	65,000	37,500	290,000
Cost of production	1,029,416	1,744,108	1,836,112	1,764,267	1,090,202	7,464,105
Tooling costs	124,963	0	0	0	0	124,963
Total cost	1,154,379	1,744,108	1,836,112	1,764,267	1,090,202	7,589,068
Desired Margin Percentage						12.5%
Revenue Required						8,673,220
Desired Unit Price Change		-2.0%	-2.0%	-2.0%	-2.0%	
Initial Unit Price	31.1000	30.4780	29.8684	29.2711	28.6856	
Shortfall (Excess) --------v (1,979)						
Annual Project Revenue	1,321,750	2,209,655	2,165,462	1,902,620	1,075,712	8,675,199
Manufacturing cost	1,029,416	1,744,108	1,836,112	1,764,267	1,090,202	7,464,105
Amortized tooling costs	18,314	31,241	31,241	28,009	16,159	124,964
Annual Project Cost	1,047,730	1,775,349	1,867,353	1,792,276	1,106,361	7,589,069
Annual Project Margin	274,020	434,306	298,109	110,344	(30,649)	1,086,130
% Gross Margin	20.73%	19.65%	13.77%	5.80%	-2.85%	12.52%

Other Costing/Pricing Considerations

As constructed, the forward-costing model provided Costa's management with the information needed to make the right pricing decision in light of their pricing strategy. Management wanted to price this one-time program using estimates of the actual indirect costing rates that would exist in the years of program performance. The model was able to provide the needed data in an efficient and timely manner.

The pricing strategy for this program, however, raised a question as to how the core business would be costed and priced during the same period. As stated on several occasions, Costa's management looked at this opportunity as a one-time event. If Costa were awarded the contract, business would return to current levels after the contract was completed. If Costa did not receive the contract, business would continue at the current level.

If Costa were to be awarded the contract under these circumstances, would it be appropriate to cost and price the core business using the rates that include the new program? Before answering, I examine what the rates for the years 1992 through 1996 would look like without the new contract. This can be done by updating the base model for each year by the inflation factors only. These are the adjustments that were made to salaries, hourly wages, health insurance, utilities, and supplies.

Using the Machine Time cost centers as examples of rate behavior, the rates with and without the new program during the period were compared as follows:

	1992	1993	1994	1995	1996
Press Operations					
With new program	32.31	33.04	34.06	35.12	35.81
Without new program	33.46	34.48	35.53	36.64	38.11
CNC Machine					
With new program	64.31	56.70	58.41	65.60	71.70
Without new program	73.12	75.44	77.90	80.43	83.83

If Costa set costs and priced the ongoing core business at the rates that include the new business, product prices would decrease considerably during the first few years, only to begin rising at a rapid pace later in the program until they would return, in 1997, to the rates that they would have been had the program never existed. Would this be a wise marketing move?

Cost is an important element in the pricing equation, but prices should not simply be established on a cost-plus-markup basis. The market and management's pricing strategy, not cost, should determine prices. Cost tells the organization at what price it can afford to sell the product, not what price it should charge. In Costa's situation, it might be wise *not* to use the rates that include the new business in developing a pricing strategy for the core business. Any benefits that might be gained during the price reduction phase might be more than lost when the period of rapid price increases is reached. This would definitely be the case with ongoing products for which customers would be extremely resistant to rapid price increases.

Being awarded the new program, however, would give Costa some product pricing flexibility. The company might find it advantageous to hold prices for a few years to increase market penetration and then begin increasing them gradually. They might consider price freezes or reductions for customers making long-term commitments. Any of a wide variety of pricing strategies could be adopted. Fortunately, the mechanics for testing the financial impact of the various strategies already exists in the cost accumulation and forward-costing models. Minor modifications can make them fit almost any set of circumstances.

Marginal Costing Possibility

Suppose that Costa's management believed that no possible advantage would be gained by using pricing as a means of improving the company's market position. The volume of Costa's core business would remain the same regardless of their efforts. The strategy might be to continue to cost and price the core business as if the new program never existed. The strategy on the one-time program could then be to determine the organization's incremental cost in executing the program and then quote double the normal margin on these incremental costs.

The cost accumulation and forward-costing models can support this strategy as well. By using the base year schedules updated

Exhibit 24.3

Year	Base Year Update with Inflation	Base Year Update with New Program	Incremental Program Costs
1992	$ 9,131,291	$10,020,460	$ 889,169
1993	9,354,630	10,674,341	1,319,711
1994	9,591,112	10,986,105	1,394,993
1995	9,837,262	11,094,603	1,257,341
1996	10,024,775	10,694,648	669,873
Total	$47,939,070	$53,470,157	$5,531,087

to include the new program developed in Chapter 22 and those updated with inflation only developed in this Chapter, we can calculate the incremental cost of the new program as shown in Exhibit 24.3.

Using Schedule 17 of the forward-costing model, Costa determined the price that meets the company's criteria by doing the following:

o Overriding the formulas in the Tooling Cost line with zeros.

o Overriding the formulas in the Cost of Production line with the incremental costs (as shown in the table above) for each year.

o Entering 25% as the desired margin.

o Entering trial Initial Unit Prices until the Shortfall (Excess) amount is near zero.

The initial unit price arrived at as a result of this process is $26.44.

As has been demonstrated by this example, the cost accumulation model coupled with a forward-costing model can accommodate almost any long-term pricing strategy and prove to be valuable tools in ensuring that an organization's pricing decisions are informed decisions.

25

Activity-Based Costing and the Small to Mid-Sized Organization

Back at the beginning of Chapter 9—a mere sixteen chapters ago—Costa Manufacturing was a $9 million organization with only the most rudimentary cost information system. Its indirect manufacturing costs were applied to products using a plantwide, direct labor–based overhead rate. Its engineering costs were distributed on the basis of the manufacturing conversion costs, and its general and administrative costs were distributed on total accumulated conversion costs.

Actually, Costa was not even as sophisticated as these three rates would imply. By following the "rate chain" backward, one finds that Costa's rate was actually an organization-wide rate of 367% of direct labor, not the three separate rates. Although management had long considered the company's cost system sufficiently detailed for both pricing and cost control, Costa's cost information was about as generalized and simplified as possible.

After designing an activity-based costing system using the methodology and tools described in Chapters 6, 7, and 8, Costa was able to build a cost accumulation model that stimulated the actual flow of costs within the organization. In the process, it created only one new data reporting requirement: the collection of

303

machine time information in CNC Machining and Press Operations. Changing the accounting system's cost centers to agree with those in the model and developing a system to collect demand information for service centers are two more changes that would enhance the activity-based system, but these changes are not required for the system to work effectively. They would merely make an already accurate system more accurate.

The accounting practices and spreadsheeting techniques employed in the design and development of the system were not difficult to comprehend or implement. There was no mysterious "black box" that took data in one end and printed out an unexplained answer at the other end. No complex software was required. All that was required was for Costa to break down its organization into logical component parts, design a means of putting those parts back together in a manner that provided a logical flow of costs, and then simulate this cost flow using basic mathematics in a cost accumulation model that was constructed as a single personal computer spreadsheet.

By Chapter 15, Costa Manufacturing had developed an "off-line" activity-based costing system and indirect cost application rates that would enable it to better determine the cost of manufacturing individual products. But that is not all it had acquired in the process. By that point the company also had a valuable decision-support tool that could be used to improve the information required by management in making a wide variety of strategic and operational decisions.

Section III of the book showed how the cost accumulation model could be used for product costing, product line profitability analyses, controlling and reducing costs, evaluating capital expenditures, making overtime versus additional manpower decisions, and supporting long-term costing and pricing decisions. In addition to the examples set forth in the book, the model could also be used as an effective tool in make versus buy decisions, budgeting, planning, forecasting, capacity planning, and many other situations where cost and resource information has a significant influence on management's decisions.

The condition of Costa Manufacturing's cost information system after Chapter 24 is far superior to its condition at the beginning of Chapter 9. Timely and accurate information is now available to Costa's management for the myriad of decisions it must make. Although the system's metamorphosis was not without cost, it was without significant cost. If Costa's effort was typical of most organizations following the approach described, less than 500 man-hours were required. When compared with the benefits to be gained by the improved cost information, the investment was very small indeed.

The principles and procedures described in this volume apply to all organizations, regardless of their purpose or size. They apply to a church, insurance company, boutique, warehouse, manufacturer, or any other organization. They apply to the $100 thousand-per-year organization and the $100 billion-per-year organization. The very smallest might find that intuition provides the answers without cost data, and the largest might prefer more detailed information, but the vast majority of organizations fall into the small and mid-sized category that are too large to be run by intuition and too small to handle masses of detailed information. The abc approach provides these organizations with an understandable and affordable method of gaining the knowledge of product and process costs necessary to prosper and grow in the 1990s without paying outrageous costs for unneeded ABC cost theories.

Costa Manufacturing was able to capitalize on the improved knowledge provided by an effective cost system without spending a small fortune. Now your company can too.

Index